The Natural Light Portrait Book

The step-by-step techniques you need to
capture amazing photographs like the pros

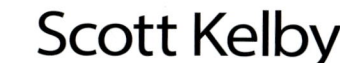

Scott Kelby

**Author of the top-selling digital photography
book ever—*The Digital Photography Book*, part 1**

The Natural Light Portrait Book Team

MANAGING EDITOR
Kim Doty

COPY EDITOR
Cindy Snyder

ART DIRECTOR
Jessica Maldonado

PHOTOGRAPHY
Scott Kelby

PRODUCTION PHOTOS
Scott Kelby
Jason Stevens
Kathy Porupski
Julio Aguilar
Brad Moore

PUBLISHED BY

Rocky Nook
1010 B Street, Suite 350
San Rafael, CA 94901

Composed in Univers and Myriad Pro by KelbyOne.

Trademarks
All terms mentioned in this book that are known to be trademarks or service marks have been appropriately capitalized. Rocky Nook cannot attest to the accuracy of this information. Use of a term in the book should not be regarded as affecting the validity of any trademark or service mark.

Photoshop and Lightroom are registered trademarks of Adobe Systems Incorporated.

Warning and Disclaimer
This book is designed to provide information about portrait photography. Every effort has been made to make this book as complete and as accurate as possible, but no warranty of fitness is implied.

The information is provided on an as-is basis. The author and Rocky Nook shall have neither the liability nor responsibility to any person or entity with respect to any loss or damages arising from the information contained in this book or from the use of the discs, videos, or programs that may accompany it.

ISBN 13: 978-1-68198-424-7

10 9 8 7 6 5 4 3 2 1

Printed and bound in the United States of America
Distributed in the UK and Europe by Publishers Group UK
Distributed in the U.S. and all other territories by
Ingram Publisher Services

Library of Congress Control Number: 2018940614

www.kelbyone.com
www.rockynook.com

*This book is dedicated to my dear friend
and colleague, Kathy Porupski.*

*I love getting to work with you on all my crazy projects.
You make every one more fun and less stressful,
and we always have lots of laughs.
Plus, you always have a way of jumping in and pulling the
nose of the plane up just in the nick of time.*

*You have been such a blessing to me and my family over the years,
and I'm honored to be able to dedicate this book to you.*

Acknowledgments

Although only one name appears on the spine of this book, it takes a team of dedicated and talented people to pull a project like this together. I'm not only delighted to be working with them, but I also get the honor and privilege of thanking them here.

To my amazing wife Kalebra: This year we celebrated our 30th anniversary and you continue to reinforce what everybody always tells me—I'm the luckiest guy in the world.

To my son Jordan: I just can't believe my "little boy" has already graduated from college. It all happened so fast, but I'm so thrilled for you, and for the many adventures, the fun, love, and laughter your future holds. If there's a dad more proud of his son than I am, I've yet to meet him. #rolltide!

To my beautiful daughter Kira: You are a little clone of your mom, and that's the best compliment I could ever give you. I love your sense of humor, your constant dancing, the hilarious faces you make, and your heart. I love the young woman you are becoming, and I particularly love when you and I go grab lunch or dinner together. Those times are so precious to me. I love you, little sweetie!

To my big brother Jeff: Your boundless generosity, kindness, positive attitude, and humility have been an inspiration to me my entire life, and I'm just so honored to be your brother.

To my editor Kim Doty: If there's a Book Editor Hall of Fame, you should truly be in it. You are so talented, organized, and awesome, and your amazing attitude, support, and ideas are what keep me going when I'm deep in the weeds. I'll be forever grateful to have you on my team. You rock!

To my book designer Jessica Maldonado: I love the way you design, and all the clever little things you add to everything you do. Our book team struck gold when we found you!

To my dear friend and business partner Jean A. Kendra: Thanks for putting up with me all these years, and for your support for all my crazy ideas. It really means a lot.

To Erik Kuna: Your suggestions, ideas, and good council have made this book, and the ones before it, that much better. I value your friendship so much, and feel very blessed to have you in my life.

To Jeanne Jilleba: Thank you for juggling my very tricky schedule in ways that give me time to write theses books. I'm very grateful to have your help, your talent, and immeasurable patience every day.

To Cindy Snyder: Thank you so much for working on my books and catching tons of little things others would have missed.

To Ted Waitt, my fantastic "Editor for life" at Rocky Nook: Boom goes the dynamite! Thanks for being such a great friend, a world-class sounding board, and for helping these ideas become a reality.

To my publisher Scott Cowlin: I'm so delighted I still get to work with you, and grateful for your open mind and vision.

To my mentors John Graden, Jack Lee, Dave Gales, Judy Farmer, and Douglas Poole: Thank you for your wisdom and whip-cracking—they have helped me immeasurably.

Most importantly, I want to thank God, and His Son Jesus Christ, for leading me to the woman of my dreams, for blessing us with such amazing children, for allowing me to make a living doing something I truly love, for always being there when I need Him, for blessing me with a wonderful, fulfilling, and happy life, and such a warm, loving family to share it with.

About the Author

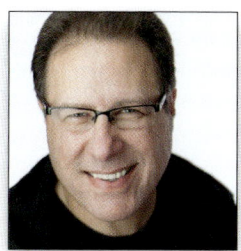

Scott Kelby

Scott is President and CEO of KelbyOne, an online educational community for learning Lightroom, Photoshop, and photography. He is Editor, Publisher, and co-founder of *Photoshop User* magazine; Editor of *Lightroom Magazine*; host of *The Grid*, the influential, live, weekly talk show for photographers; and is founder of the annual Scott Kelby's Worldwide Photo Walk.®

Scott is a photographer, designer, and award-winning author of more than 90 books, including *The Landscape Photography Book*; *Light It, Shoot It, Retouch It*; *The Adobe Photoshop Book for Digital Photographers*; *Photoshop for Lightroom Users*; *How Do I Do That In Lightroom?*; *The Flash Book*; and his landmark, *The Digital Photography Book* series. The first book in this series, *The Digital Photography Book*, part 1, has become the #1 top-selling book ever on digital photography.

His books have been translated into dozens of different languages, including Chinese, Russian, Spanish, Korean, Polish, Taiwanese, French, German, Italian, Japanese, Hebrew, Dutch, Swedish, Turkish, and Portuguese, among many others. He is a recipient of the prestigious ASP International Award, presented annually by the American Society of Photographers for "…contributions in a special or significant way to the ideals of Professional Photography as an art and a science," and the HIPA award, presented for his contributions to photography education worldwide.

Scott is Conference Technical Chair for the annual Photoshop World Conference and a frequent speaker at conferences and trade shows around the world. He is featured in a series of online learning courses at KelbyOne.com and has been training Photoshop users and photographers since 1993.

For more information on Scott, visit him at:

His daily Lightroom blog: **lightroomkillertips.com**

His personal blog: **scottkelby.com**

Twitter: **@scottkelby**

Facebook: **facebook.com/skelby**

Instagram: **@scottkelby**

Contents

Chapter One

PORTRAIT LENSES   1

It All Starts Here

A 70–200mm f/2.8 or f/4 Zoom Lens 2

An 85mm f/1.8 Lens 3

A Fast 135mm Portrait Lens 4

Avoid Wide-Angle Lenses
for Most Portraits 5

Should You Ever Shoot Portraits
with a Wide-Angle Lens? 6

Why I Avoid 50mm Lenses
for Close-Up Portraits 7

Yes, You Need That Lens Hood 8

It's These Three Things That Create
Soft Backgrounds 9

Minimum Focusing Distance 10

How Lens Choice Affects Your Background 11

Shoot 'Em at What You Bought 'Em For! 12

Should You Buy a Lens with IS or VR?
Well, That Depends 13

Chapter Two

CAMERA SETTINGS   15

F-Stop, Shutter Speed & ISO

Shoot with Your Camera Set to RAW Format 16

Choosing Your Shooting Mode 17

Which Aperture (F-Stop) to Use 18

Why Your Shutter Speed Is Important 19

How to Stop Worrying about
Slow Shutter Speeds 20

When to Shoot at Your Lowest ISO 21

What If Your Camera Chooses
the Wrong Exposure? 22

How to Keep from Damaging
Your Highlights 23

Choosing the Right White Balance 24

How to Focus for Sharp Portraits 25

Contents

How to Focus f/1.8 Lenses or Faster 26

Which Eye to Focus On. 27

Why the Eye Autofocus Feature Rocks 28

Shooting Group Shots at Wide-Open F-Stops 29

Where to Focus for Multi-Row Group Shots. 30

Image Stabilization: On or Off?. 31

Chapter Three

WINDOW LIGHT PORTRAITS 33

Working That Window Like a Dutch Master

Why Direct Window Light
Is Often Bad Light 34

Turn Off Any Room Lights 35

Move Away from the Window. 36

Move Behind a Window or Doorway 37

For the Love of North-Facing Windows 38

Use a Shower Curtain Liner 39

Close the Sheers for Better Light. 40

How to Position Your Subject for
a Window Light Portrait 41

Rembrandt Window Lighting 42

Highlight Profile Portrait 43

What If You Don't Want the
Classic Window Light Look?. 44

Shooting with Your Subject
Facing the Window. 45

What Kind of Window Am I Looking For? 46

Watch Out for Changing Window Light 47

Using an Open Doorway for Light 48

Using Hard Light Shadow Patterns 49

Shooting with Painted Backdrops 50

Adding a Reflector 51

Choosing the Right White Balance 52

It Might Be Tripod Time 53

Contents

Chapter Four

SHOOTING OUTSIDE   55
Making the Bright Beautiful

My Outdoor Photography
Secret Weapon.. 56

A Small Tri-Grip 1-Stop Diffuser
and Stand... 57

When to Use a Gold Reflector............................... 58

When to Use a White Reflector.............................. 59

Use a Black Reflector on Cloudy Days.................... 60

Where to Position a Reflector 61

Use a Reflector to Create Shade........................... 62

Diffusing Group Shots 63

Avoid Dappled Light.. 64

Find Shade Near the Edge
of Bright Sunlight 65

Another Great Option:
Shooting in Full Shade... 66

Shooting on Cloudy Days 67

Position Your Subject to Have Directional Light 68

Nailing Your White Balance Outdoors 69

Chapter Five

SHOOTING IN DIRECT LIGHT   71
Taming the Beast

The Advantages of Shooting with
the Sun Behind Your Subject 72

Watch Out for Light Spilling
on Their Face.. 73

Using the Sun as a Rim Light
or Hair Light... 74

Getting Sun Flare Effects..................................... 75

The "Overexposing by a Stop or More" Trick 76

The Best Time to Shoot, Hands-Down 77

Look for Contrasting Backgrounds 78

What to Have Your Subjects Wear......................... 79

Contents

Chapter Six

COMPOSITION 81

Gettin' It All in the Frame

Composing for a More Intimate Portrait 82

Eyes Go in the Top Third of the Frame 83

Don't Center Your Subject in the Frame 84

Cut Off the Top of Their Head 85

Don't Leave Too Much Space
Above Their Head 86

Compose So There Is Space for
Your Subject to Look Into 87

You Want to See Catchlights 88

Avoid Distracting Background Elements 89

Keep the Scene Simple 90

Avoid Bright Spots in the Background 91

Get Low for Full-Length Shots 92

Shoot from a Slightly Higher Angle 93

Avoid This Framing Mistake 94

Don't Cut Off Their Feet 95

Environmental Portraits 96

Photographing Kids 97

Chapter Seven

POSING 99

How to Be a Poser

What Makes a Truly Memorable Portrait? 100

Photographing Photogenic People 101

Build a Posing List 102

Build Rapport 103

Which Outfit Should They Wear First? 104

Stop and Review Five Minutes into the Shoot 105

The Shots between Poses 106

Directing Your Subject during the Shoot 107

Looking Directly Toward the Camera 108

Looking Off-Camera 109

The Eyes Have It 110

Avoid Seeing Too Much Whites in the Eyes 111

Contents

If They Have a Roundish Face, Do This 112

If They Have a Thin Face, Do This Instead 113

Peter Hurley's Famous Jawline Trick 114

Chin Down for Better Eyes and Much More 115

Thinning the Nose 116

Tilt Their Face Up toward the Light 117

Don't Let Their Expression Go Blank 118

Add Volume and Movement to Hair 119

Turn Their Shoulders for a More Flattering Look 120

Don't Shoot Flat-Footed with Straight Legs 121

Another Trick for Thinner Waistlines 122

Making Legs Look Thinner 123

Keep Their Arms Away from Their Sides 124

Sitting? Put Them on the Edge 125

Keep Arms, Legs, Fingers, Everything Bent 126

Avoid Showing an Open Palm 127

Keep Fingers Closed, Not Open 128

Add Simple Props 129

Chapter Eight

POST-PROCESSING   131

The Important Lightroom & Photoshop Stuff

Adding a Sunburst Effect 132

Adding a Soft Glow Effect 133

Adding a Sun Flare Effect 134

Desaturating Skin 135

Removing Blemishes 136

Reducing Wrinkles or Moles 137

Reducing Shiny Spots on the Skin 138

Enhancing the Irises 139

Sharpening Portraits 140

Brightening the Eyes 141

The Perfectly Clear Retouching Plug-In 142

Cinematic Color Grading for Portraits 143

Using Liquify's Face-Aware Feature 144

Removing Fly-Away Hairs along the Outside 145

Brightening the Face, So It's the Focal Point 146

Adding a Subtle Vignette 147

Adding a Spotlight Effect 148

Adding Texture to Solid Backgrounds 149

Brightening Skin 150

Smoothing Skin 151

Contents

Chapter Nine

PORTRAIT RECIPES 153

The Ingredients for Making Great Portraits

Overhead Sun Portrait with Diffuser
BTS 154
Final Image 155

Large Area Portrait with Diffuser
BTS 156
Final Image 157

Backlit Sun Flare Portrait
BTS 158
Final Image 159

Backlit Indoor Window Light Portrait
BTS 160
Final Image 161

Direct Sun Location Portrait with Diffuser
BTS 162
Final Images 163

Harsh Direct Light Portrait with Diffuser
BTS 164
Final Image 165

Dramatic Window Light Portrait
BTS 166
Final Image 167

Classic Window Light Portrait
BTS 168
Final Image 169

Cloudy Outdoor Portrait
BTS 170
Final Image 171

Direct Sunlight Portrait
BTS 172
Final Image 173

Glass Door Light Portrait with Diffuser
BTS 174
Final Image 175

Window Light Bridal Portrait
BTS 176
Final Image 177

Low-Perspective Bridal Portrait
BTS 178
Final Image 179

Open Shade Portrait
BTS 180
Final Image 181

Epic-Style Indoor Window Light Portrait
BTS 182
Final Image 183

INDEX **184**

Five Things You Need to Know Up Front…

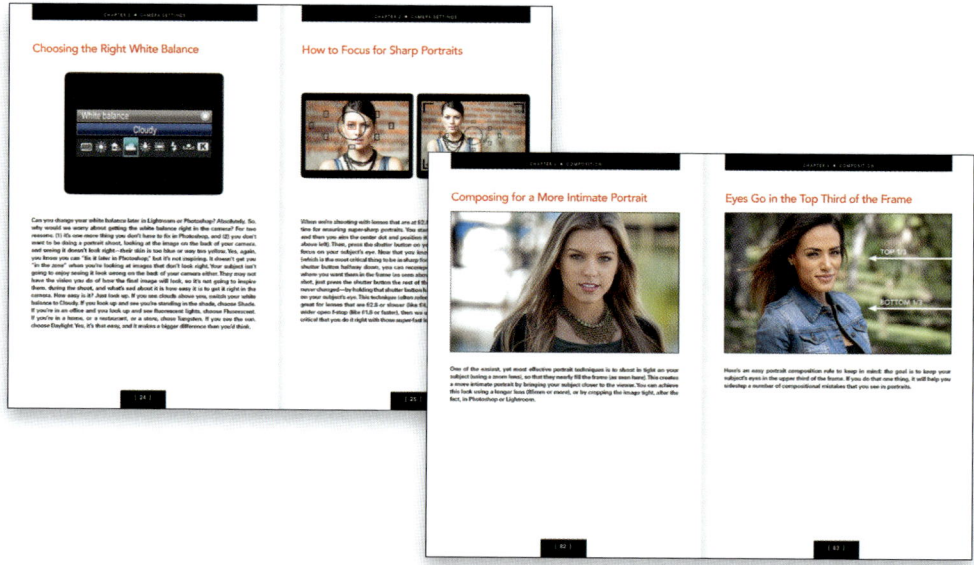

(1) Okay, that headline may be slightly overstating it, but it's so important that you read these five things that I had to create an attention-getting headline to make certain you did, in fact, read them. Now, what kind of stuff would be so important that if you missed it, it would be bad? Well, if you skipped this, you wouldn't know that there's a special webpage with some videos I created just for you that will help you big time. Here's the link to that webpage: **kelbyone.com/books/nlpbook**. Now, let's get on with the other four riveting things (stop snickering).

(2) Here's how this book works: Basically, it's you and me together at a shoot, and I'm giving you the same tips, the same advice, and sharing the same techniques I've learned over the years from some of the top working pros as I would a friend. When I'm with a friend, I skip all the technical stuff, so for example, if you turned to me and said, "Hey Scott, where am I supposed to focus so this portrait is tack sharp?" I wouldn't give you a lecture about hyperfocal distance or depth of field zones for acceptable sharpness. In real life, I'd just turn to you and say, "Aim your focus point on whichever eye is closest to the camera, then hold your shutter button halfway down, lock focus, compose the shot any way you want, and then press the shutter button down all the way." I'd tell you short and right to the point like that, so that's pretty much what I do throughout this book.

(3) You don't have to read this book in order. This is a jump-in-anywhere book, so if there's a particular area of portrait photography you want to read first, you can just jump to that chapter and dive right in, no sweat. If you're brand new to all of this, then it would probably be helpful to start up front, because later chapters build on earlier chapters, but you don't have to read it in order.

To Keep You from Destroying Your Life, or Worse!

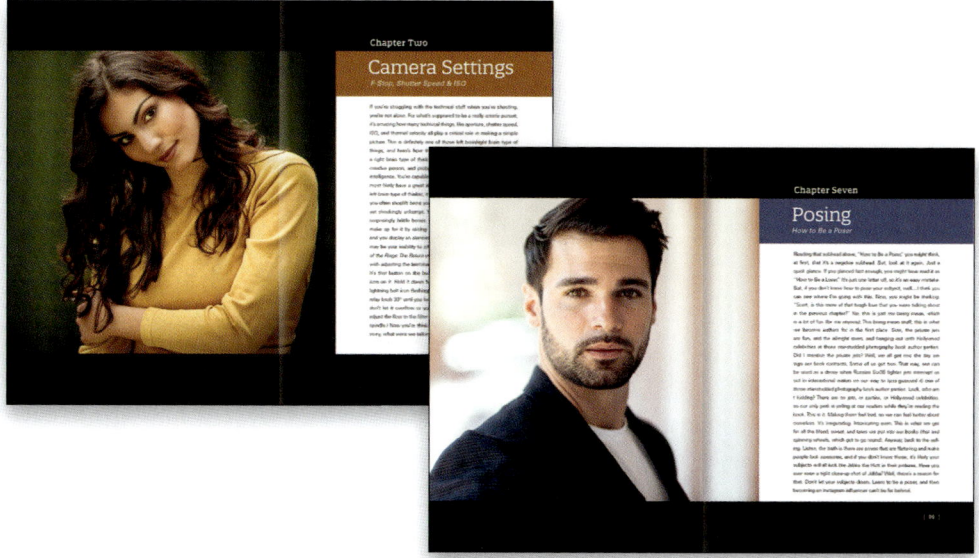

(4) If you're shooting with a Sony, or Olympus, or a Fuji digital camera, don't let it throw you that a Canon or Nikon camera is often pictured in the book—it's only because that's what I had access to. Most of the techniques in this book apply to any DSLR or mirrorless camera, and a bunch of them will even help if you only shoot with your smartphone's camera. So, don't let brands, makes, or models throw you off—this is about the bigger picture of portrait photography.

(5) Should you read the intro page to each chapter? I have a tradition in all my books that either delights my readers, or sends them into fits of anger. It's how I write the introduction to each chapter. In a normal book, these brief intros would give you some important insight into the coming chapter. But, mine…um…well…don't. These quirky, rambling intros have little, if anything, to do with what's actually in the chapter. They're designed to simply be a mental break between chapters, and a lot of folks really love them (so much so, that we actually published a whole book of nothing but chapter intros from my various books. I am not making this up), however some "serious type" folks hate them with the passion of a thousand burning suns. Luckily, I've relegated the "crazy stuff" to just those few intro pages—the rest of the book is just straight-to-the-point stuff. But, I had to warn you just in case you're a Mr. Grumpypants, and if that sounds like you, I'm begging you, please just skip the chapter intros altogether. Okay, thanks for taking the time to read these two pages, and now you're ready to launch into this puppy and make the very most of it. Turn the page and let's get to work!

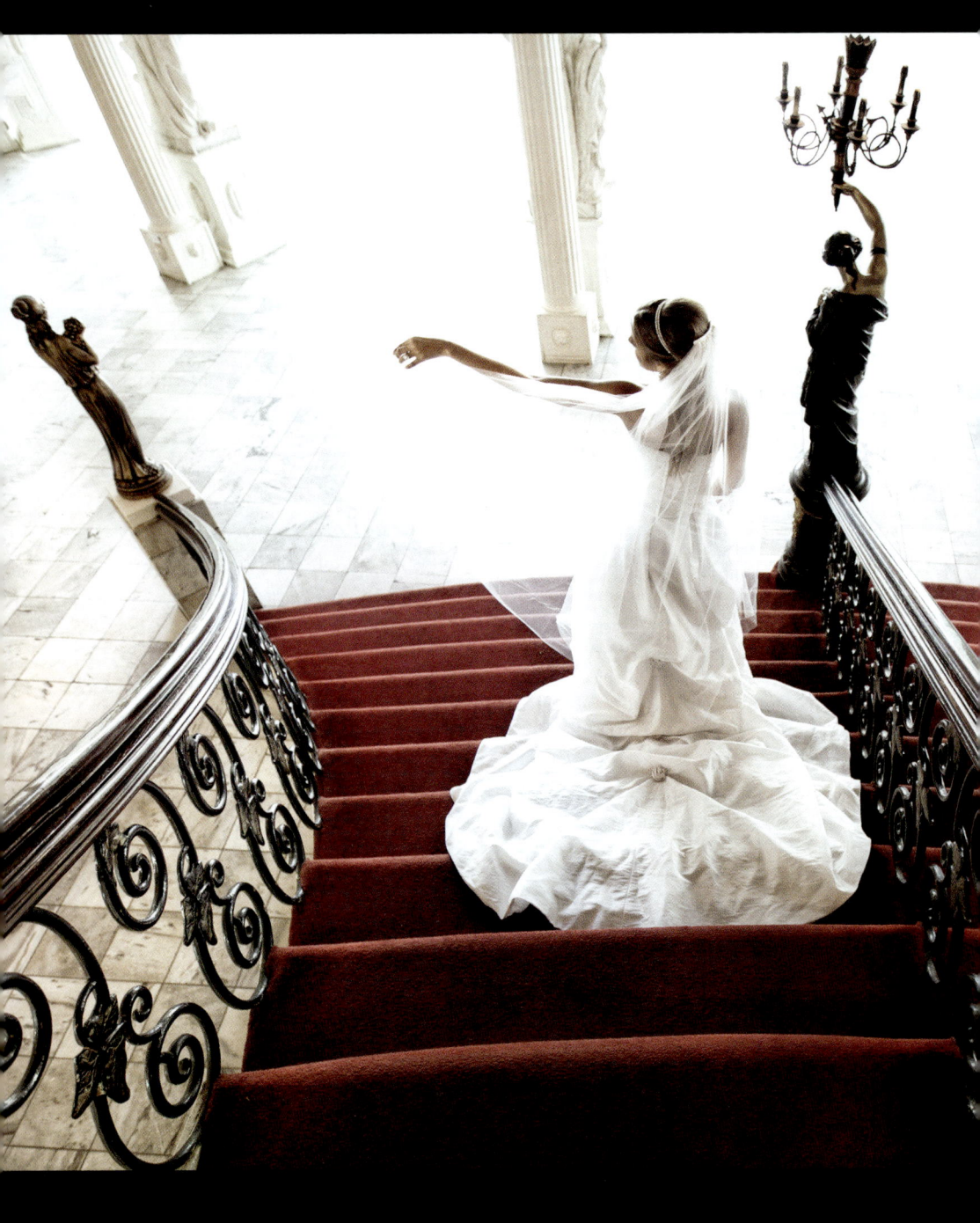

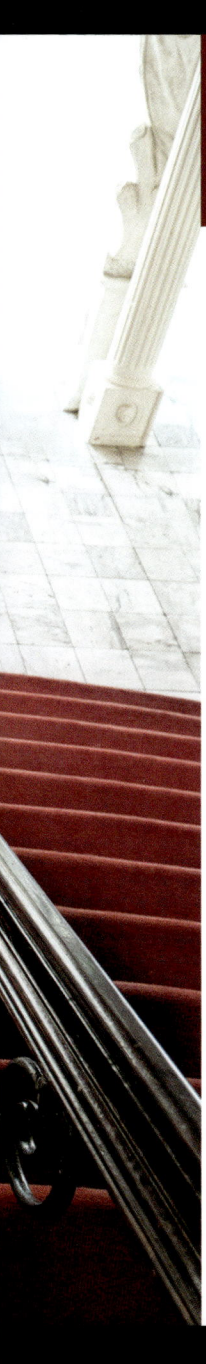

Chapter One

Portrait Lenses

It All Starts Here

Before we start, it is absolutely imperative that you stop here, go back, and read #5 in the "Five Things You Need to Know Up Front..." on page xiii. Once you've done that, you're cleared to come back and pick up reading right here. Okay, lenses. They are not cheap! But have you ever stopped to think about why some lenses actually cost more than the camera bodies themselves? I know, right? It's crazy. Especially since all that's in a lens is some die-cast machine-engineered aluminum for the barrel, and then some finely ground glass, and it's probably recycled glass at that. Interesting side note here on the origins of the word "lens": I was surprised to learn that "lens" is not a word at all. It was originally an acronym used in the mid-1820s when the Daguerreotype process (considered the first documented successful use of a camera) was invented and the acronym LENS actually stood for "Light Emitting Numinous Sphere," which of course was a reference to the circular glass used in photographic lenses. Although Nicéphore Niépce gets a lot of the credit for creating the first actual working camera, it was his assistant Louis-Jacques-Mandé Daguerre who actually came up with the term LENS. But, perhaps more importantly, it was Daguerre's Italian confidential secretary, Julia Louis-Dreyfus, who not only recorded the historical event, erroneously crediting Niépce with originally coining the term LENS, but some years later she went on to play the character Elaine on *Seinfeld*, and the rest, as they say, is made up history.

A 70–200mm f/2.8 or f/4 Zoom Lens

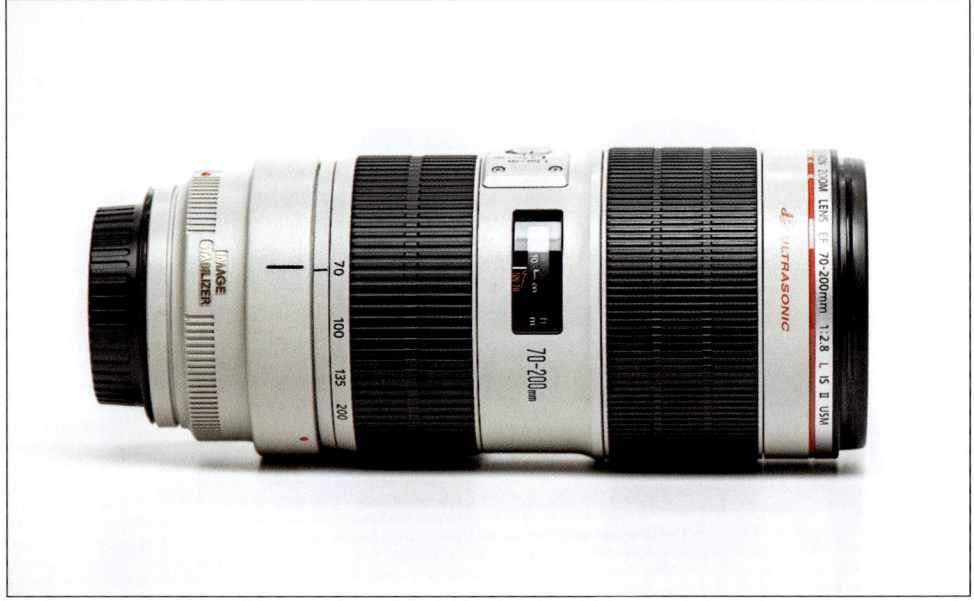

This is my #1 go-to lens for natural light portraits, and whether you choose the f/2.8 version or the f/4 version, they are both sharp, flattering lenses (pretty much every lens manufacturer's 70–200mm is a very solid lens—Sony, Nikon, Canon, Sigma, Tamron). This lens does three great things: (1) It makes people look awesome! When you shoot at its longer focal lengths—for me, I like anywhere from 120mm to 200mm—the lens compression creates a very flattering look for faces. Although I like the 120mm to 200mm range, really anything around 100mm or more will do the trick. Using a longer lens like this is one of the nicest, most flattering things you can do for your subject. (2) Having a wide zoom range like 70–200mm gives you lots of different compositional options without having to move from your shooting position a bunch. (3) By shooting farther back, it makes your subject feel more comfortable—you're not right on top of them, shooting two feet from their face, like you might wind up doing with a shorter lens. If you're working with a professional model, it won't faze them at all that you're shooting up close like that—they're used to it. But, if you're doing a portrait of the vice president of marketing for a company, or a high school student for a senior portrait, having the photographer so close tends to make them uncomfortable, and that's the last thing you want in a portrait session. One more thing to consider: How much of a difference will you see between an f/2.8 lens and the f/4 version? To the eye? Not much at all, but you'll feel the difference in your hand (the f/2.8 version weighs a lot more), and in your pocket (it literally costs about twice as much). So, if you don't shoot in low-light situations often, where that one extra stop of light might make a difference, go with the f/4.

An 85mm f/1.8 Lens

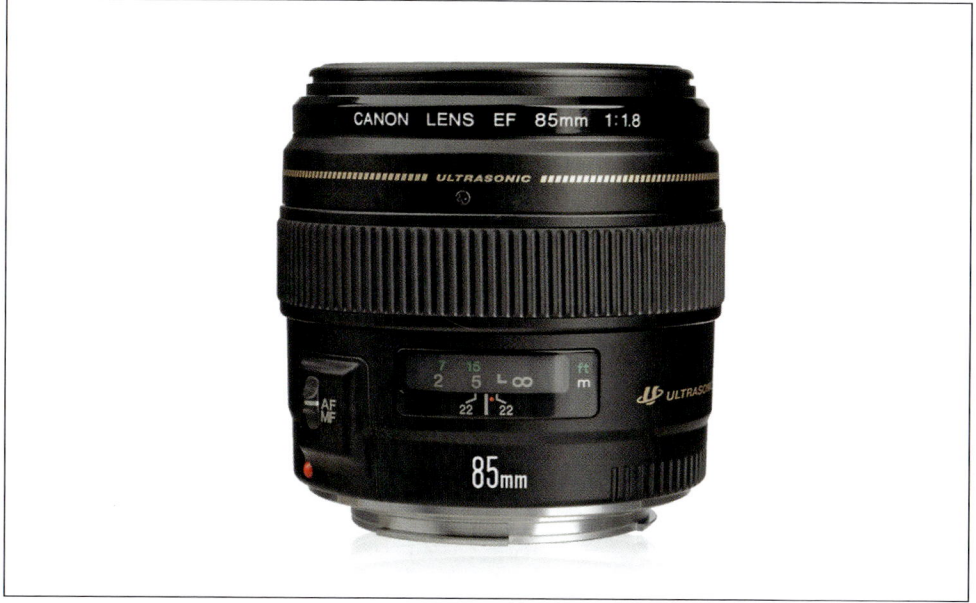

If I'm not shooting my 70–200mm, it's only because I'm shooting my second go-to lens for portraits: the 85mm f/1.8, which lets you get the background behind your subject even softer and more luscious (there's a word you don't get to use every day) thanks to that f/1.8 f-stop. The general rule is: the lower the number, the more out of focus the background will be. Well, if that's the case, you might be wondering why I'm not using an 85mm f/1.4 or even an f/1.2. It's because at those super-wide-open f-stops, the depth of field is so shallow (the part that's in focus is so thin) that it's easy to take an out-of-focus portrait if you're not careful. I don't want to have to be deadly precise, especially since no one is really going to be able to tell the difference whether I used an f/1.8 or an f/1.4. I've done side-by-side tests, shooting the same subject at f/1.8 and f/1.4, and nobody could reliably tell me which was shot with which—they'd have to guess and half the time they were wrong. But, it's not just the "be careful when you focus" thing (more on that later in this chapter), it's the price and weight. A Nikon 85mm f/1.4 costs $1,597 (when I wrote this), but a Nikon 85mm f/1.8 only costs $477 and weighs about a third less. So, it's less than a third the cost, and it weighs a third less. Just sayin'. One more thing: Everybody kinda needs at least one "fast lens" in their kit—that one lens that you can hand-hold in really low-light situations and still get a sharp shot (a "fast lens" is any lens that lets you shoot at very low-numbered f-stops, like f/2.8, f/2, f.1/8, f/1.4, or f/1.2). The lower the number, generally, the more expensive the lens, but like the Nikon f/1.8, there are some great deals out there, like the Canon 85mm f/1.8, which is only $369. That's a pretty darn fast lens at a really great price (well, it's a great price for a nice lens anyway), and you'll always have a sharp, fast lens in your bag when you need it.

A Fast 135mm Portrait Lens

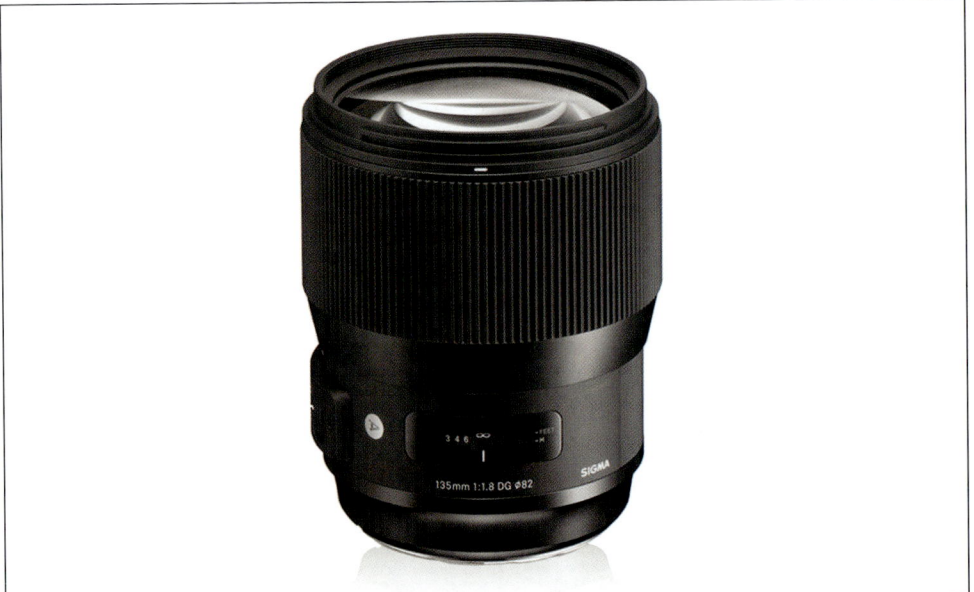

You now know that my two go-to lenses for portraits are the 70–200mm f/2.8 and the 85mm f/1.8, but there's another lens that's also quite popular with portrait shooters, so I wanted to include it here, as well, even though I don't use it myself. The 135mm lens is considered by some portrait photographers to be the absolute perfect focal length for portraits, and it's right in that flattering lens compression range (you don't see much visible difference in lens compression once you get above 135mm), so for some, it's just too perfect. The Canon 135mm f/2 is actually a good deal because it's f/2 (which is awesome for creating soft, creamy backgrounds), but it's only $999. If you're a Sony shooter, the Sony 135mm f/1.8 costs twice as much, just over $2,000, so you might want to consider the Sigma Art lens (shown above), which is also f.1/8 and really sharp, but it's more than $600 cheaper. They make one for Nikon too, for around the same price. Nikon makes their own, but it's kind of an old-school lens (it looks old school), so for the same price, I think I'd go with the newer Sigma Art lens.

Avoid Wide-Angle Lenses for Most Portraits

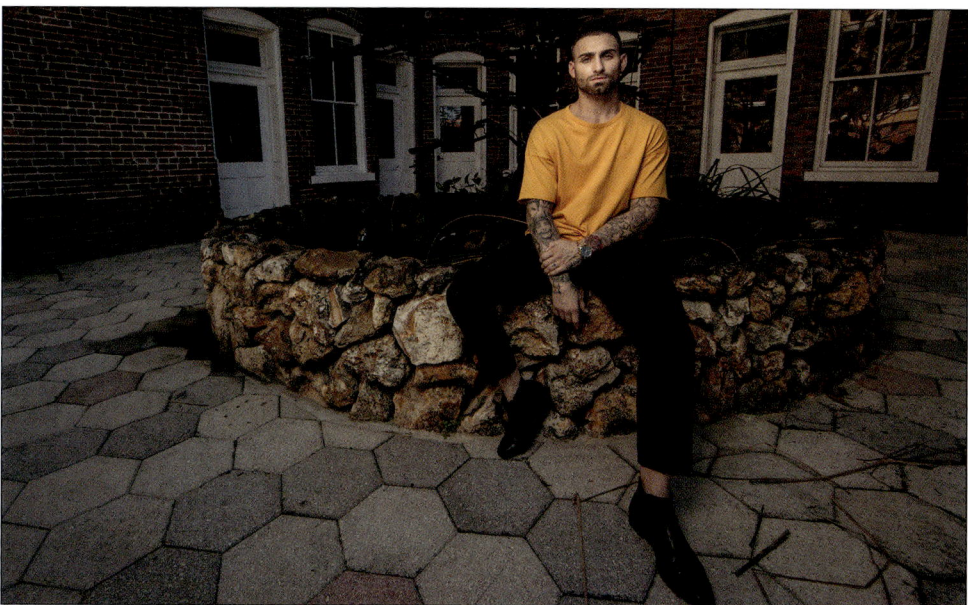

If your goal is to make people look their very best, I would tell you what I would tell a friend: avoid wide-angle lenses. They generally create distortion and people's faces usually don't look very good when they're distorted. Plus, if any part of your subject gets near the edges of the image, those parts will get elongated (like the subject's foot above), so you pretty much have to get your subject right in the center of the frame. That's why I recommend sticking with telephoto or longer zoom lenses (think at least 85mm or longer) for more flattering results. Now, you might have instances where you need a wide-angle lens, like when you're doing an environmental portrait where the location is important to the overall picture. For example, if you were shooting a portrait of a NASCAR driver, posing in front of their car, it might be important to the story to include the car, and maybe even the track. So, in that case, you might need to go with a wide-angle lens. You're doing this knowing that the overall scene and story is as important as the subject, and what you're giving up in a more flattering rendition of their facial features, you're getting back in showing an epic and bigger scene that takes it all in. Just remember, as I mentioned, the distortion is worse at the edges of the frame, so if you need to shoot a portrait with a wide-angle lens, try to keep your subject, and all their limbs, as close to the center of the frame as possible to keep from exaggerating those body parts.

Should You Ever Shoot Portraits with a Wide-Angle Lens?

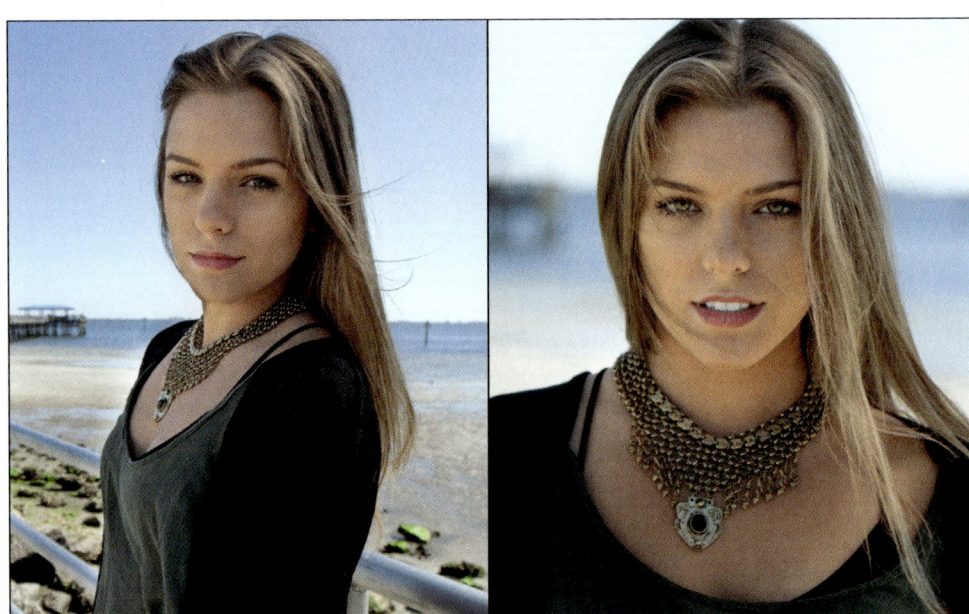

Now, there are photographers out there who are very successful shooting portraits with a wide-angle lens, and they choose to shoot wide angle because they're after a very specific look. That being said, these photographers are definitely more advanced in their portrait skills, so they know the rules (using longer lenses, which are considered "portrait lenses," will give you more flattering results), but they are intentionally breaking these rules to get the specific look they're after. They fully understand the limitations of shooting wide-angle portraits and they work within them. Now, you may come to a point where you want to break the rules as well, but I hope that's after you've mastered shooting with longer, more flattering lenses first. That way, you're breaking the rules because you know the rules, and need to break them to achieve a look—not because you don't know any better. I see lots of pretty horrible portraits taken by people who never mastered the longer lenses—they don't know what they don't know—and it shows in their images. Take a look at the images above. The shot on the left was taken with a wide-angle lens. The shot on the right is the same subject, taken moments later at the same location, but with a longer, more flattering lens. The shot on the left isn't terrible, and the subject doesn't look awful, but it doesn't look as flattering as the one shot with a more flattering lens (an actual portrait-length lens). Don't fall into that trap—stick with the longer, more flattering lenses for now, and then down the road, you can decide if you want to take that wide-angle fork in the road or not.

Why I Avoid 50mm Lenses for Close-Up Portraits

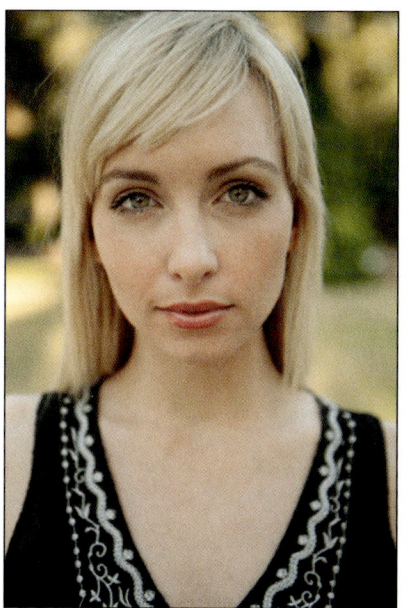

50mm at f/2.8

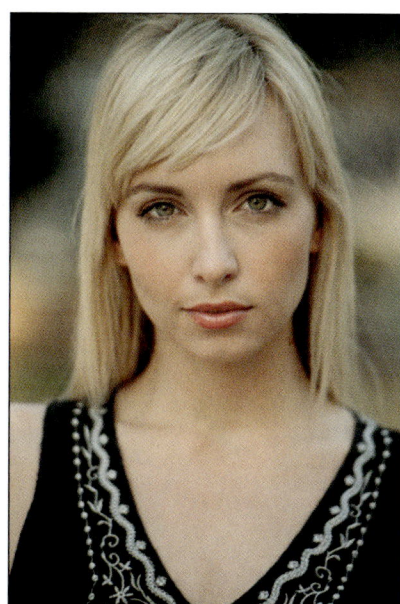

200mm at f/2.8

The 50mm lenses are handy if you're doing full-length fashion, but if it's a headshot, or head and shoulders, or anything the least bit close in, the distortion those lenses create is not at all flattering to your subject (see above—the only thing I changed was the lens). I get that people are drawn to a 50mm lens—you can get an f/1.8 for around $100 to $125, which is insanely low for a sharp, fast lens you can shoot in low light and/or put the background out of focus. However, to get the background out of focus with a 50mm, you have to get fairly close to your subject, which means you'll have some unflattering facial distortion (again, see above left). You'll find plenty of photographers on the web (myself included) telling you not to shoot portraits with a 50mm. But, it's the Internet, right? So, you'll find differing opinions, including YouTube videos, like "Why You Need a 50mm Lens for Portraits." Here are a couple things to consider: (1) Often, the photographers I see shooting 50mm portraits are actually street photographers, and they've got great 50mm shots of an old man in the park with rough, weather-worn skin. This is more like documentary-style portraiture; it's not about making a flattering portrait. These type of shots do look cool, but shooting that style takes a lot of practice and lots of post-production. (2) On the other side of the coin, 50mm lenses have a particular look to them. There are photographers who love that look, and they've learned how to get good results. So, would I recommend to a friend to shoot portraits with a 50mm? No, I would not. Because of the lens distortion, it's more challenging to get a flattering portrait—but it can be done. Here's what I want you to consider: While you'll find lots of pro photographers warning you not to use a 50mm lens for portraits, you won't find any telling you not to use an 85mm or longer lens for portraits. That speaks volumes. Those longer lenses are referred to as "portrait lenses" for a reason.

Yes, You Need That Lens Hood

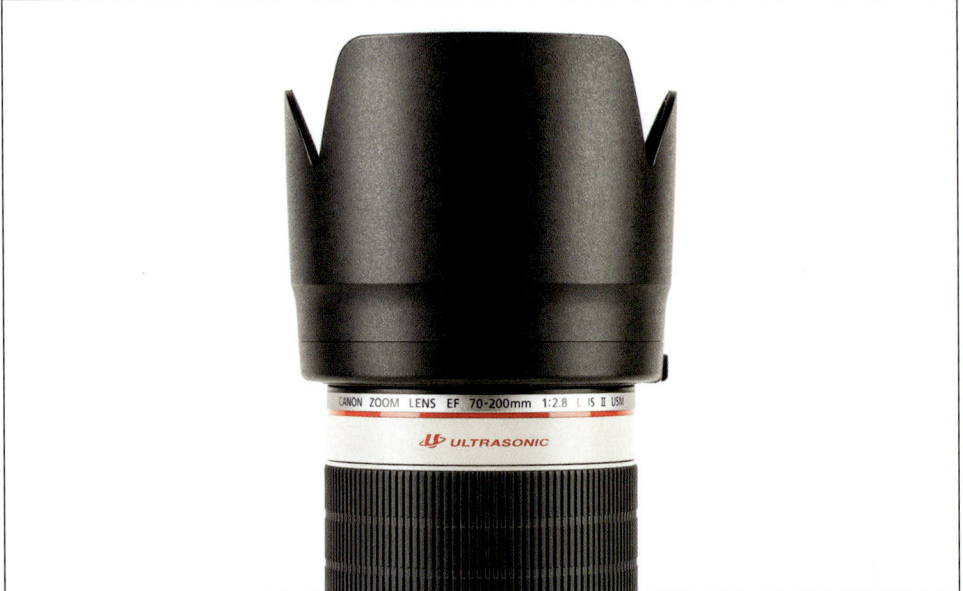

There are three reasons why you want to use that lens hood that came with your lens: (1) It's actually specially designed for your lens to reduce the lens flare that we're likely to encounter while shooting portraits outdoors. Lens flare is bad for all sorts of reasons, like putting big color rings over part of your photo, but one of the biggies is that you lose overall contrast in your portrait. So, the lens hood helps big time in reducing lens flare, which is good. (2) It protects your lens from getting scratched. That hood has kept the face of my lens from getting scratched more times than I can count, so I always leave it on. And, (3) it looks cool. I'm sorry, but it does. You put a lens hood on a 70–200mm and it makes the lens look so much longer that other photographers instinctively step out of your way and let you pass right by. Admittedly, this last reason probably only pertains to guys, so if you're a woman reading this and you're shaking your head and thinking, "Guys. Pssfft!" I can't say you're not right.

It's These Three Things That Create Soft Backgrounds

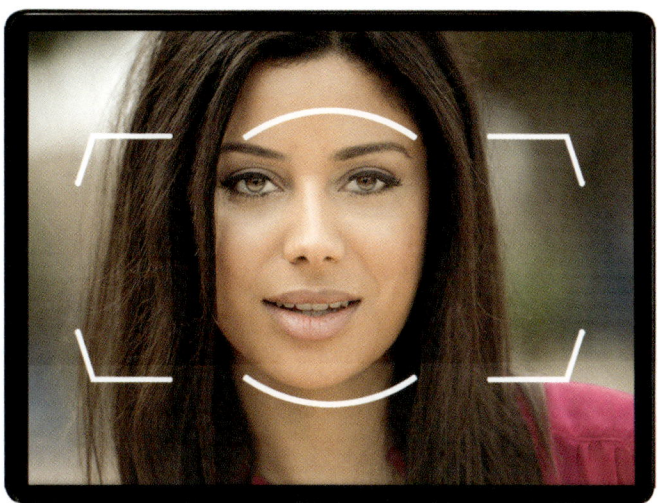

It's not just the f-stop, it's getting in tight on your subject, getting them away from the background, *and* the f-stop. In fact, if I had to choose between zooming in tight or using a low-numbered f-stop to create a soft, blurry background, I'd go with the zooming. Here's why: I can take a zoom lens, zoom in tight on my subject at f/5.6 or f/6.3, and still get a nice soft background, as long as the background they're standing in front of isn't right up against my subject. Now, if I'm not zoomed in relatively tight on my subject, and I used an f-stop of f/2.8, even with that low f-stop, the background would only be minimally out of focus, if at all. It's the combination of zooming in on your subject, getting as much space between them and the background as you can, and the low-numbered f-stop that gives you that awesome out-of-focus background that creates the separation of your subject from the background (the farther they are from the background, the more separation you'll get).

Minimum Focusing Distance

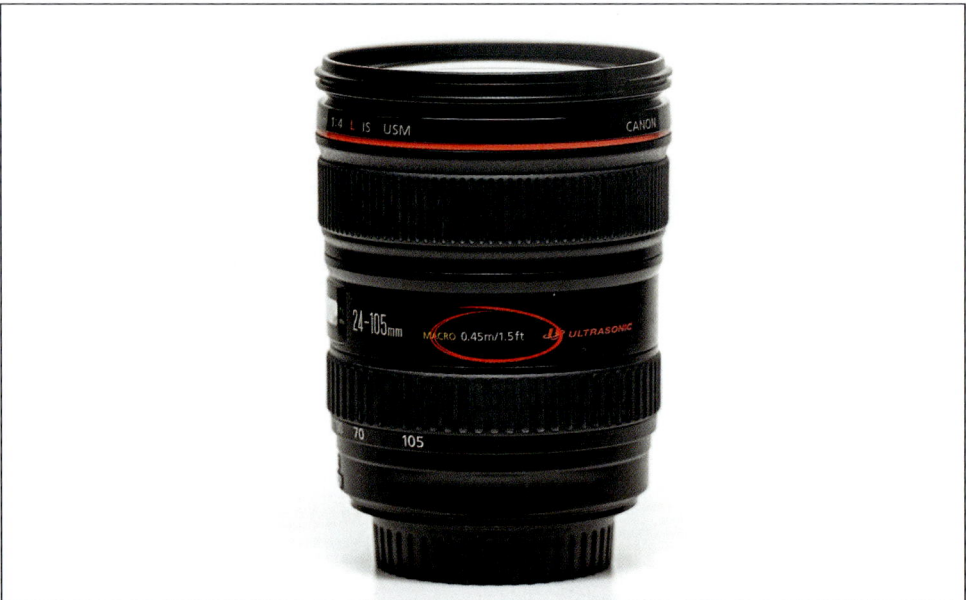

If you go to shoot a portrait and your lens won't focus, it's probably because you're standing so close to your subject that your lens can't focus. Lenses have a thing called Minimum Focusing Distance, and if your lens won't focus, it means that you're trying to shoot inside that Minimum Focusing Distance range so it can't focus. Just step back a couple feet, and then zoom in to get the same basic composition (this is why I like a zoom lens so much). How do you find out what your Minimum Focusing Distance is? Sometimes it's printed right on the barrel of your lens (as seen above), or right on the front where you would screw a filter onto it (you might see something like "1.5 ft" — that's telling you the Minimum Focusing Distance). Interesting, semi-weird tidbit: You'd assume that the measurement is taken from the end of your lens, right? Nope. That would be too easy. Too obvious. It's taken from the focal plane of your camera body, and that spot where it's measured from is usually marked right on the body of your camera, using a straight line with a circle in the center. That's the focal plane they measure the distance from. Go figure. Well, now ya know.

How Lens Choice Affects Your Background

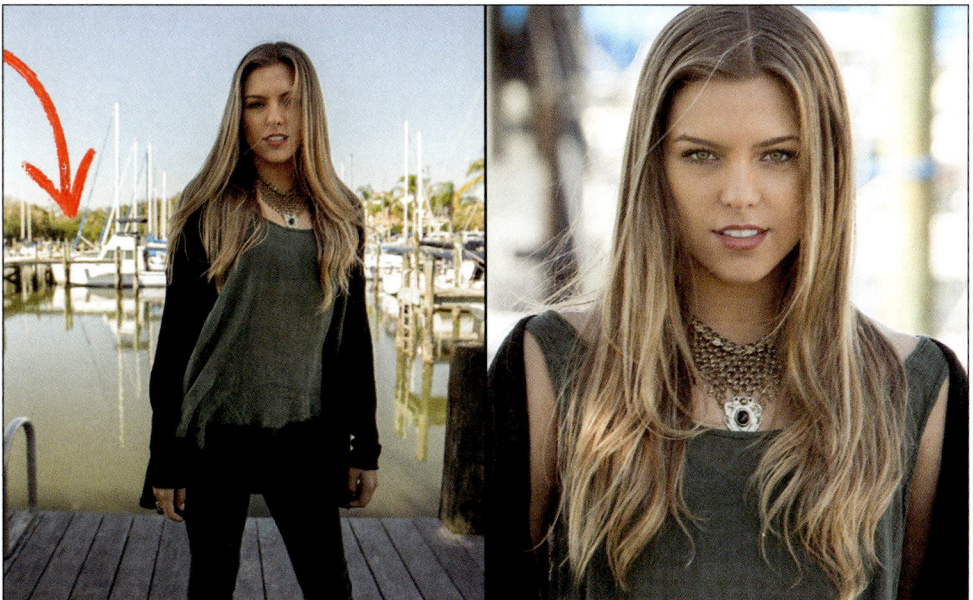

You've heard me talk about lens compression and how flattering that is for portraits, but lens compression actually affects more than people's faces—it affects how your background is rendered in the shot. For example, when you use a wide-angle lens—let's say a 24mm lens (the shot you see above left)—it pushes the scene away, so the background behind your subject looks farther away in the photo than it actually is in real life. That's great when you want to make a scene look big and epic—you're making a scene look bigger than it really is. Now, if you were to change lenses to a long telephoto or zoom lens (like I did here, where I switched to a 70–200mm), and not change any of your camera settings, and you zoomed in tight on your subject, the background would not only appear out of focus, it would appear much, much closer to your subject, like it was right behind them (like you see above right). So, think about this: When you reach into your bag to choose a lens, you're actually making a big composition decision. You're pretty much deciding whether your background will be in focus and farther away from your subject, or out of focus and closer to your subject. Choose wisely, young Padawan.

Shoot 'Em at What You Bought 'Em For!

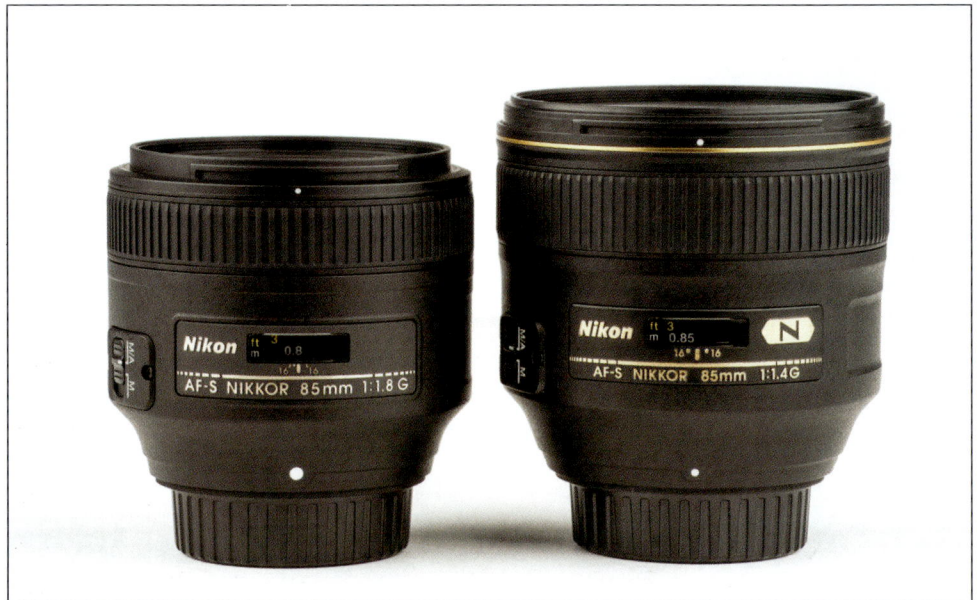

Like I mentioned earlier in this chapter, fast lenses (lenses that have really low-numbered f-stops, like f/2.8, f/2, f/1.8, and lower) are expensive, and if you're going to be spending that kind of money, shoot them at the f-stop you bought them for or you're wasting your money. If you bought an 85mm f/1.8, and you find yourself shooting at f/4 or f/5.6 or f/11 or any f-stop other than f/1.8, you're missing the entire reason you bought that lens. Every lens you already own has f/5.6, and f/8, and f/11. For portraits, use the f-stop you bought the lens for, and you'll get the best effect that lens can deliver.

Should You Buy a Lens with IS or VR? Well, That Depends

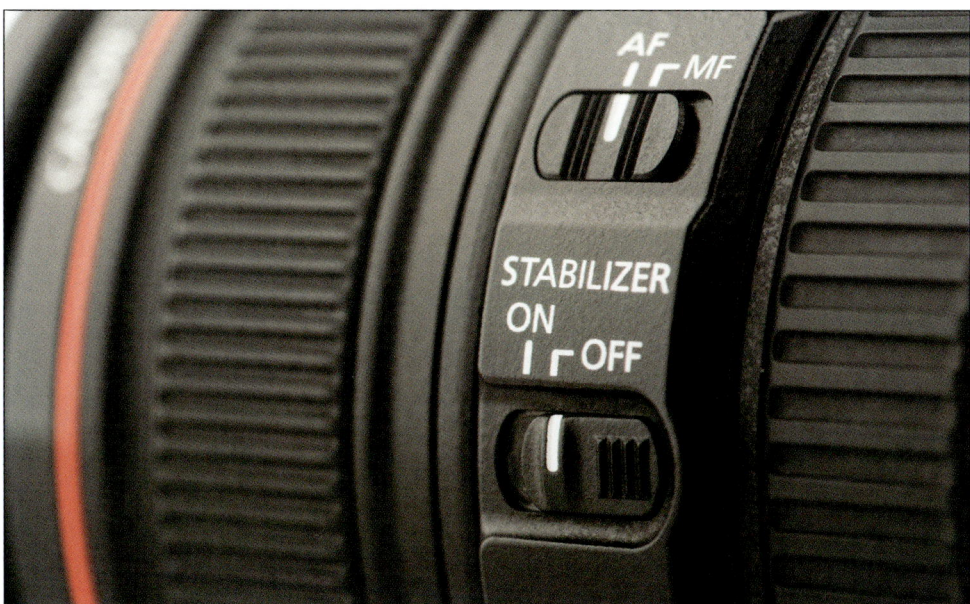

When you're looking at lenses, you'll notice that many of them have either IS (Image Stabilization) or VR (Vibration Reduction) built right into the lens. You'll also notice when you're shopping that lenses with these features built-in cost more, but it might be worth it depending on where you shoot your natural light portraits. If you find you shoot a lot at sunrise, sunset, or in low-light situations, this is when IS and VR actually help. They don't help if you're shooting out in the middle of the day with shutter speeds over 1/500 of a second because you don't need image stabilization with those fast shutter speeds. Where you need IS or VR is when you're in a low-light situation, which means your shutter speeds get really slow, like 1/30 of a second, or 1/8, or even slower. In those situations, IS or VR helps stabilize your lens so you don't get camera shake, which gives you blurry photos. So, in short, they help in low-light situations, and if your lens has IS or VR, you should definitely turn it on in those situations. If you don't shoot in low-light, you won't need IS or VR, and you can save yourself enough money to probably buy another lens. Think about the type of portrait shooting you do, and you'll know if IS or VR is something you need to pay for or not.

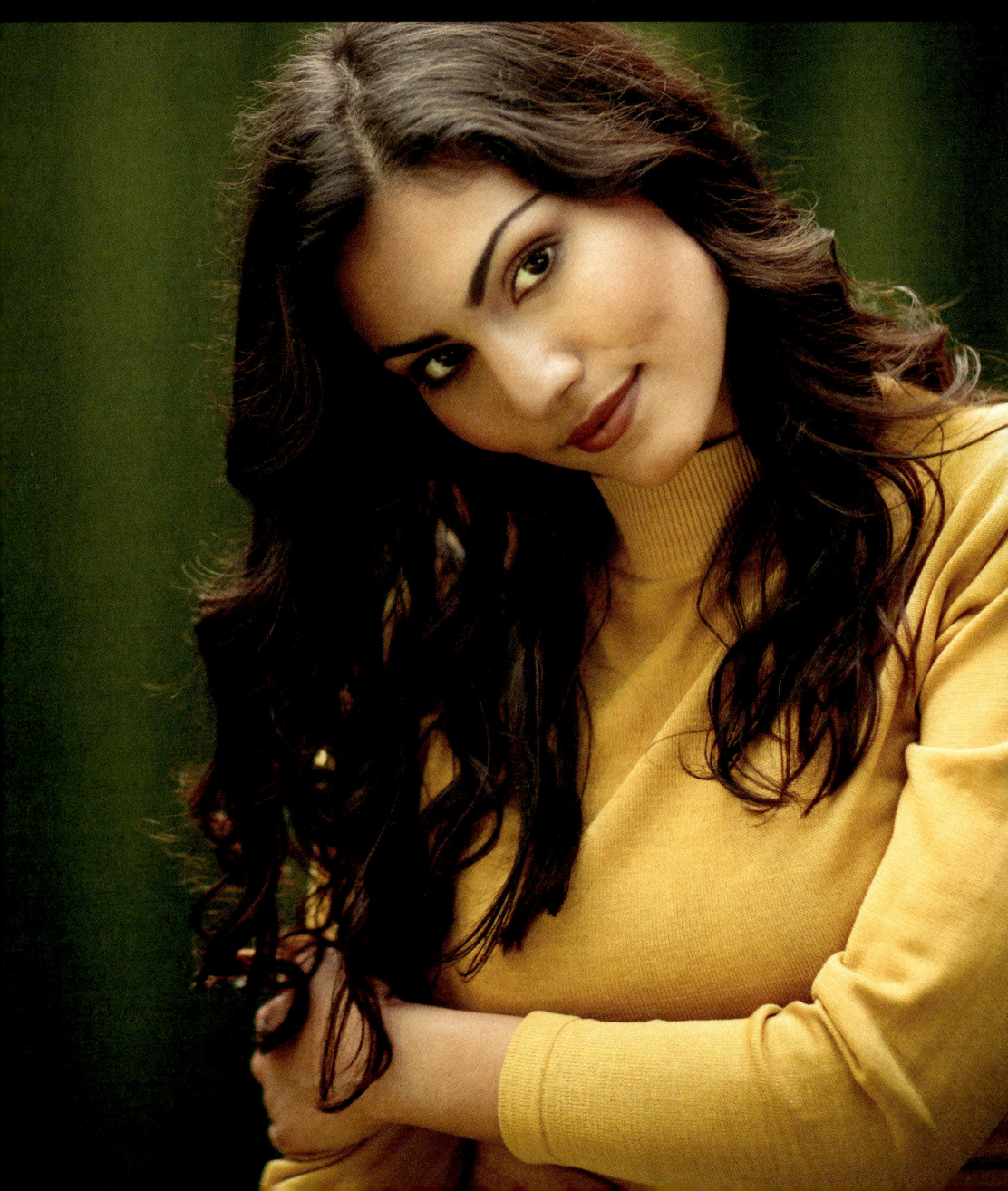

Chapter Two

Camera Settings

F-Stop, Shutter Speed & ISO

If you're struggling with the technical stuff when you're shooting, you're not alone. For what's supposed to be a really artistic pursuit, it's amazing how many technical things, like aperture, shutter speed, ISO, and thermal velocity all play a critical role in making a simple picture. This is definitely one of those left brain/right brain type of things, and here's how that translates to photography: If you're a right brain type of thinker, that generally means you're more a creative person, and probably have a highly developed emotional intelligence. You're capable of a wide range of expression, and you most likely have a great imagination, as well. If you're more of a left brain type of thinker, it means you're probably dehydrated, and you often shoplift items you don't really need. You're sophisticated, yet shockingly unkempt. You're cruel to small animals, and have surprisingly brittle bones. You lack an inner monologue, but you make up for it by raising wild boar. You're a dilettante, a debutante, and you display an alarming lack of purity, but your greatest failing may be your inability to sit through the entirety of the movie *The Lord of the Rings: The Return of the King.* Is it any wonder you struggle with adjusting the terminal velocity of your camera? (Spoiler alert: It's that button on the back of your camera with a lightning bolt icon on it. Hold it down for three seconds or so, until you see a lightning bolt icon flashing in your viewfinder, then rotate the C30 relay knob 30° until you hear a loud click. Fill the brew gasket, but don't let it overflow or you'll overheat the internal whisk. Lastly, adjust the flow to the filter pod until the end of the film catches the spindle.) Now you're thinking like a right-brainer there, Bunky! I'm sorry, what were we talking about?

Shoot with Your Camera Set to RAW Format

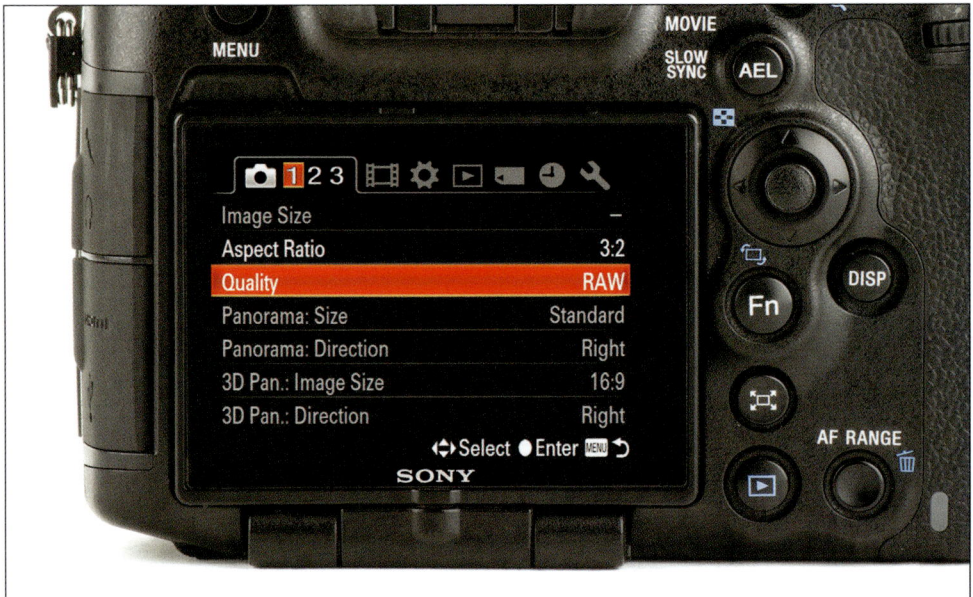

You're probably already doing this, but if you're not, now is your chance to switch off JPEG and start shooting in RAW format. It's a higher-quality format that captures a wider tonal range. It's much more forgiving if you make any mistakes with exposure or white balance, and you'll wind up with better-looking images even if you messed up when you took the shot. You'll have less clipping of the highlights in your image, and your original RAW image will always be protected (you don't ever wind up editing the original by accident, like you can with a JPEG file). There are a ton of advantages and very little downside, which is that your file sizes will be larger when you shoot in RAW, so your memory card will fill up a bit quicker.

Choosing Your Shooting Mode

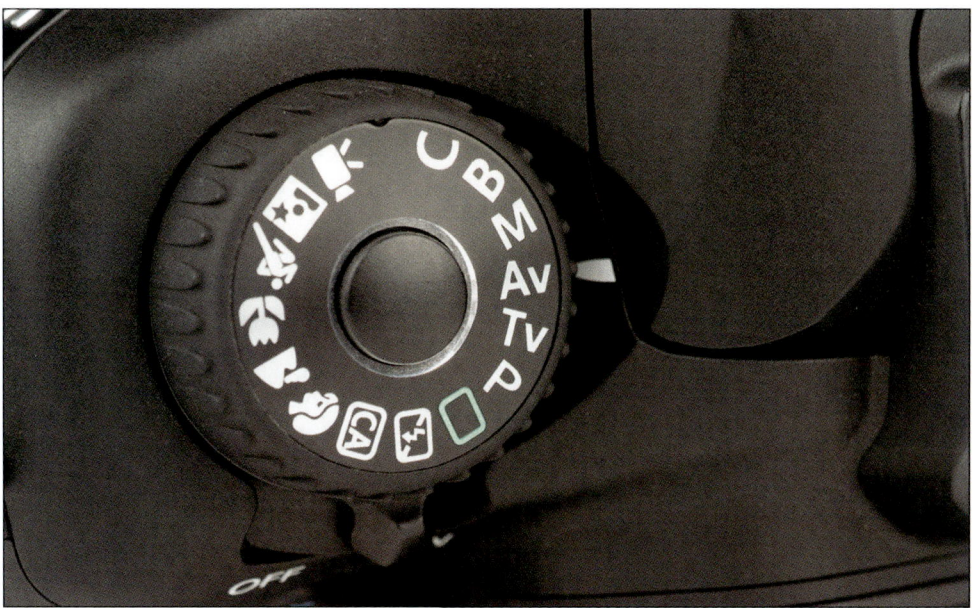

For me, this is an easy decision because I shoot all my natural light portraits in aperture priority mode. On most cameras that appears as "Av" or "A" on the mode dial, and I totally recommend it for natural light portrait shooting. Here's why: What Av mode does is it lets me choose my f-stop (which for portraits is a key decision), and then the camera will automatically choose the right shutter speed for me to get a proper exposure. It limits me having to think so much about the camera settings, so I can focus on working with my subject. I choose my f-stop and forget about everything else, so I'm not futzing with dials or settings during the shoot. Highly recommend shooting in aperture priority mode.

Which Aperture (F-Stop) to Use

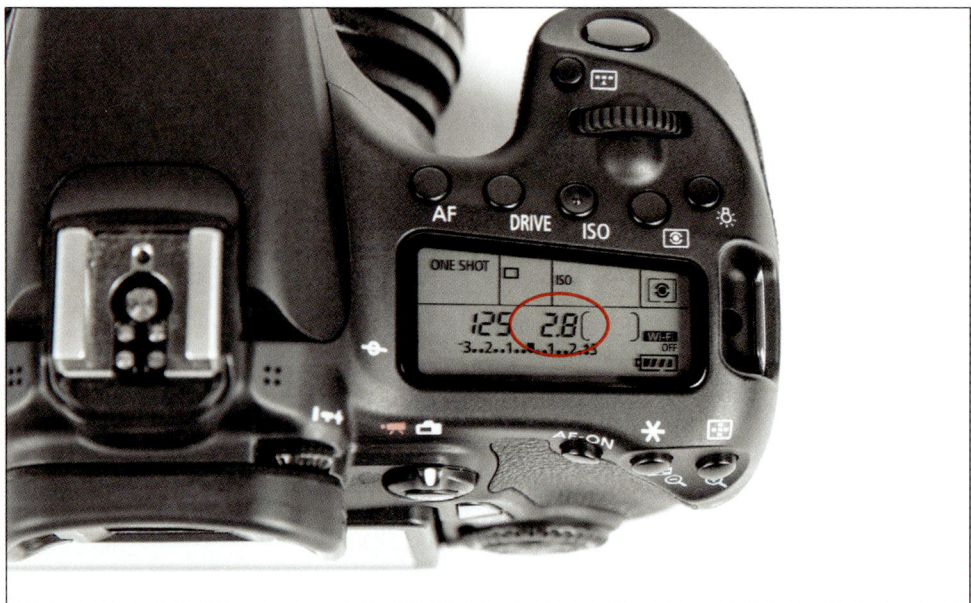

For natural light portraits, this is a pretty easy choice—I use the lowest numbered f-stop my lens will allow. So, if the lowest number my lens will allow me to use is f/4, that's what I use. Using the lowest numbered f-stop like this will help create that separation from the background by giving you that out-of-focus background that you generally want in natural light portraits. Plus, these low-numbered f-stops allow more light in the camera, and help a lot when you're shooting in the shade, or under a tree, or in any low-light situation. So, when I'm shooting natural light portraits with my 70–200mm f/2.8, for my f-stop, I choose f/2.8. If I'm shooting my 85mm f/1.8, I shoot it at f/1.8. It's an easy choice.

Why Your Shutter Speed Is Important

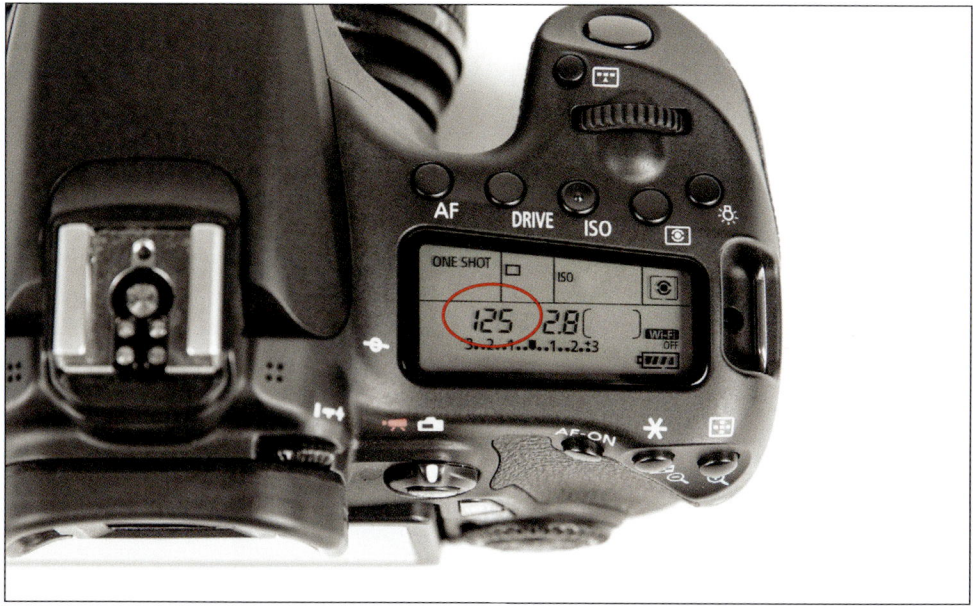

As I mentioned earlier, I don't set my shutter speed—the camera does it for me, once I choose my f-stop—but I do keep an eye on the shutter speed for one simple reason: if my shutter speed gets too low, I'm going to wind up with some out-of-focus photos. Okay, so how low is "too low?" I can usually hand-hold my camera pretty steady as long as my shutter speed is 1/60 of a second or faster. To be quite honest, I'd prefer 1/125 of a second or faster. At that speed, I can pretty much be sure my shot will be sharp and in focus, and if I'm shooting in bright light, or in the middle of the day, my shutter speed usually won't be an issue. I'll look in the viewfinder at my shutter speed and it will be something like 1/2000 of a second, or even 1/4000 of a second, which means even if I don't hold the camera perfectly still while I'm shooting, the shutter is only open for such a short time that it really won't matter—the shots will still be sharp. However, as it gets later in the day and closer to sunset and the light gets darker, or if it starts to get really cloudy outside, my shutter speed will fall pretty dramatically. If I see it go below 1/60 of a second, I jump into action, and by that I mean I raise my ISO setting, which, in turn, raises my shutter speed for me because I'm shooting in aperture priority mode, which is another reason I love Av mode. So, I might go from 100 ISO to 400 ISO to get my shutter speed up over that 1/60 of a second mark to hopefully something like 1/125 of a second. Once I hit that, I know my shot will be sharp again. If I ignore it, there's a pretty good chance that my shot will be either a little soft or just downright out of focus.

How to Stop Worrying about Slow Shutter Speeds

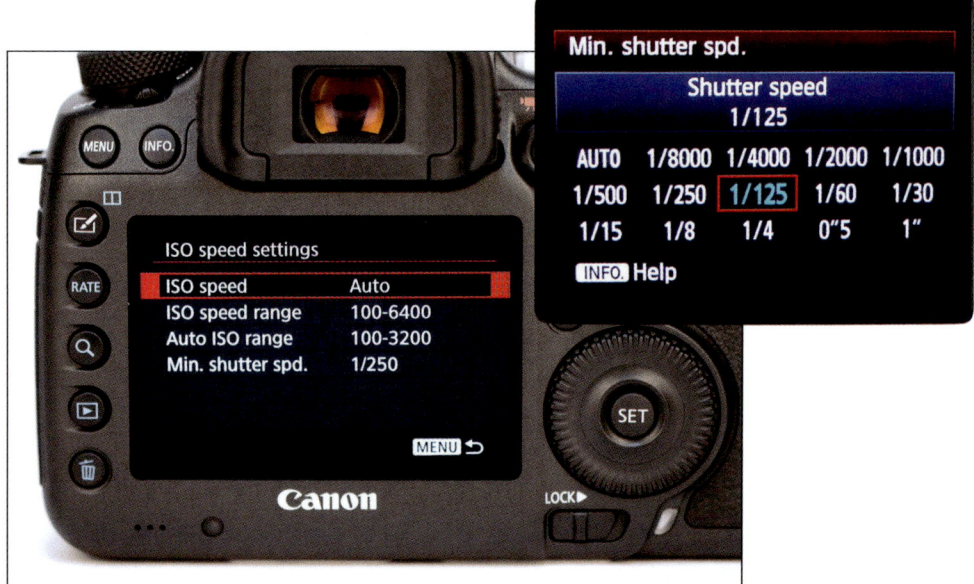

Okay, so on the previous page, I talked about having to keep an eye on my shutter speed, which I do, unless I turn on one of the greatest features ever for portrait photographers, and that is Auto ISO. What this little marvel of a menu command does is automatically raises your ISO to make sure your shutter speed doesn't fall below a minimum amount you choose. So, do you remember what shutter speed I ideally don't want to fall below? Right, 1/125 of a second! So, after I turn on my camera's Auto ISO setting, I then go into my camera's menu and set my Minimum Shutter Speed to 1/125 of a second. That way, no matter how low my shutter speed falls due to the lighting situation I'm shooting in (maybe I'm in the shade, or under a tree, or it's getting close to dusk), my camera will automatically cover my back by raising the ISO just enough to get me back up to that glorious 1/125 of a second, so I get a sharp shot no matter how dark it gets outside. It's important to note that raising the ISO, especially on some older cameras, is going to add some noise to your photos (higher ISO creates noise—those red, green, and blue dots and specks on your image, like we commonly had back in the film days). If you bought your camera in the past year or two, you'll probably hardly notice it, especially if you bought a full-frame or mirrorless camera, because they have much less noticeable noise. If you have a bit of an older camera, you might see a little noise, or even a lot if you're shooting in low light, but if you have the choice between a blurry photo or a sharp photo that's a little noisy, we'll take a little noise every time!

When to Shoot at Your Lowest ISO

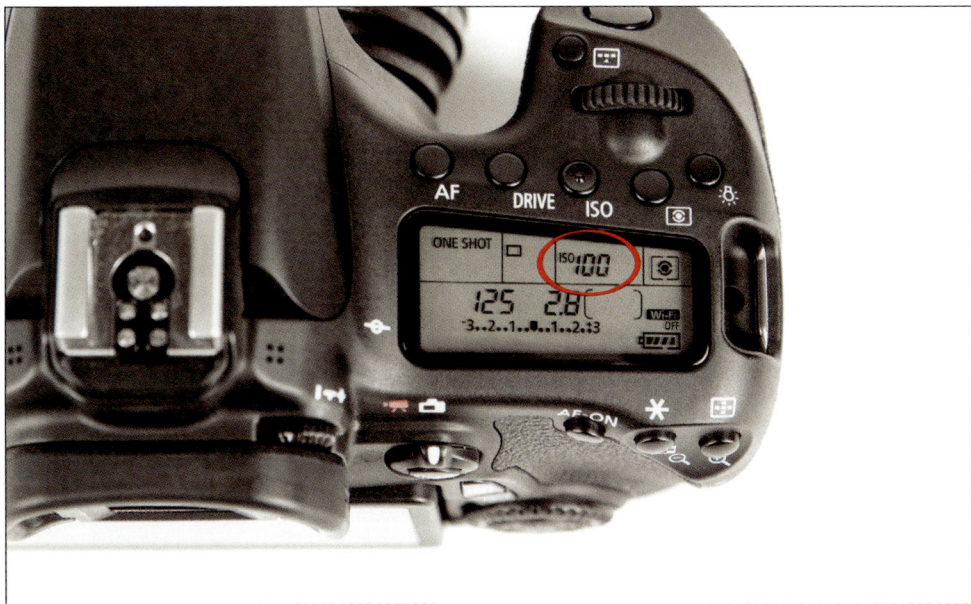

Now, if you're shooting in bright light, shutter speed won't be an issue, so you'll want to use the lowest, cleanest native ISO for your camera. The ISO where you'll have the lowest noise and, therefore, the cleanest image files. For most cameras, that will be 100 ISO, but it might be as low as 64 ISO or as high as 200 ISO on some older Nikons. The important thing is that you use the lowest number—not a letter and number, like "L01." If you're not shooting in bright light, and you need to use an ISO that will increase your shutter speed to a speed that will allow you to hand-hold and still get sharp shots, then go back to the previous page for how to set your camera to Auto ISO and let it choose the right ISO for you.

What If Your Camera Chooses the Wrong Exposure?

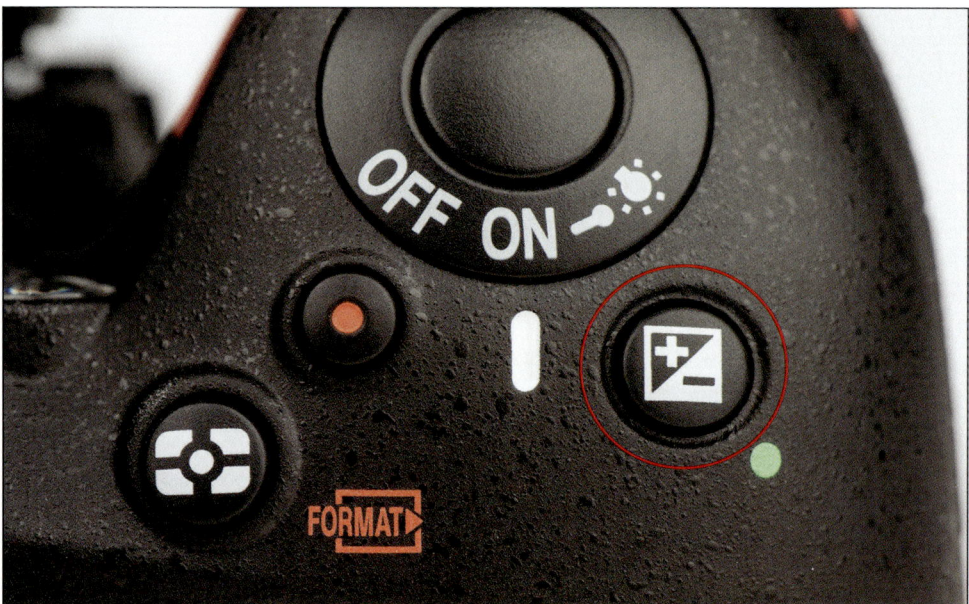

Hey, it happens. You're in aperture priority (Av or A) mode and you take the shot, you look at the screen on the back of your camera, and you don't agree with the exposure the camera thought was right. Maybe you think it's too dark, or it's overexposed, but whatever the issue is, it's easy to fix when you're in aperture priority mode thanks to a feature called "exposure compensation." For example, if you look at the shot and you think it's too dark, you can override what the camera thought was right and make it brighter, simply by turning a dial. Generally, they move in 1/3-stop increments, so if you think it needs to be a little brighter, you'd increase the exposure compensation by 1/3 and take another shot. Look at the back of the camera again, and if that's not bright enough, you'd increase it another 1/3 (so now it's 2/3 of a stop brighter) and take another test shot. If that wasn't enough, you'd go another 1/3 (so, at this point, you would have increased the brightness by a full stop), and so on. That's basically how it works. If you need to override what the camera thought was right, you'd make it brighter or darker using this exposure compensation feature.

How to Keep from Damaging Your Highlights

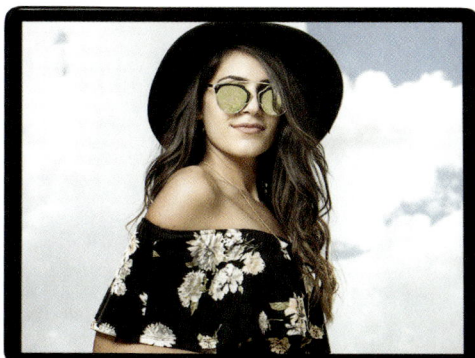 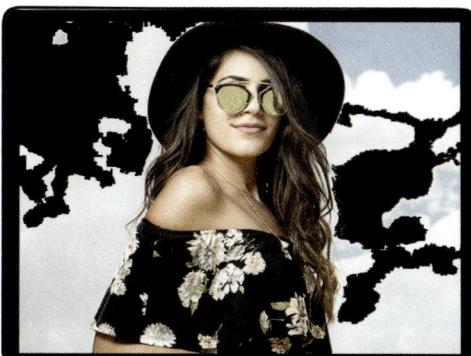

There is one big thing we need to look out for when shooting portraits, especially if we're outdoors, and that's blowing out the highlights (also known as "clipping the highlights" or just "clipping"). This occurs when something in your image gets so bright (like clouds, a white blouse, a wedding dress, etc.) it "blows out" the pixels, and you'll have no pixels in those areas, no detail, no nuthin.' Seriously. If you were to make a print of the image, there would literally be no ink on the paper in those blown-out areas. That's how bad an issue it is. So bad that there's a warning you can turn on (nearly every make and model of camera has it) called either Highlight Warning or Clipping Warning. When you turn this on, it shows you which areas in your image have gotten so bright that they're clipping (losing detail). Depending on your camera's make and model, you'll either see it when you view your image on the back of the camera or (like with some mirrorless cameras) beforehand. You'll either see the blown-out areas blink on/off like a strobe light, or on some mirrorless cameras, it displays a zebra-like, black-and-white pattern of lines over areas that are blown out. The first step is to turn the clipping warning on, and then if you see clipping after you've taken the shot (or before), all you have to do is darken your exposure. If you're in aperture priority mode, just use exposure compensation (see the previous page) to darken it by 1/3 of a stop, and then take a test shot to see if that did the trick. If it's still clipping, drop it another 1/3, take another test shot, and so on, until the "blinkies" go away. If you miss fixing it in-camera, both Lightroom and Photoshop's Camera Raw have a slider that can usually fix the problem: simply drag the Highlights slider to the left until the missing detail comes back.

Choosing the Right White Balance

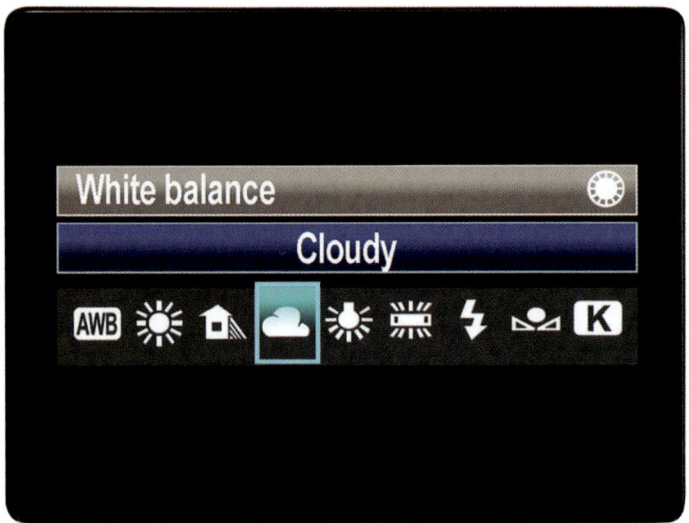

Can you change your white balance later in Lightroom or Photoshop? Absolutely. So, why would we worry about getting the white balance right in the camera? For two reasons: (1) it's one more thing you don't have to fix in Photoshop, and (2) you don't want to be doing a portrait shoot, looking at the image on the back of your camera, and seeing it doesn't look right—their skin is too blue or way too yellow. Yes, again, you know you can "fix it later in Photoshop," but it's not inspiring. It doesn't get you "in the zone" when you're looking at images that don't look right. Your subject isn't going to enjoy seeing it look wrong on the back of your camera either. They may not have the vision you do of how the final image will look, so it's not going to inspire them, during the shoot, and what's sad about it is how easy it is to get it right in the camera. How easy is it? Just look up. If you see clouds above you, switch your white balance to Cloudy. If you look up and see you're standing in the shade, choose Shade. If you're in an office and you look up and see fluorescent lights, choose Fluorescent. If you're in a home, or a restaurant, or a store, chose Tungsten. If you see the sun, choose Daylight. Yes, it's that easy, and it makes a bigger difference than you'd think.

How to Focus for Sharp Portraits

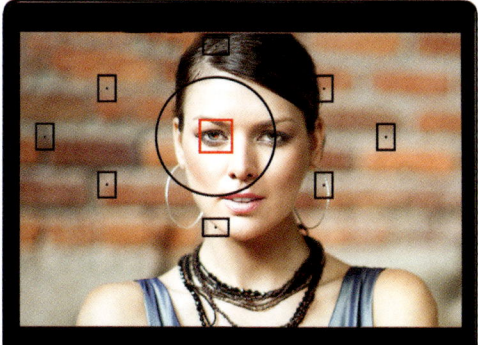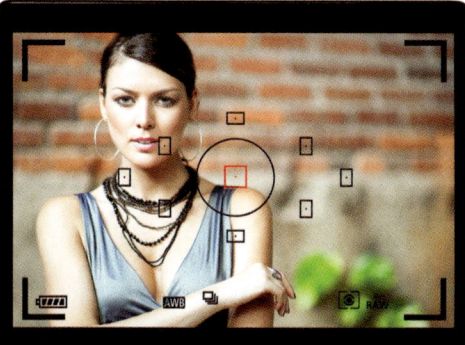

When we're shooting with lenses that are at f/2.8 or above, we have a very simple rou-tine for ensuring super-sharp portraits. You start by looking through your viewfinder, and then you aim the center dot and position it right over your subject's eye (as seen above left). Then, press the shutter button on your camera halfway down to lock your focus on your subject's eye. Now that you know your subject's eyes will be in focus (which is the most critical thing to be in sharp focus in a portrait), while still holding that shutter button halfway down, you can recompose the shot, putting the subject right where you want them in the frame (as seen above right). When you're ready to take the shot, just press the shutter button the rest of the way down. During all this, the focus never changed—by holding that shutter button halfway down, you kept the focus locked on your subject's eye. This technique (often referred to as "focus and compose") works great for lenses that are f/2.8 or slower (like f/4, f/5.6, etc.), but if you're shooting at a wider open f-stop (like f/1.8 or faster), then we use a different technique (and it's more critical that you do it right with those super-fast lenses). That's covered on the next page.

How to Focus f/1.8 Lenses or Faster

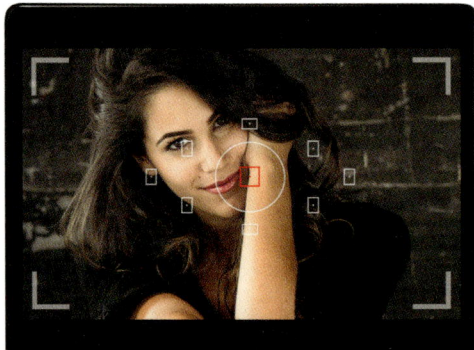 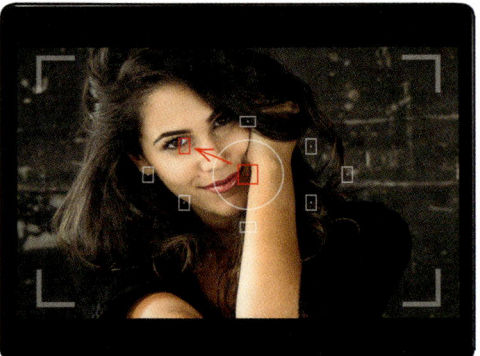

Focusing is a totally different technique with f/1.8, f/1.4, and f/1.2 lenses, and if you don't use it, since the depth of field is so shallow with these super-fast lenses, you'll wind up with a ton of out-of-focus shots, and if you want to use these types of lenses, that would be a shame. The technique is pretty much the opposite of the technique you just learned on the previous page (the one you use for regular lenses). In this case, you'll need to turn off your camera's multi-point focusing feature (it's usually on by default) and choose single-point focusing mode because you need to choose the focus point manually. Once you've switched to the single-point focusing mode, start by composing the shot. Look through the viewfinder and position your subject exactly where you want them in the frame (as seen above left). Now, use the joystick (or dial) on the back of your camera to manually move the focus point directly over their eye (as seen above right) and take the shot. That way, once you've composed the shot, the camera doesn't move—just the focus point—and that helps keep the shot in focus. It's important to note that with these super-fast lenses, you shouldn't expect all your shots to be in sharp focus. When you're dealing with such razor-thin areas that are in focus, you can't expect to nail every one of them—some are just going to be out of focus because of moving the camera while shooting. Also, if you're aiming the camera up or down at your subject (rather than straight on), it makes the shallow depth of field even more shallow. So, keep that in mind if you're getting a lot of out-of-focus shots.

Which Eye to Focus On

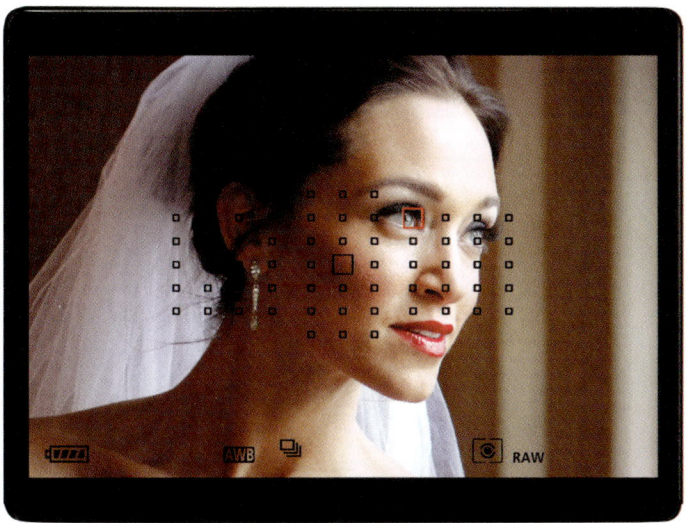

If they're not facing straight on to the camera, there's a simple guideline: always focus on the eye that's closest to the camera. Since that was short, here's a bonus tip: if your subject's face is obstructed for any reason (there's hair covering their eyes, or it's an athlete and their face is covered, or if they're wearing a mask, etc.), then you can focus on their chest. Their chest is roughly in line with their eyes, so this is your backup focal point if you can't get a clear view of their eyes.

Why the Eye Autofocus Feature Rocks

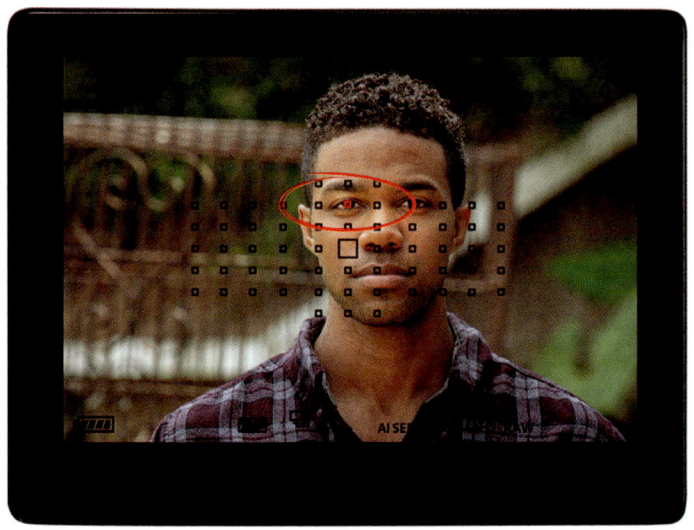

There's a feature, first made popular on Sony digital cameras, that's becoming more popular as the latest cameras from Sony, Nikon, and Canon now have it. It's an eye autofocus feature (also known as "Eye AF"). This feature is made for portrait photographers because it goes beyond the standard facial recognition feature that has been around for years, as it detects your subject's eyes and it focuses right on them for you automatically. The nice thing is, even though this technology is fairly new, it actually works amazingly well. This makes the job of getting sharp portraits so much easier, especially if you're using very wide-open f-stops, like f/1.8, f/1.4, or faster. The camera does all the work of nailing the most critical focus area in portraits for you. Again, this feature is only on newer cameras, so to see if your camera has the Eye AF feature, download the free PDF for your camera manual and use the find feature to search for the term "Auto Eye AF" or just "eye" in the PDF. If you get a hit, it's in your camera. If it doesn't come up, well, you'll be using the techniques back on pages 25 and 26.

Shooting Group Shots at Wide-Open F-Stops

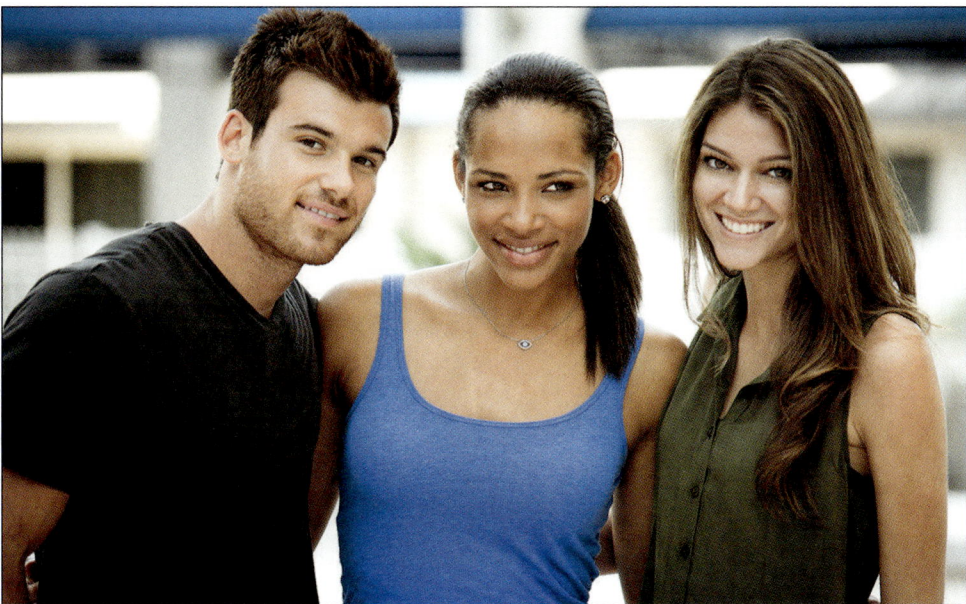

If you're shooting a group with a super-fast lens, the key to getting everybody in focus is to get everybody on the same plane. Everybody pretty much has to be in a straight row beside each other, with nobody behind, nobody in front—everybody on the same plane. That way, when you focus on the person's eyes in the center, everybody else's eyes will be in focus as well, since (say it with me now) they're all on the same plane.

Where to Focus for Multi-Row Group Shots

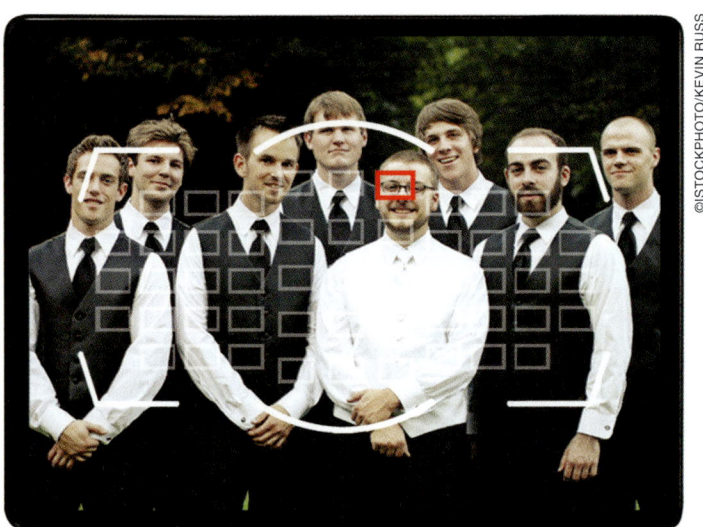

There's a simple rule for larger group shots: focus on the eyes of the people in the front row (not everybody's eyes—you have to pick one main person's eyes). It's important that the row closest to the camera is in focus, and that will give the overall appearance of the entire shot being in focus, even though the second and/or third rows won't be in as sharp a focus. When it comes to multi-row group shots, I tend to shoot a little less fast, so instead of shooting with my f-stop at f/2.8, like I would with one or two people, I'd shoot at something like f/5.6 to get a little wider depth of field for those folks in the second or third rows. If you really want to shoot at wide-open f-stops, like f/1.8 or f/1.4, you actually can—the trick is to get everyone to stand in a straight row, and all on the same plane, so across that single row, all their eyes are essentially the same distance from the camera (see the previous page for more on this).

Image Stabilization: On or Off?

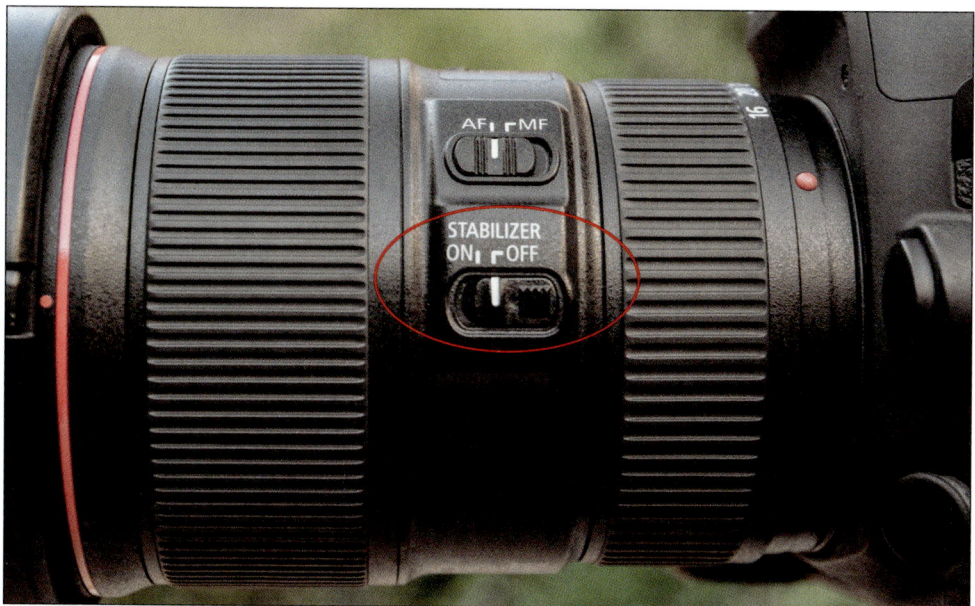

There's an easy rule about this one: if you're shooting on a tripod, turn it off. That's because it's designed for when we're hand-holding—it has a motor inside that detects movement, and if it finds movement, the motor stabilizes the lens. It works amazingly well when you're hand-holding. It works against you when you're on a tripod because that motor doesn't know you're on a tripod, so it keeps searching for movement even though there is none, but (get this) that searching causes (wait for it...wait for it...) a small amount of movement. Just enough to keep your images from being tack sharp. So, if you're on a tripod, turn IS or VR off. If you're hand-holding, turn it on. Easy peasy.

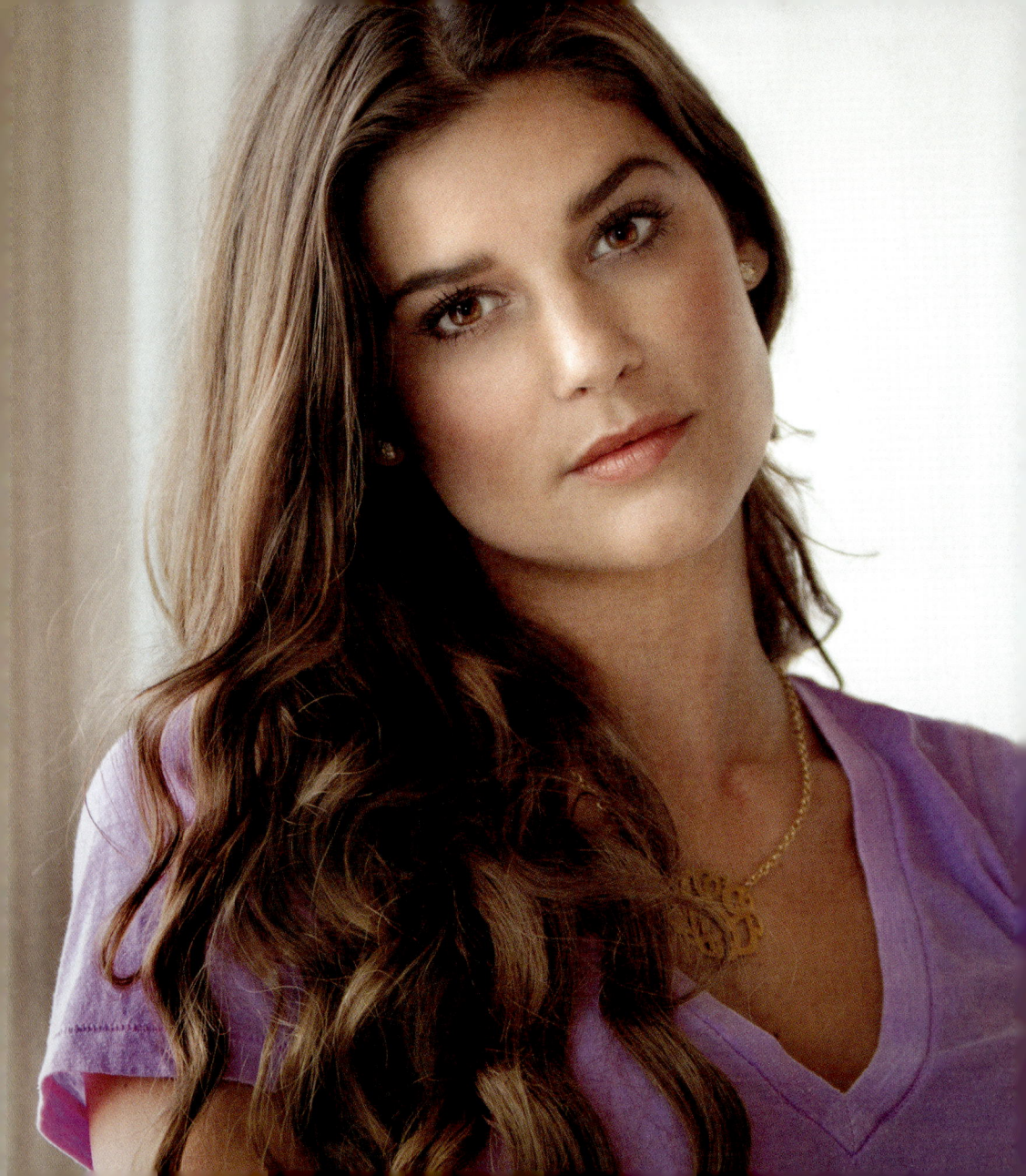

Chapter Three

Window Light Portraits

Working That Window Like a Dutch Master

As a photographer, even if you're pretty new to all this, I'll bet you've already heard that window light is the most beautiful light. But, in reality, that's not actually true. The whole window light myth started with the famous Dutch masters, Han and Chewy. But, it's not like a clear piece of glass is suddenly going to take sunlight and somehow mold it into soft, beautiful light. It's not the glass; it's the type of window. And, in my experience, there's only one type of window that works, and that would be (full disclosure: this is a paid endorsement) the energy efficient Renewal by Andersen® replacement windows, which offer the elegance, strength, and stability of wood, with the low-maintenance features of vinyl. Those are the only windows that produce the quality of light that was made famous by other Dutch masters, like Penn & Teller or Bartles & Jaymes, so if you want your images to look like that, you must buy Renewal by Andersen. Available at your local Lowe's or Home Depot. Evening appointments available by request. (Full disclosure: that was not actually a paid endorsement from Andersen because, seriously, why in the world would a window replacement company offer a paid endorsement opportunity to me when they could actually pay an endorsement to some of the living Dutch masters, like Mario & Luigi?) Anyway, the point is simple: there will come a time where you have to replace your windows, so why not buy windows that have the elegance, strength, and stability of wood, with the low-maintenance features of vinyl? Feel free to use my discount code for 15% off your next installation. That's all I'm saying. #windowdiscount

Why Direct Window Light Is Often Bad Light

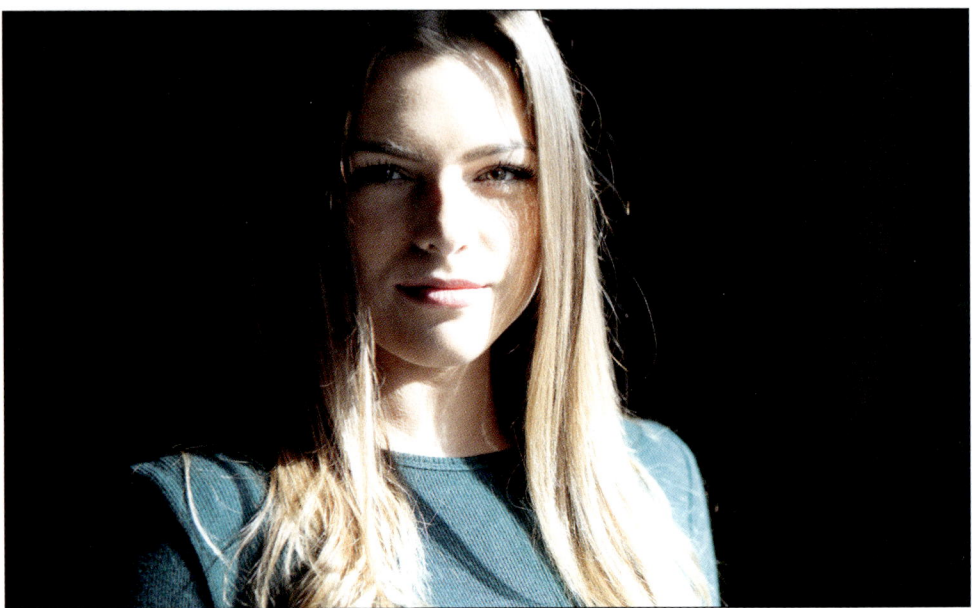

If you've ever been outside and looked up at the sun, you already know it's a pretty harsh source of light. When that harsh sunlight hits people you're trying to photograph, it's not pretty. You get squinting, and ugly, hard shadows on your subject's face, and it's mighty unflattering, to say the least. Now, what if you put a clear piece of glass between your subject and the sun? Well, sadly, that wouldn't change a dang thing, as harsh sunlight has no problem traveling right through that clear glass, and when it does, it's just as harsh and nasty as ever. This really throws a lot of photographers because you've probably heard for years that window light can be the most beautiful light for portraits. It's what the classic Dutch master artists from the 1600s used to light the subjects of their paintings, and their light was legendary, right? Right. But, that's because they did things to make the light from that window soft and beautiful. That's a lot of what this chapter teaches you—how to take that harsh, nasty sunlight and make it soft and beautiful—but it all starts with the understanding that window light, in most instances, is not soft, beautiful light. Once you understand that, and you understand that you are in charge of making the light from the sun soft and beautiful, you're on your way to some of the best-lit portraits you'll ever make.

Turn Off Any Room Lights

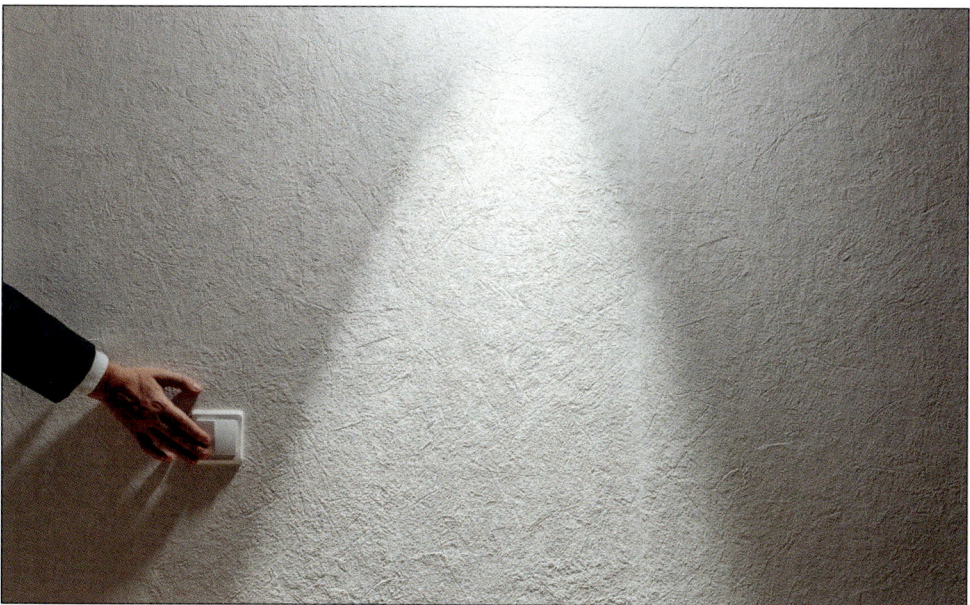

If you're shooting indoors, you want your subject to only be lit by the natural light in the room. So, to keep from having conflicting light sources, and multiple shadows, and different colors of light in your shot, go ahead and turn off any existing room lights or lamps. Having those mixed lighting sources can give you some real headaches that are often surprisingly hard to fix in post (that's short for "fixing in it Photoshop").

Move Away from the Window

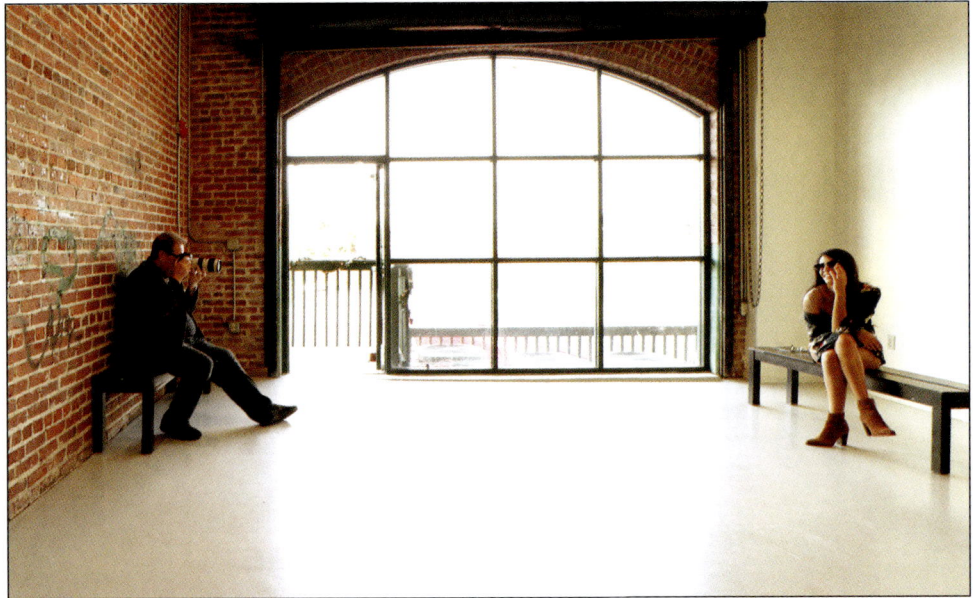

If you have harsh sunlight coming through the window, one quick and easy thing you can do to get much better quality light is to simply move your subject farther away from the window. When your subject is right up close to the window, they are getting the full force of the light. Harsh city (as I mentioned earlier). So, by simply moving your subject farther away from the light, that harshness trails off, and the farther you get from the window, the softer and more beautiful the light becomes. Start by moving around six feet away from the window, and then take a test shot. Really take a look at the shadows falling on your subject's face and make sure they're soft shadows. If they're still harsh, you're not far enough away from the window. As you move away from the window, the light from it gets softer and more beautiful, but it also gets darker (just like it does when you walk away from a room lamp—the farther you are from the lamp, the darker the light gets, right?). So, just keep an eye on your shutter speed, so it doesn't fall so low that you wind up with soft, beautifully-lit, but out-of-focus shots.

Move Behind a Window or Doorway

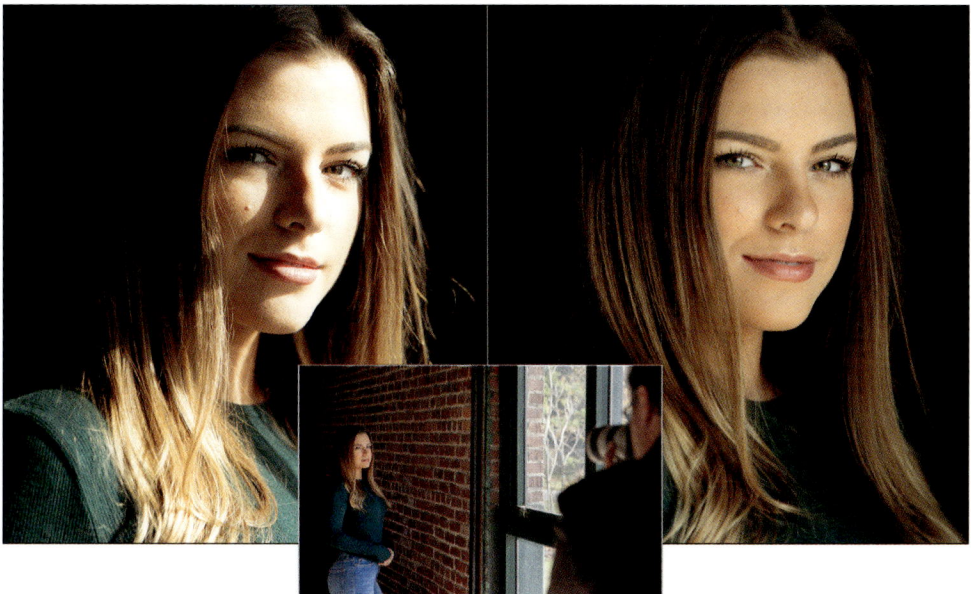

Depending on the room you're shooting in, you may not always be able to do this, but if you want even softer light than just moving away from the light, move your subject right behind the window or doorway (we'll talk more about doorways in a bit), so they're literally standing a few feet before the window even begins. Do that, and also move them a few feet back from the wall where the window is, and you've got some amazingly beautiful light. Take a look at the side-by-side examples above. The one on the left was taken with her right in front of the window. The image on the right was taken after repositioning her a few feet behind the window and a few feet back from the wall (as seen in the inset in the center). The difference in the quality of light is pretty dramatic. Remember, we're looking for soft shadows and beautiful, flattering light, and this is an easy way to get there—if you have room behind the window.

For the Love of North-Facing Windows

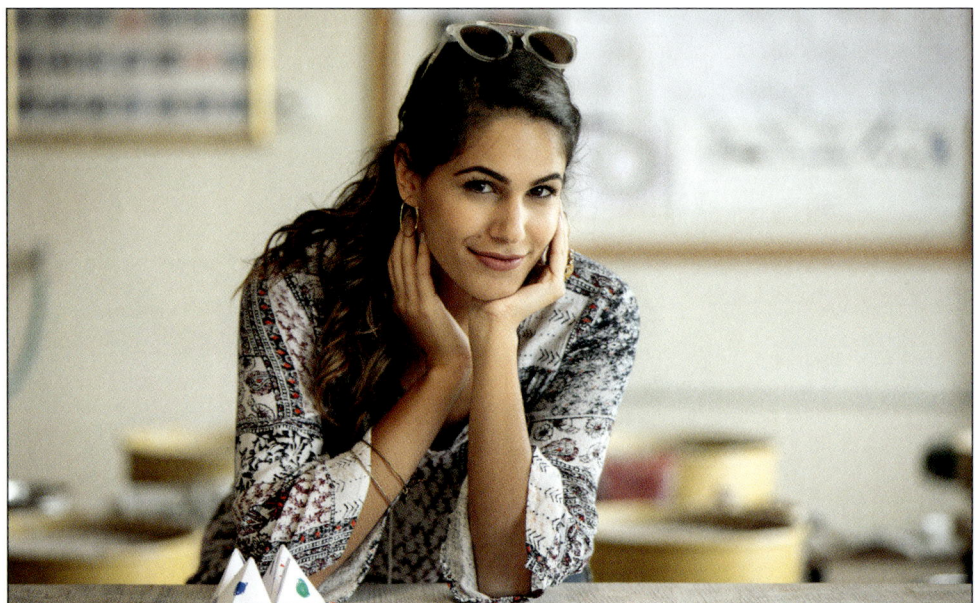

The holy grail of all window light is north-facing window light (well, at least it is in the Northern Hemisphere). This is the light the Dutch masters used to seek out because a big north-facing window doesn't have harsh sunlight directly beaming in. The light from it is soft and even. It's that beautiful window light we all dream of, but of course, the problem is finding a north-facing window (not everybody has one, and even if they do, it may not be in an ideal place for making portraits). Even after I find a north-facing window, I'm still keeping my subject six or more feet back from the window to get the softest, most-wrapping light possible (the large north-facing window in the shot above is to the right of my camera).

Use a Shower Curtain Liner

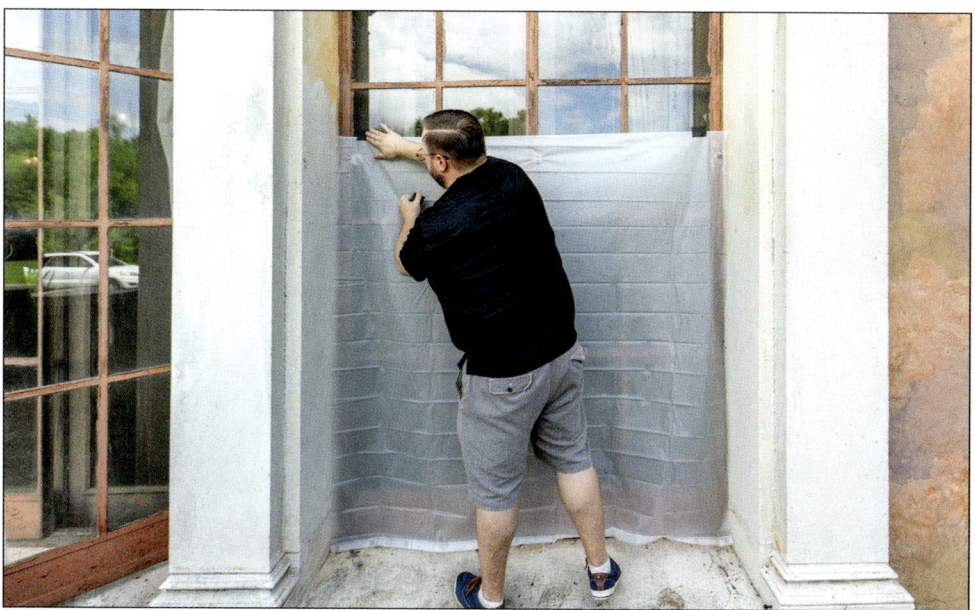

If you don't have north-facing window light to shoot with, then you can create your own big, beautiful light source from any large window by putting a frosted shower curtain liner over the window (as seen above, where we're using gaffer's tape on the outside of the house to cover the window with the shower curtain liner). These are very inexpensive (anywhere from $1.99 at Walmart to around $4.00 at Target)—just remember to get a shower curtain liner, not a shower curtain. By the way, we use gaffer's tape to attach the shower curtain liner to either the inside or outside window frame because when you remove gaffer's tape, it doesn't remove the paint or wallpaper like other tapes do—it pretty much comes right off without messing up the surface or leaving a sticky residue. It gets its name from Hollywood, where it was developed for use on movie and TV sets, and the stuff is like magic. You can pick up a roll cheap at B&H Photo, and you'll wind up using it for much more than just sticking up shower curtain liners. I recommend that every photographer keep a small roll in their camera bag—you'll wind up using it more than you'd ever dream, and it can save the day when you really need it.

Close the Sheers for Better Light

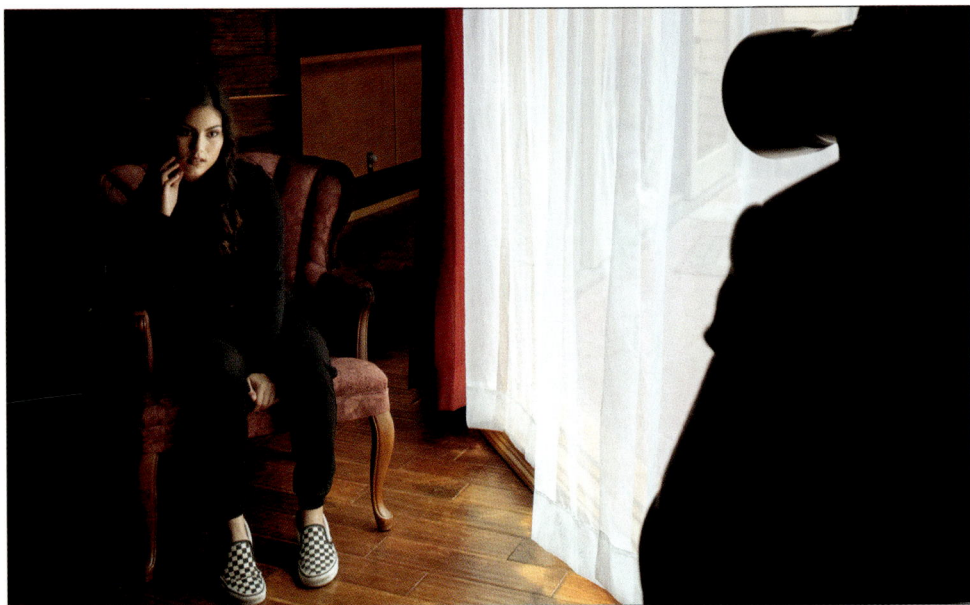

Unless you're shooting with a north-facing window, your challenge will usually be taming the light. But, it might not be much of a challenge at all if the windows you're shooting in front of have either sheers or a translucent shade. Either one of those will help soften and diffuse the light big time. So, if your windows have sheers or a shade, close 'em. Don't forget that doing this makes the light softer and more beautiful, but it also cuts the amount of light coming in, so keep an eye on your shutter speed (you don't want it falling to less than around 1/125 of a second. If it does fall lower, you'll either need to raise your ISO to get it back to around 1/125 or you can lower your f-stop. If you were using f/4, try f/2.8 to let more light in). If your lens won't go any faster, grab your faster lens (see page 3), or it's raise-the-ISO time because when it comes to hand-holding, a fast shutter speed can (and probably will) be the difference between a sharp shot and one that's a bit soft or even just plain out of focus.

How to Position Your Subject for a Window Light Portrait

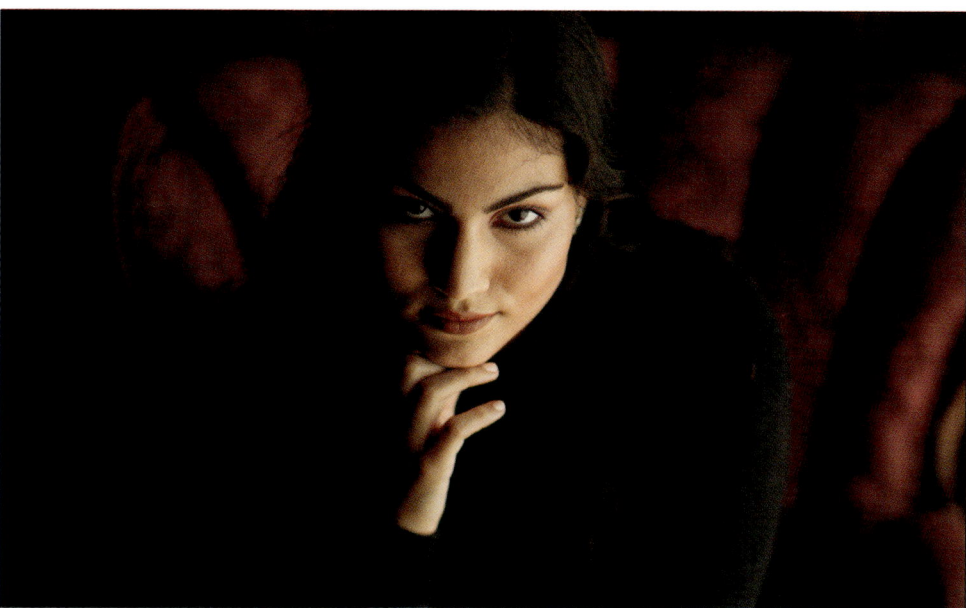

For most window light portraits, we don't have the subject facing directly toward the window (after all, if we did, we'd have to be standing outside to shoot them). Instead, we position them parallel to the window, so it is mostly side-lighting them. This usually creates a split-lighting look where half of their face is lit from the window and the other half is in shadows, which is great for movie posters, but not particularly awesome for everyday portraits. Ideally, we like to let some of the window light spill over to the other side of their face, and you can do that by simply having your subject turn their head a little bit toward the window. However, generally, what I prefer is to (1) have my subject turn their body away from the window, and then (2) turn their head back toward the window, so the light starts to fall on the shadow side of their face, and then (3) I have them look back toward the camera, mostly just moving their eyes and not their head too much. I'm usually standing closer to the window and shooting back toward my subject, and that shooting angle also helps you see a little more of the shadow side of their face.

Rembrandt Window Lighting

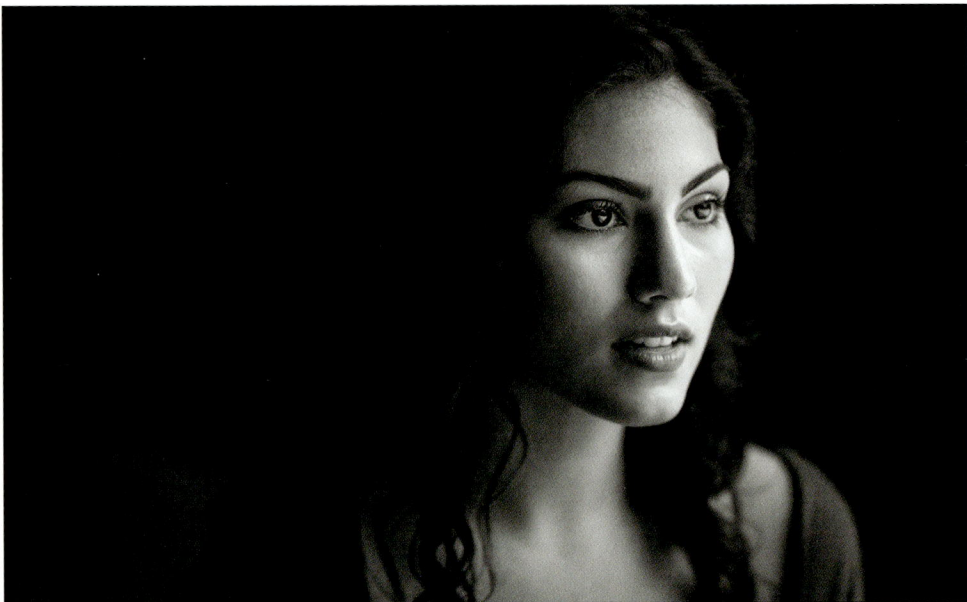

Like I just mentioned, for most window light portraits, we don't have the subject facing directly toward the window. Instead, we position them so the window light is mostly side-lighting them. However, to get that classic, dramatic window light portrait, we position our subject so a little of that window light spills onto the side of their face that is facing away from the window in the shape of an upside-down triangle. This is called "Rembrandt lighting," and while it's originally from the Baroque period of the 1600s, it is still an incredibly popular style of lighting used today. In the example seen above, the right side of her face (from the camera position) is lit by the window on the right side of the image, but a little bit of that light is also falling on the other side of her cheek, creating an upside down triangle of light below her eye.

Highlight Profile Portrait

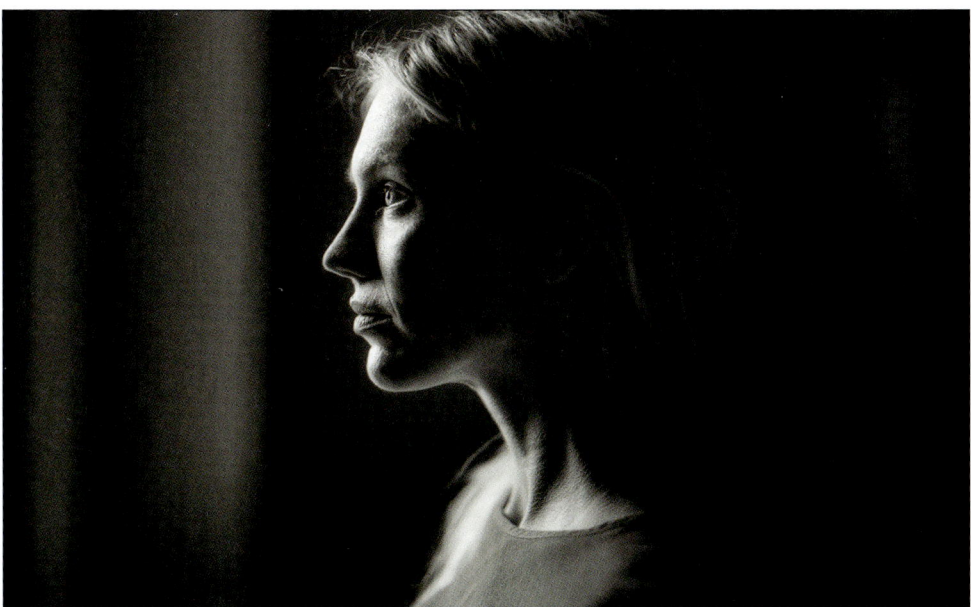

For this look, you're going to shoot a profile shot of your subject where they are actually facing directly toward the window. You're going to position them directly in front of the window, and then have them side-step over toward the camera—a few feet in front of where the window starts, so the light isn't hitting them directly. In fact, you'll want them to move over enough, so that only a little bit of light spills over onto the shadow side of their face (like you see here), and they are mostly back lit. You might have to have them side-step closer toward where the window starts on the wall or farther away from the window until you have just a little bit of rim light falling on them. So, don't get frustrated if you have to tell your subject, "Okay, take another side-step toward me. Okay, another. One more. Keep going," etc. But, once you hit that sweet spot, it's pretty sweet. I love to convert this particular type of portrait to black and white for added drama.

What If You Don't Want the Classic Window Light Look?

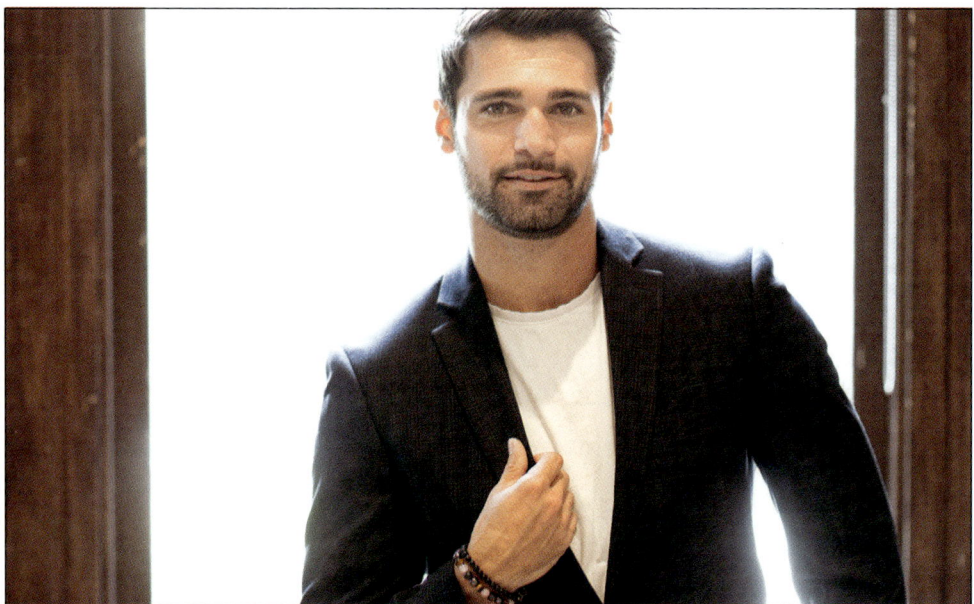

If you want the classic window light look, you'll be shooting parallel to the window, with your subject looking toward camera or toward the window (so they're kind of side-lit). But, if you don't want that classic look, here is another way to position your subject: have them stand with their back toward the window (as shown here). They will wind up being backlit, they'll look like a silhouette for the most part, and the windows behind them will be so bright you're going to wind up blowing them out (losing detail as that area turns mostly solid white). You can either go with this blown-out look (I see it often), and then use exposure compensation to overexpose the image by a stop or so, so their face will appear lit, or you can expose for the light outside. First, have your subject step away from the window and get a shot of what it looks like outside, as if you were shooting a cityscape or real estate-type shot out the window. Once you get that dialed in, now put your subject in front of the window, so the sunlight from it creates a backlight or rim light around them. Of course, exposing like this for the light behind them is pretty much going to make them a silhouette, so to get them out of the shadows we bounce some of that window light coming in with a reflector. Use the silver side of the reflector if you need a lot of light bouncing back, or use the white side if you just need a little bit of light to fill in the shadows (you won't really know which side to use until you try it, but I'd start with silver as that's probably what you'll wind up using). Just another option to try if you don't want the classic window-light look.

Shooting with Your Subject Facing the Window

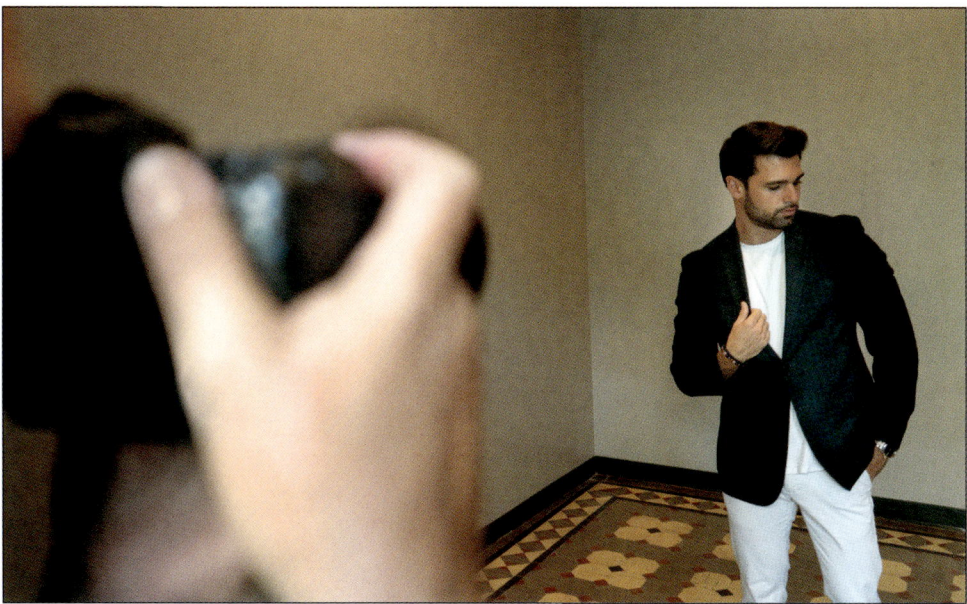

For yet another window light scenario, you could put your (the photographer's) back toward the window and have your subject face the window. This isn't the "classic window shot" look, because the straight-on window shot doesn't have any side shadows, so your subject's face won't have much dimension and you'll have more of a flat look. But, if your subject is back at least six or eight feet from the window, it can still have a nice look. If you're doing something to diffuse the light from the window (anything from sheers to a diffuser), you may be able to move your subject closer to the window.

What Kind of Window Am I Looking For?

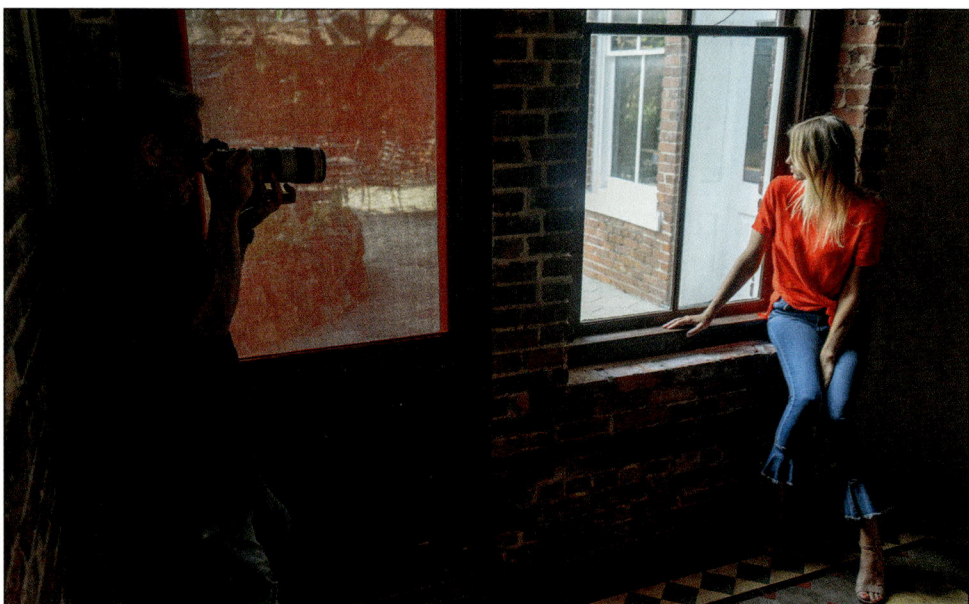

Well, ideally, you'll want a large window, so that the light it produces is soft and even. But, also, if you have a choice, look for a window that is a bit higher than your subject. You want the light to come from the top and side, but not up too high or you'll start getting weird shadows under the eyes and nose. Also, if you have a choice between squeaky clean windows or dirty ones that need cleaning, take the dirty windows every time (they give you softer, more diffused light). I have a friend that has windows that he intentionally hasn't cleaned in like 11 years because the light from them is so awesome.

Watch Out for Changing Window Light

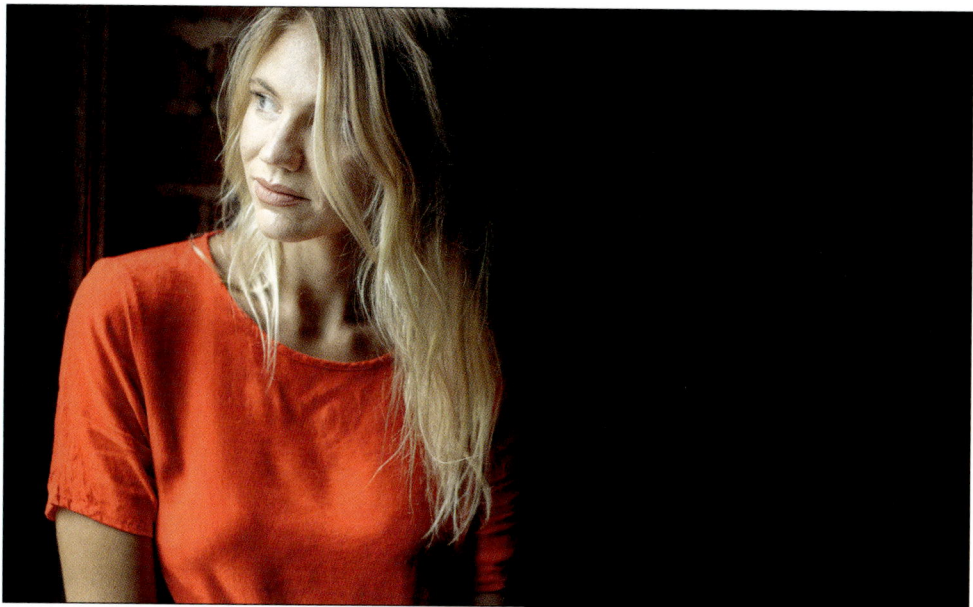

Anytime you're dealing with natural light it's subject to change. As the sun moves across the sky, it's going to change the angle and intensity of the light, and it seems (at least to me) like this change is more noticeable when you're shooting with window light. You start out the shoot with one setting, and 30 or 45 minutes later, that setting isn't right any longer, so you need to keep an eye on your shutter speed throughout the shoot. You don't want to start out at 1/125 or 1/200 of a second and find out later that, when the light changed, it dropped to 1/30 of a second, and you have a bunch of shots that are out of focus later in the shoot.

Using an Open Doorway for Light

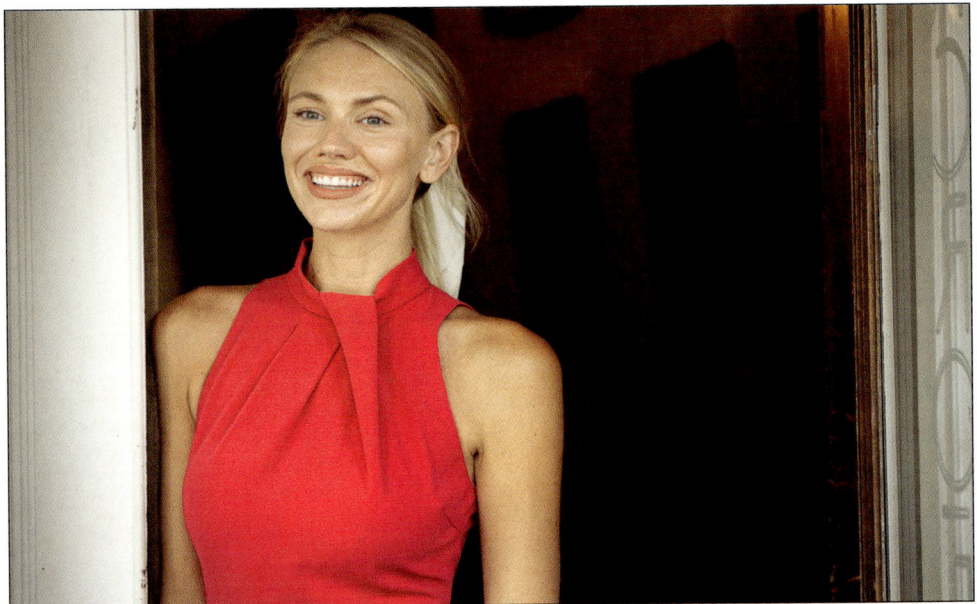

Another spot to consider with potentially really nice light is the window's cousin: an open doorway. This sometimes works really nicely because there's often a roof over-hang above a doorway. So you can be standing outside, shooting back toward the house or building, with your subject in that doorway safely shaded from harsh light. Of course, this doorway has to be on the shaded side of the house or building, and away from direct light, but it's something to keep in mind when you're on location and searching for some nice soft light.

Using Hard Light Shadow Patterns

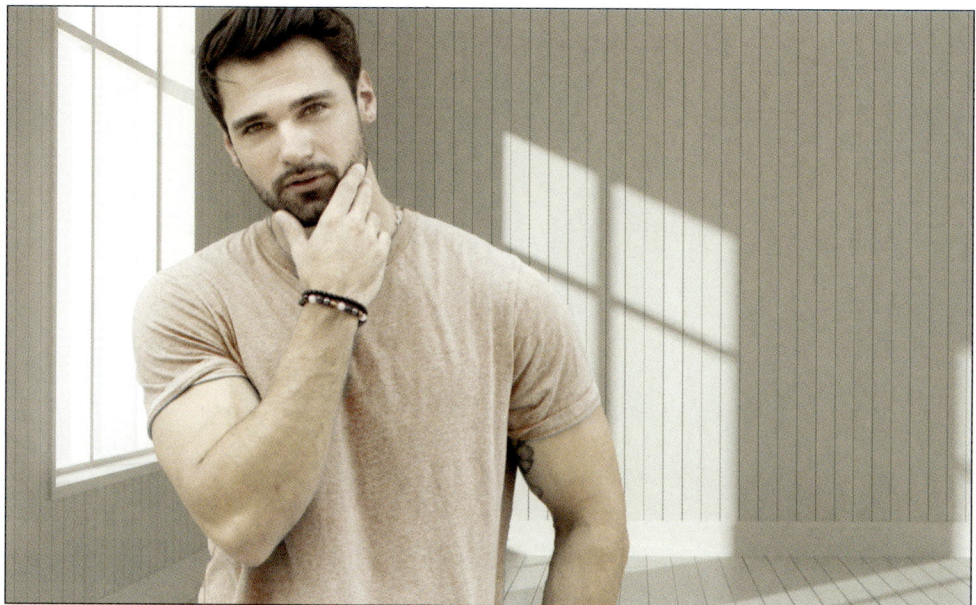

If you have a window that casts an interesting pattern on the wall, you might consider using that as a background pattern behind your subject. This may put your subject in harder light, but if your subject has pretty decent skin (or you're pretty decent at retouching skin in Photoshop), you can absolutely get away with it.

Shooting with Painted Backdrops

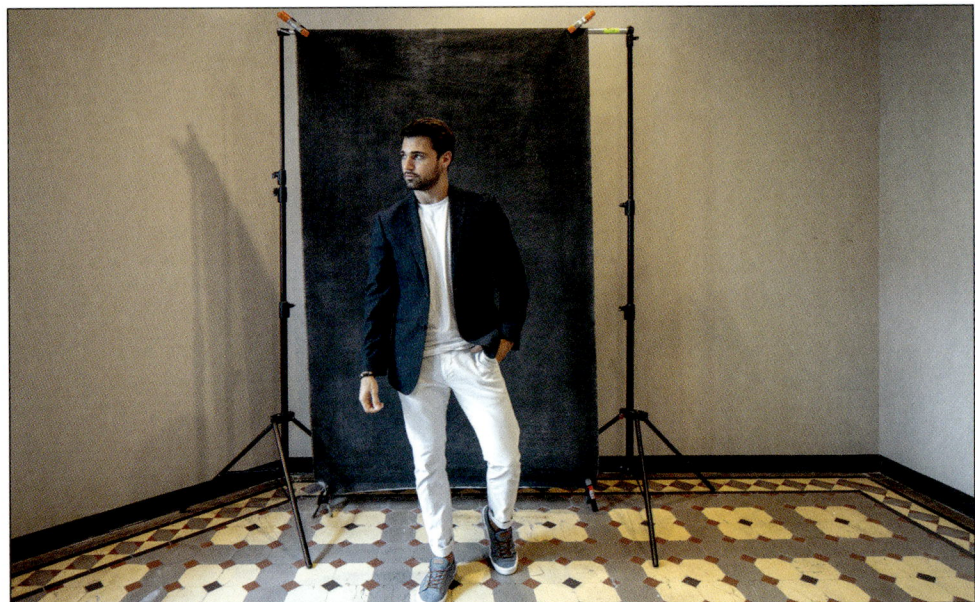

If you really want that "old masters" look for your portraits, you might want to consider shooting with a painted backdrop behind your subject. Like Rembrandt-style lighting, using painted backdrops is also still very popular and, in fact, it's kind of a "thing" right now (the ones I use are from GravityBackDrops.com, and I love them like you can't believe, mostly because I can buy a backdrop from them at a price I would have to pay someplace else to rent a high-end painted backdrop for a weekend. Can't say enough about them). Anyway, the idea is you let the window light that's lighting your subject also spill onto and light your background, and it creates a very dynamic-looking portrait. You can pick up a background stand set and the pole that goes between them (the one that holds up your backdrop roll) for around $110 at B&H Photo. The two clamps holding up our background are steel spring clamps from Home Depot (about $5 each).

Adding a Reflector

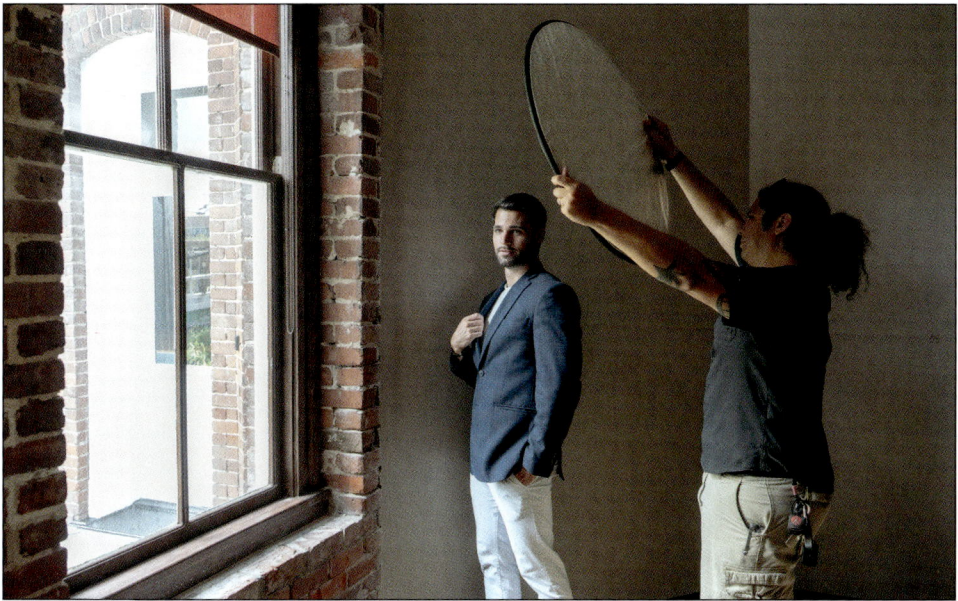

Using window light is a "one-light shoot." You only have one light source (the window), so the side of your subject's face that is facing away from the window will be in shadows (a lot or a little, depending on how they're facing). Personally, I love shadows, even dark shadows—I love the depth, dimension, and drama they add to a portrait (it's one of the things I love best about window portraits). But, if you feel like the shadows are too dark on the shadow side of your subject's face, you can open them up and reveal more detail by simply putting a reflector on the opposite side of your subject (the shadow side) to bounce some of the window light back into your subject's face. This will open up those shadows big time, almost like you added a soft fill light, and best of all, these reflectors are fairly inexpensive (you can buy a 22" two-sided [gold and silver] collapsible reflector for $9.58 at B&H Photo. That's cheaper than the chicken wings appetizer at Applebee's). To bounce light indoors from a window, you'd use the silver side of the reflector (the gold side is for use outdoors later in the day). If you think the silver side might be reflecting too much, instead of a gold/silver reflector, get a silver/white one and use the white side as it reflects much less light.

Choosing the Right White Balance

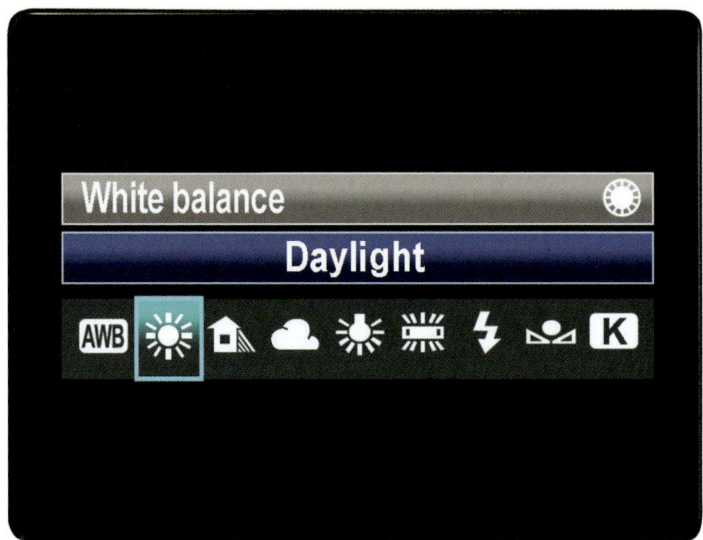

This might sound kinda obvious, but generally, to get the best skin tones in your image from a window light shot, set the white balance on your camera to Daylight. If you do a test shot and the image looks too blue, it might be that you're doing more of a dramatic window light portrait, or that it's cloudy outside and that affects the color of the light. In that case, you might try switching your white balance to Shade, but again, only do this if you notice in your image that your subject has a bit of a bluish tint. Switching your white balance to Shade will warm the image and offset that blue tint.

It Might Be Tripod Time

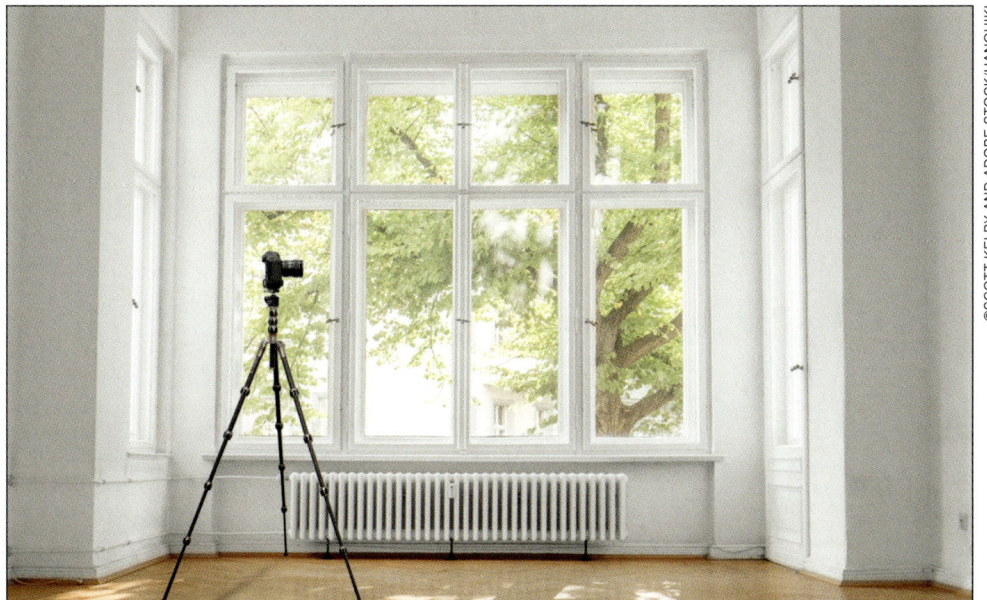

©SCOTT KELBY AND ADOBE STOCK/HANOHIKI

Because we're going to be shooting away from the direct light (either back from the window, or behind it, or from a north-facing window), the light we'll be shooting in isn't terribly bright (it's soft and beautiful, but not super-bright). So, if you're shooting in kind of a low-light situation like this, you might consider shooting on a tripod. Without a tripod, you run the risk of getting blurry images because the light from the window is so low, which could make your shutter speed drop to a speed that would make it hard to get a really sharp shot by just hand-holding. Each window light scenario is different, so I can't say you'll *have* to shoot on a tripod, but I would throw one in your trunk on the way to the shoot just in case you wind up needing it. Better to have it with you and not have to use it, than need a tripod and not have one.

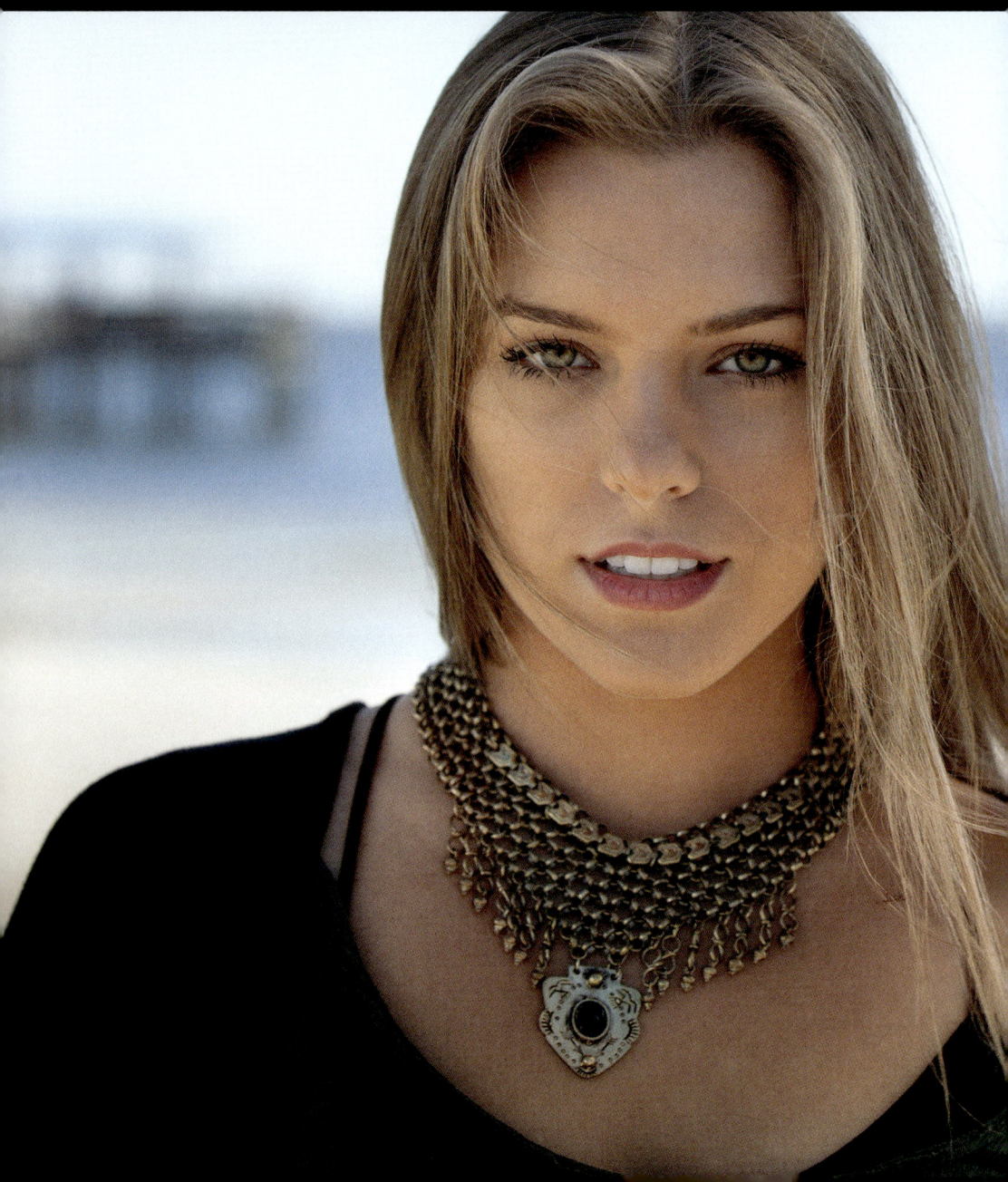

Chapter Four

Shooting Outside
Making the Bright Beautiful

Here we are, four chapters in, and if you're still reading, I think you and I are ready to break some new ground for a chapter intro. I think you're ready for me to write my first "rap" intro. Don't worry, I'm going to go "old school" with my rap, so it will be less Kanye and more Sugarhill Gang. Less like Kendrick Lamar, and more like Run-DMC. By the way, for years, I've been wanting to use my rap name (yes, I'm not ashamed to admit that I came up with my own rap name, and the reason I'm not ashamed is because it's such a good one) and this is probably my best opportunity (or perhaps, my only opportunity) to become the old-school rapper it has always been my destiny to become. Ladies and gentlemen, please welcome to the stage, Plain White Rapper! [insert crowd cheering sound effect here] My rap is about taking portraits outside, and I call it "Shootin' and Pollutin'." Here we go: "That sun outside is really bright, and you want to get your lighting right. I hope you're picking up on what I'm hinting, 'cause you don't want to see your subject squinting. You've gotta find a way to diffuse that sun, or when you see the shots it won't be fun. You don't wanna tell the art director that you can't take the pic because you forgot a reflector. That smooth even light will get you paid, so you better get your subject to some open shade. Please heed the tips that are in this chapter, and shooting outside won't become a factor, and if you want to be cruising in a new Audi, you'd better have a black reflector when it's cloudy. This is how you make portraits that your clients will like, that's my devastating rap, and now I drop the mic." That's it. That's my first chapter intro rap ever. Though, I have to admit, it sounded a lot better in my head (I had a lot more bass and a dope trap beat. That's rap guy talk. You wouldn't understand). #illin #def #phat #bling #fresh #wack #dis #diffuser

My Outdoor Photography Secret Weapon

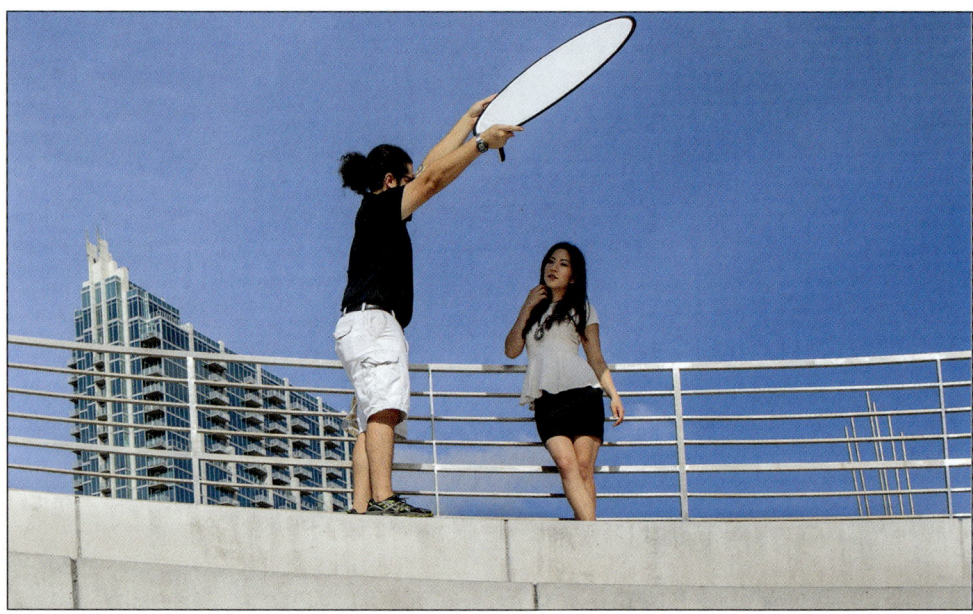

It's one of the cheapest photography accessories you can buy, yet one of the most powerful for outdoor photography. It's called a "1-stop diffuser," and this little collapsible wonder lets you shoot outdoors in direct sunlight and still have soft, gorgeous light. You simply pop it open (it folds up into a small disc, and when you open it, it pops into its full shape, which is about 30" for the one I use), have a friend (or an assistant) put it between the sun and your subject (as seen above), and it spreads and diffuses that harsh sunlight. It doesn't just put your subject in the shade—it's actually better because the diffuser is translucent, so the sunlight still comes through to light your subject, but the light that comes through is much softer. It works like magic. You can find them online for around $9.99, but I recommend going with something like Westcott's 5-in-1 Reflector Disc. You're going to need to own a reflector or two as well, and this one has a 1-stop diffuser and then a reversible cover with silver, white, gold, and black sides. So, for the money (around $39), it's hard to beat.

A Small Tri-Grip 1-Stop Diffuser and Stand

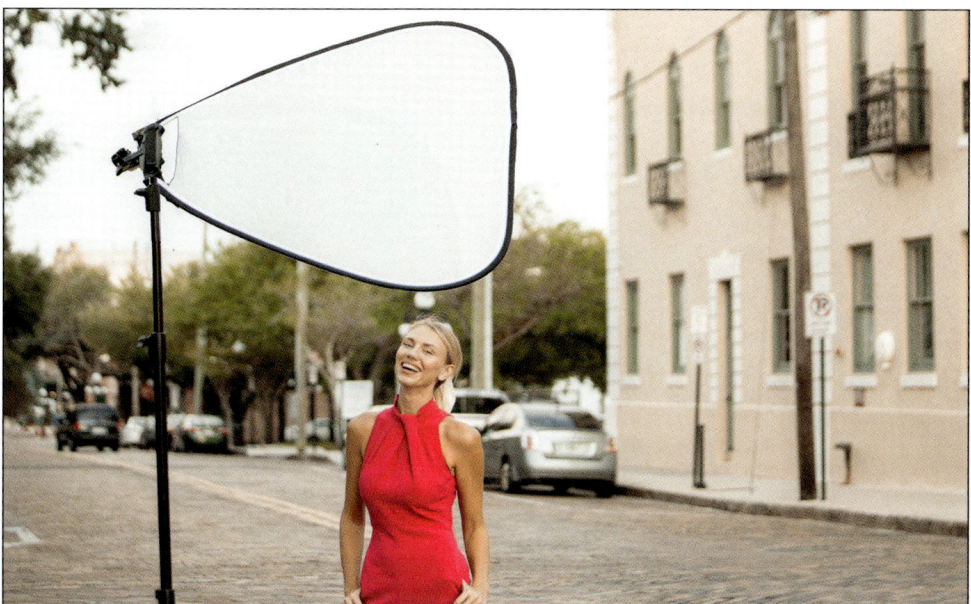

There's another type of 1-stop diffuser that's designed for pros (spoiler alert: it's more expensive because, well…it's for pros) that has a built-in handle and a different shape (more on that in a moment). The handle, of course, makes the diffuser easier for your friend or assistant to hold, but it also allows you to hold the diffuser yourself, which is handy if you don't have a friend or assistant around to hold it for you. Rather than a round shape, it has a long triangular shape, so you can hold it up in one hand to diffuse the sun over your subject, and then hold your camera with your other hand to take the shot, so you can kind of be your own one-man band. You can also buy a specially made clamp, called a TriGrip Bracket, that attaches to any standard light stand to hold your TriGrip diffuser. This works great as long as it's not windy outside where you're shooting because even a medium gust of wind will send that bad boy flying. If that's a concern, you can put a sandbag over one of the light stand's legs to keep it from taking off. If wind is a real concern, use more than one sandbag—maybe one on each leg (you can get sandbags from B&H Photo).

When to Use a Gold Reflector

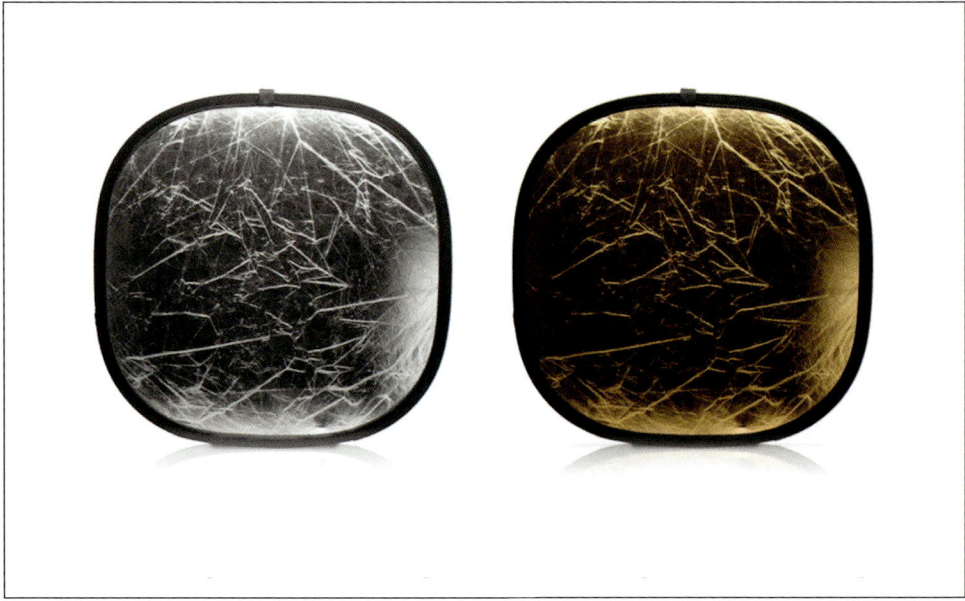

Two of the most popular colors for reflectors are silver and gold, but they are used outdoors at very different times. Reflectors take the sunlight and bounce it back toward your subject, and the light that hits your reflector is going to pick up the color of what it bounces off of. Most of the time, we use a silver reflector outdoors because the light color it bounces is kind of neutral outdoors in daylight. However, if you hold up a gold reflector, when the sunlight hits that gold, what comes off it is gold-colored light. For that reason, we generally only use gold reflectors later in the day, toward sunset, when the natural color of the sunlight would be warmer due to the setting sun, so that gold reflected light looks natural on your subject. If you use the silver side at sunset, the light that comes off that reflector would be kinda white, which would look odd with the setting sun. So, think silver for daylight, and then gold as we start to get toward sunrise or sunset.

When to Use a White Reflector

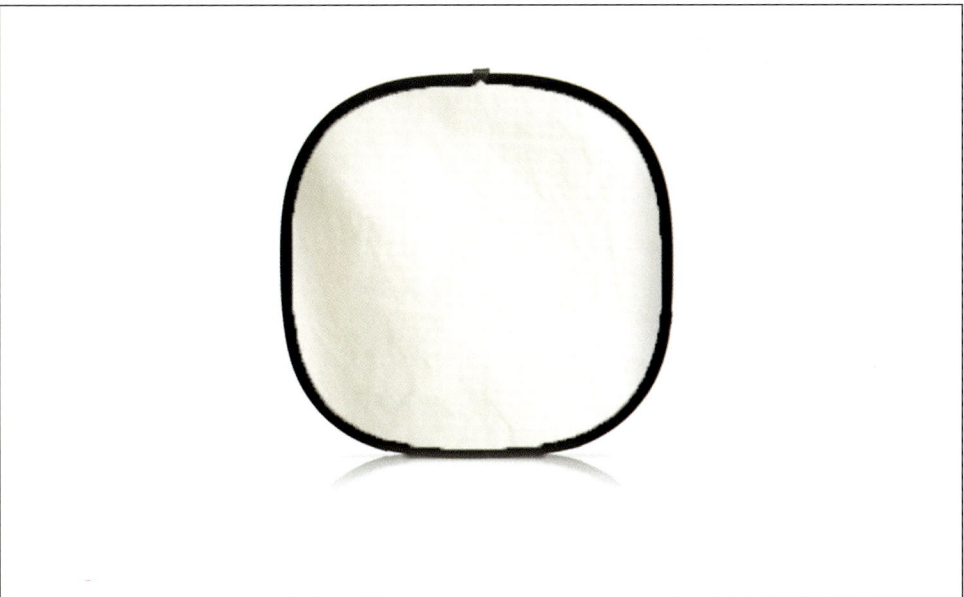

As I mentioned, a silver reflector is going to be our go-to reflector for shooting in day-light because it reflects and bounces a lot of light back toward your subject, but what if it's too much light, or too bright? That's when we switch to the white reflector. It doesn't bounce nearly as much light back at your subject, so it kind of tones down the power of the reflector. You probably won't use it as much as the silver side, but there will be times when you're so glad you have it.

Use a Black Reflector on Cloudy Days

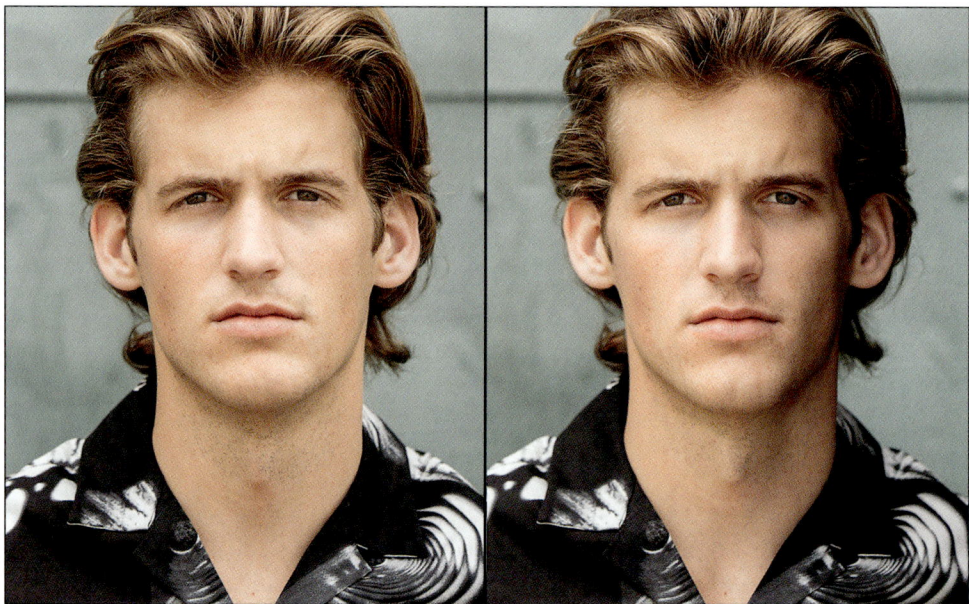

There's a real benefit to shooting outdoors on cloudy or overcast days: you don't have that harsh, direct sunlight. But, there's also a real downside and that is the light is usually very flat and boring. You don't have the all-important shadows you get with the directional light of sunlight, but that's when a black reflector is so incredibly helpful. Just put it right up beside your subject and it creates those missing shadows, so your portrait can still have depth and dimension even on overcast days. Take a look at the shot above on the left—it was taken under an overcast sky and the light is very flat. Now, look at the shot on the right where all I did was hold up a black reflector, so his face would now have those wonderful shadows (camera right). This also works when you're shooting in the shade and you notice the lighting looks flat—just add that black reflector. It's a super-easy trick, but it works wonders.

Where to Position a Reflector

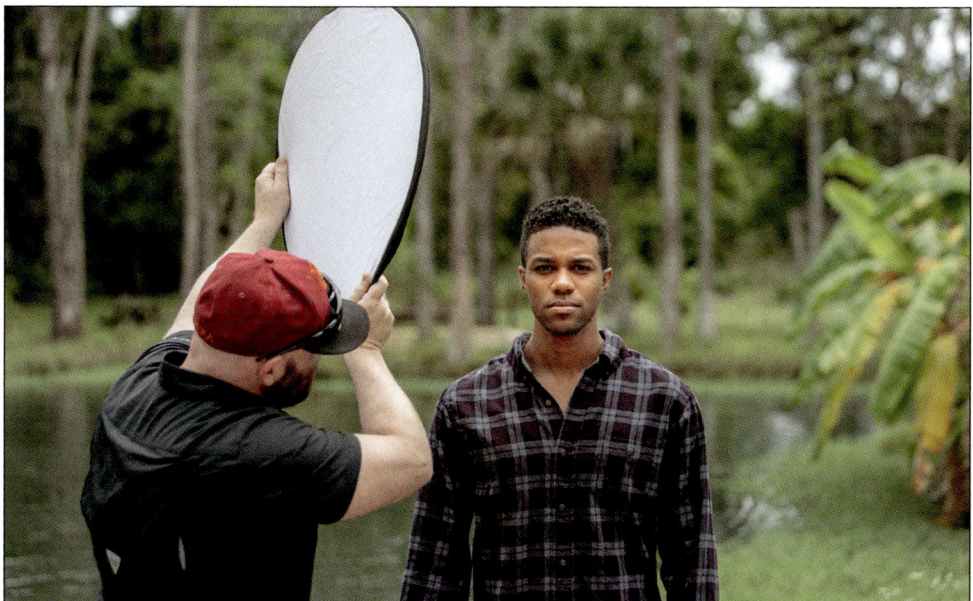

The most comfortable position for your friend or assistant to hold a reflector is down low around their hips, but unfortunately that's about the worst possible place to hold a reflector. Here's why: When it's down low like that it bounces the sunlight from down low up at your subject. Under-lighting people like this is what you do to make them look angry or aggressive, like if you're lighting a football player or wrestler and you want them to look really tough and aggressive. For most of our portraits, we're not going for "tough and aggressive"—we're trying to create beautiful light that flatters our subject. This is why the appropriate place to hold a reflector is up high (like you see here), so the reflected sunlight angles down at your subject from above, like the sun. This angle for your bounced light is much more flattering. It's definitely not as comfortable for your friend or assistant to hold the reflector up high like this, but once you see the difference it makes, you'll give your friend a bonus for doing it the right way.

Use a Reflector to Create Shade

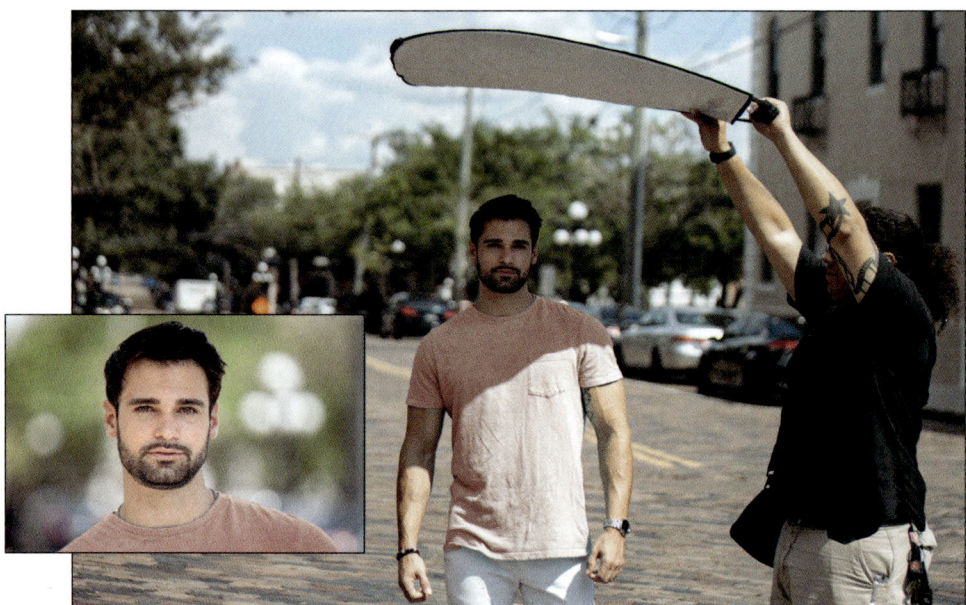

If you can't find a shady spot to shoot, and you don't have a 1-stop diffuser with you (hey, it happens), you can simply hold a reflector over your subject to create shade. You're not doing any reflecting or bouncing here—you're using it to simply block out the light, just like an overhang on a house or a porch or some trees would. That way, you're not shooting in direct sunlight. It's kind of "shade on demand." In case you're wondering how this is different from using a diffuser, the difference would be that a diffuser lets in the sunlight and makes it soft and beautiful (and it's preferable, if you've got one), so you still get directional light and shadows and all that. Using a reflector like this is simply blocking the harsh light, like you're walking into the shade, but of course, you'd only use this trick if there isn't any usable or available shade where you are.

Diffusing Group Shots

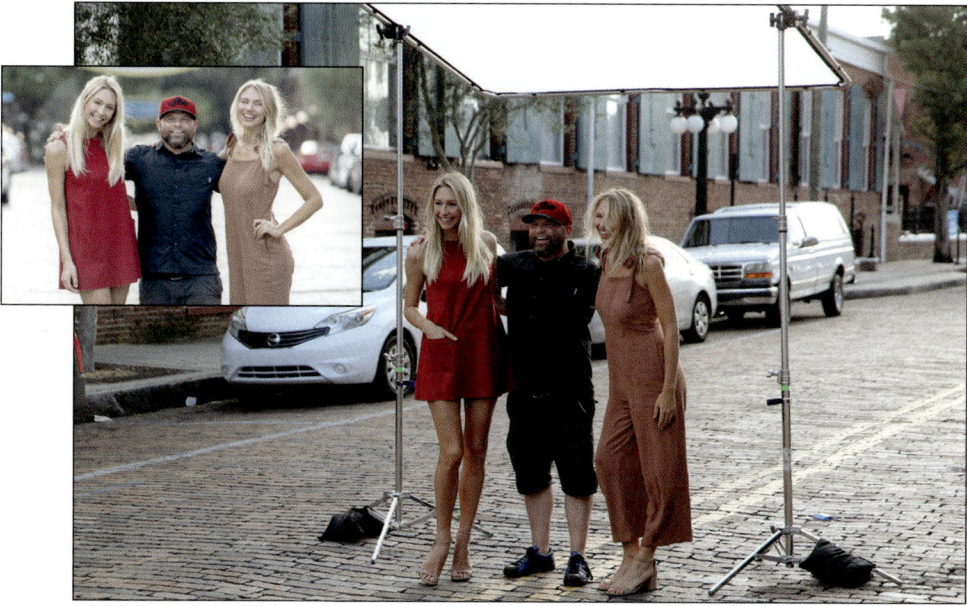

If you're going to be shooting a group outside—maybe you're doing a family portrait, or a family reunion, or the group formals for a wedding—a small 30" 1-stop diffuser isn't going to do the job. You're going to need something much bigger—a scrim. A scrim is essentially a really large 1-stop diffuser, so large that they usually have an aluminum frame built around them, and you'll generally need a couple of light stands to support the scrim and a few sandbags to keep your scrim from taking flight. Also, depending on which setup you get, you'll probably also want a socket to allow you to tilt the scrim, so you can position it between the sun and your subjects. I know this sounds like a lot of work, but you can have it up and running in just a few minutes, and it collapses down into a small bag, so it's easy to transport and fairly lightweight (well, everything but the sandbags, they're...ya know...filled with sand). The scrim shown here is a Lastolite Skylite 6.6x6.6' (the frame and diffuser together run around $295). Another popular large-sized diffuser is the 6x6' Scrim Jim from F.J. Westcott for around $439 for the frame and the 1-1/4-stop diffuser.

Avoid Dappled Light

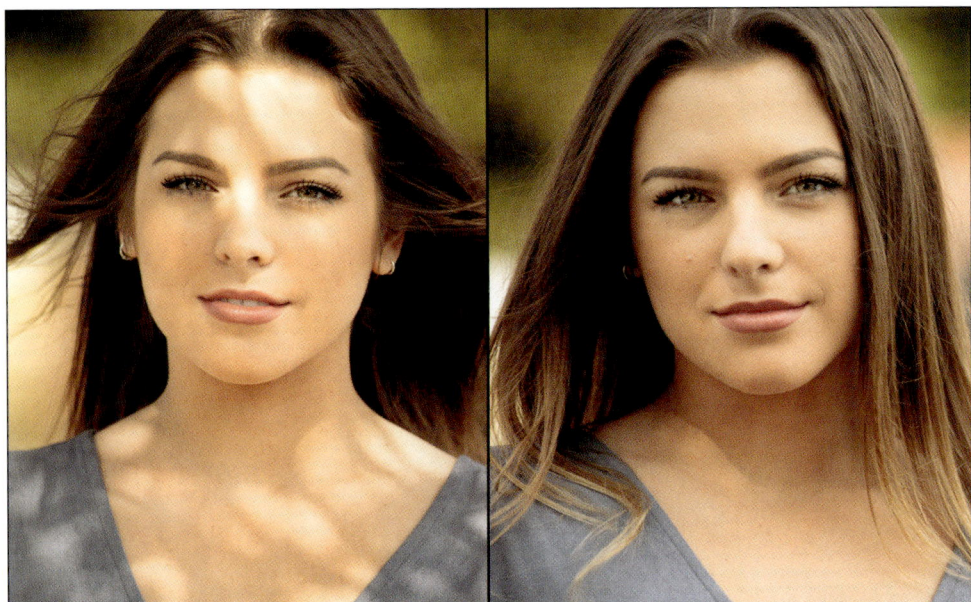

Dappled light usually happens when you're shooting outdoors in the shade of a tree, where little speckles of light wind up hitting your subject (as seen above left), and ruining the shot. Luckily, it's an easy fix. If you see this dappled light situation happening, put your eye up to the viewfinder and have your subject move either to their left or right, or take a step forward or backward, until they are clear of the speckles (as seen above right). You'll be able to find a spot where your subject is in solid shadows without a dapple in sight.

Find Shade Near the Edge of Bright Sunlight

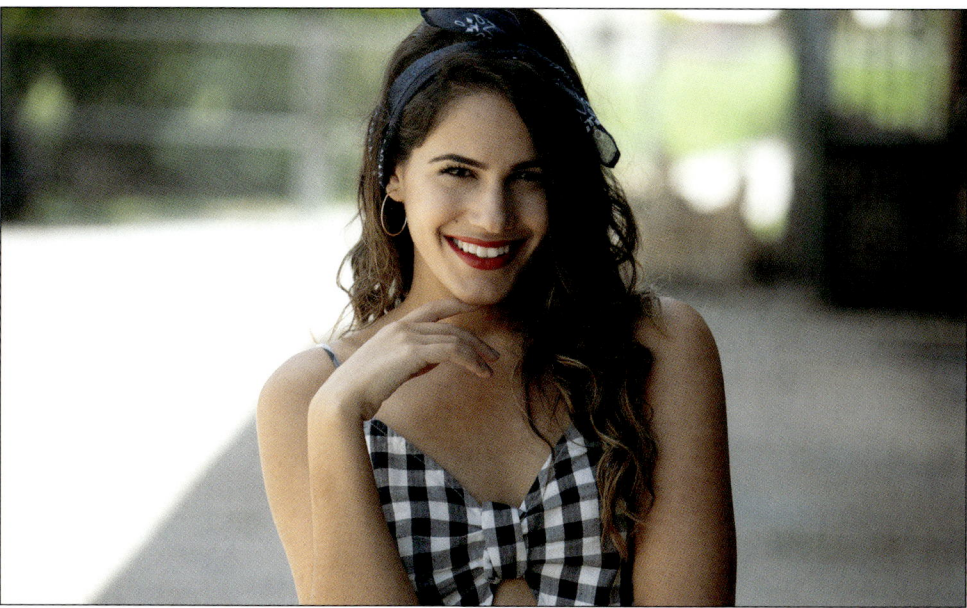

If you're stuck for finding an area with good light outside, here's something you can keep an eye out for: look for a shady area that's right next to a bright, sunny area. We're not looking for deep shade here—we want to position our subject right at the edge of that shade. Because you're close to the sunny area, you'll have some soft, beautiful light, and there will be enough light at the edge of that shade to keep you from having to really crank your ISO to get a decent shutter speed. Make sure none of that bright light nearby actually hits your subject. You still want to be fully in shade—just a couple of feet from the edge of the shade. Remember, some really nice light is waiting right there for you.

Another Great Option: Shooting in Full Shade

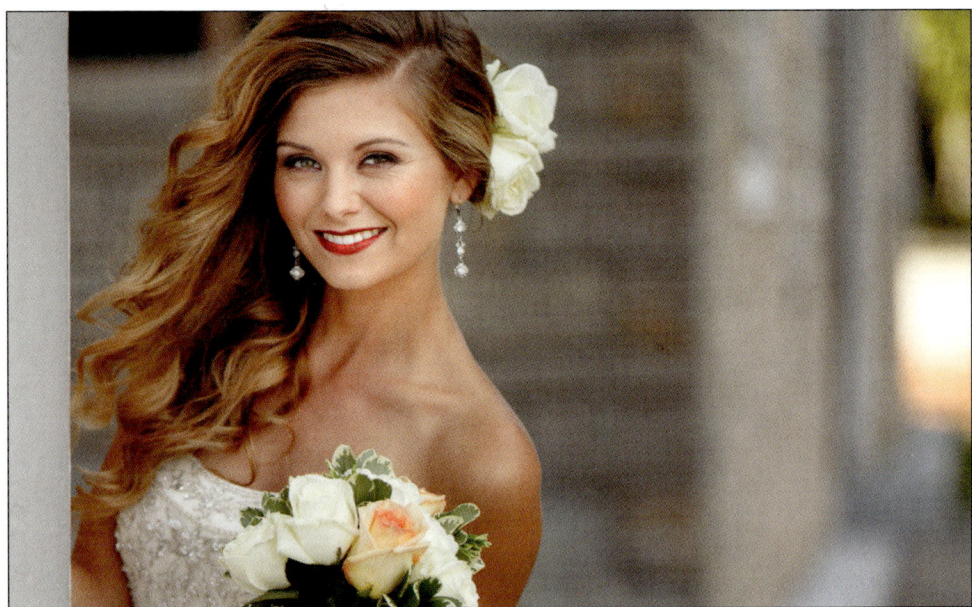

Another option you can use, instead of shooting out in the direct sun, is to look for an area with some full shade. We're talking a front porch, or an overhang on a building, under a really shady tree, that kind of thing. In the example here, our bride is standing under an overhang outside of the church. There's generally nice, soft light in the shade, so just make sure your subject is in full shade and there are no slivers of light sneaking in on their shoulder or on their clothing (see page 64 on dappled light). It needs to be full shade. Often, the light in full shade will be kind of flat (not a lot of shadows on the face), but depending on where the sun is in the sky when you do this, sometimes even in the shade, you can get some nice shadows. So, keep an eye out once your subject is standing in that shade, turning their body a little bit one way or the other might bring some nice shadows, depth, and dimension to their face.

Shooting on Cloudy Days

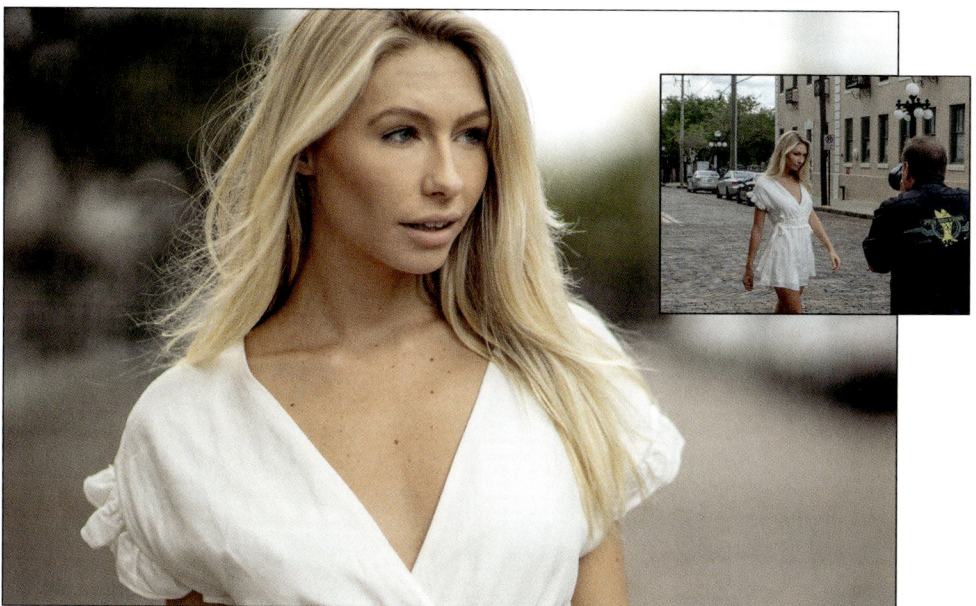

Don't cancel the shoot if it's a cloudy day—those clouds act like a natural diffuser, like nature's giant softbox, so you won't have to deal with harsh sunlight and all that entails. In fact, many portrait pros prefer to shoot on cloudy days, but just keep in mind that while the sunlight won't be harsh, it may not be very directional either. So, the light will be kind of boring, depending on how cloudy it is. (*Note:* Here we were still able to get some shadows on one side of our subject's face, which is ideal, but not always possible. You can see from the behind-the-scenes shot that we are right out in the middle of the street—no diffusion—just making the most of the few minutes when the sun went into a large bank of clouds.) It's important to change the white balance setting on your camera to Cloudy, otherwise your subject's skin tone will have a bit of a blue tint (and bluish skin is the tone they use in movies and on TV when they want someone to look dead, so…this is a setting worth changing). Also, if you're going to be shooting in this type of light, make sure you check out the technique on page 60 about using a black reflector.

Position Your Subject to Have Directional Light

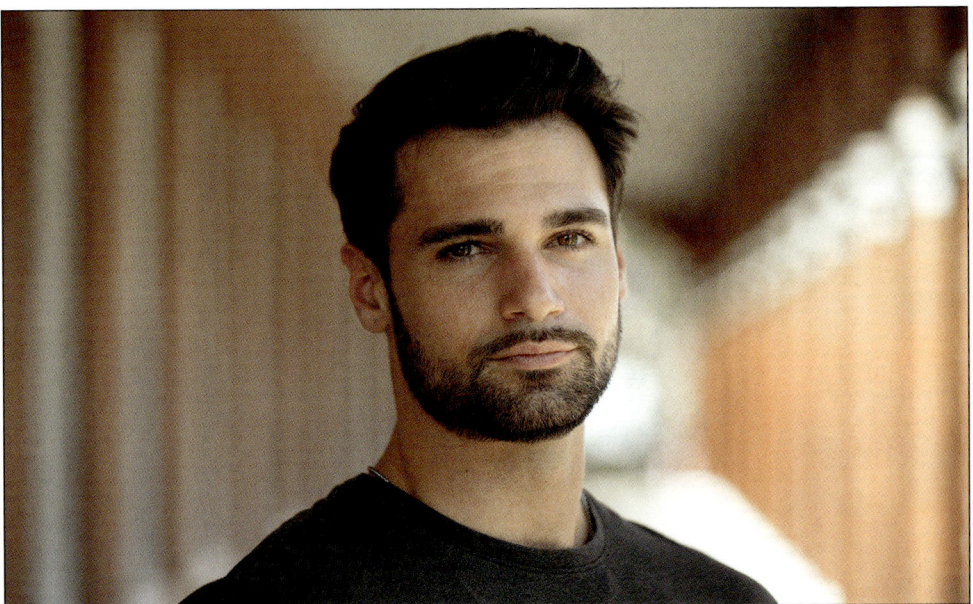

The thing that adds depth and dimension to our portraits (and helps to keep them from looking like flat 2D art) is the shadow on your subject's face. So, when you're shooting outdoors, it's a balancing act because we're trying to keep our subject out of the direct sunlight (so they're not squinting and they don't have hard shadows), but at the same time, we don't want flat light. We want directional light—light that produces shadows and highlights and gives our subject's face depth and dimension (like you see above, where we have those nice, soft shadows on his face, camera left, courtesy of the light coming in from the front on the right side. Even though he's in full shade, the light is still directional). Keep an eye out if you see the light looking really flat (without those shadows) and try to position your subject so you are getting soft shadows on one side of their face, like you see above.

Nailing Your White Balance Outdoors

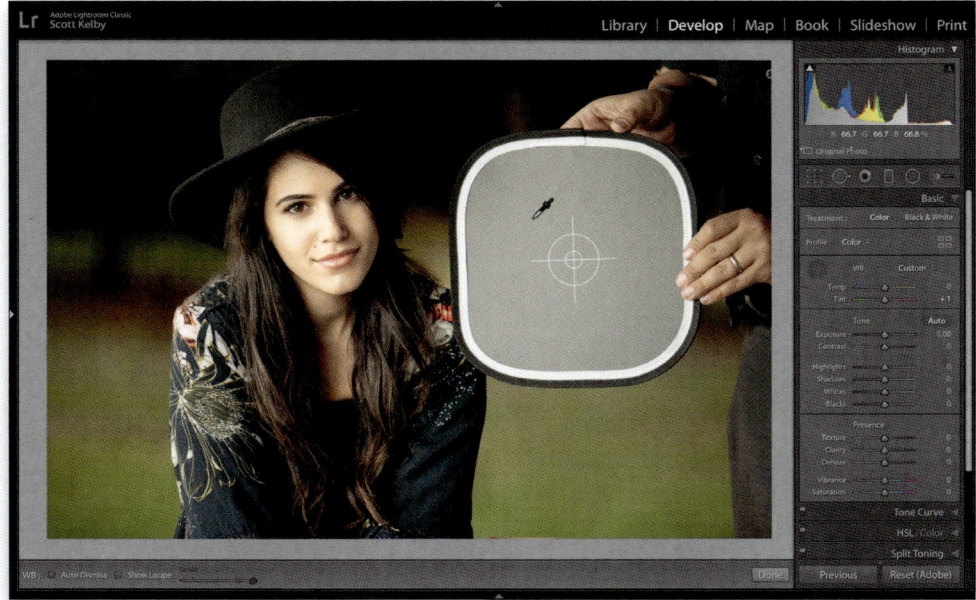

If you're concerned about getting your skin tones just right outdoors, there's something that can really help. It's called a "gray card," and you can pick one up at any camera store (the one shown above is the Lastolite EZYBalance Collapsible 18% Gray/White Balance Card that I got from B&H Photo). These make getting your white balance right (and therefore, your skin tones) incredibly easy. You just hold the gray card in the frame (or have your subject or assistant hold it) and take a shot. Now you can use that shot to fix the white balance on all your other shots from that spot. Here's how:

In Lightroom: In the Develop module, click on the image where you have a gray card visible in the shot, and then select all the other images that were taken in that same spot. At the bottom of the right side Panels area, click on the button to the left of Sync to turn on Auto Sync, so any changes you make to that gray card image are automatically applied to all the other selected images. Now, get the White Balance Selector tool **(W)** from the Basic panel (it's near the top and looks like an eyedropper), click it once on the gray card (as shown above), and it corrects the white balance for not only that image, but for all your other selected images.

In Photoshop: In Camera Raw, open all the images that need their white balance corrected. Click on the gray card image, then press **Command-A (PC: Ctrl-A)** to select all the other images in the Filmstrip on the left, and now any changes you make to that gray card image are automatically applied to all your other selected images. Get the White Balance tool **(I)** from the toolbar at the top of the window, and then click it once on the gray card to correct the white balance in all your selected images.

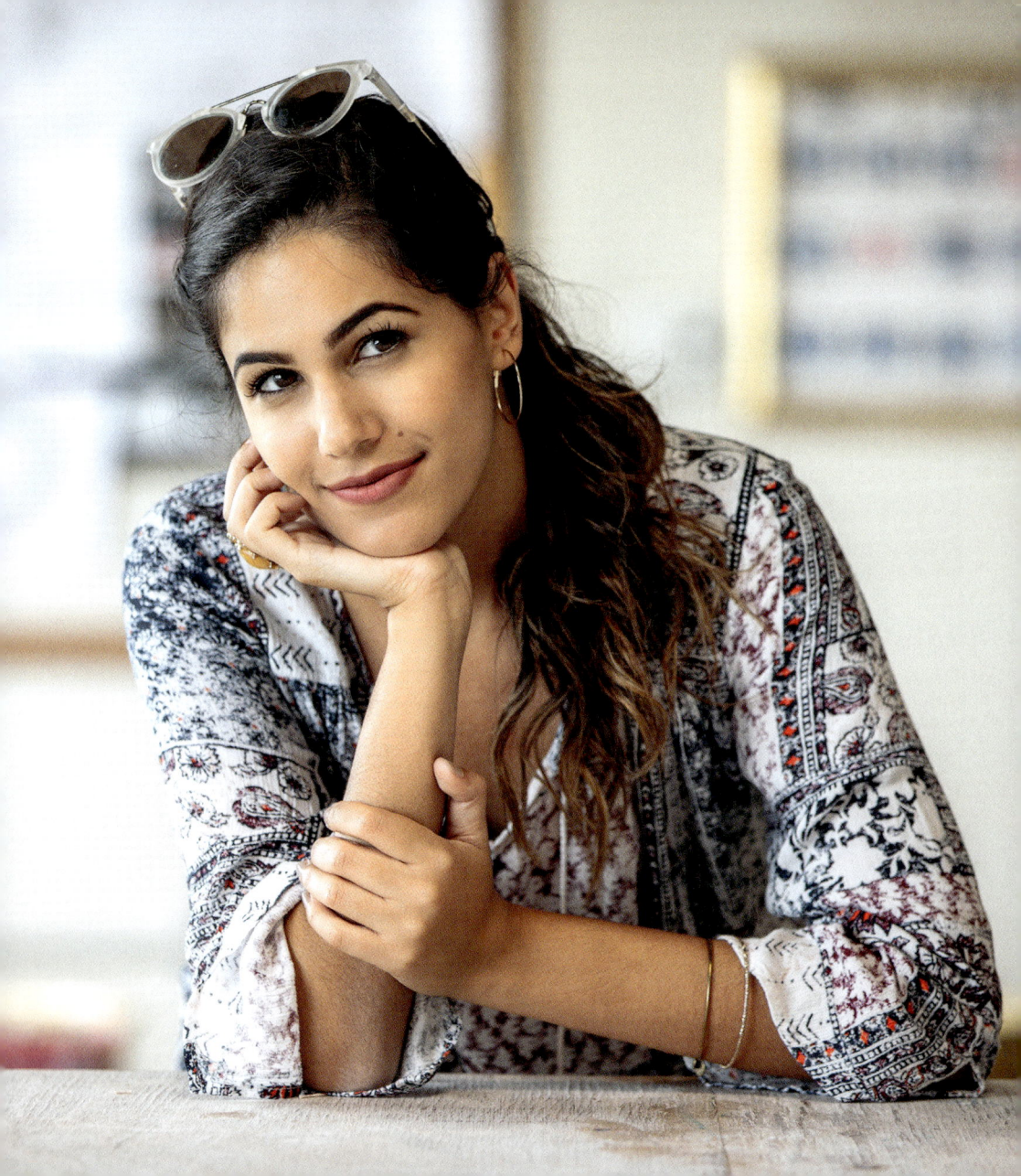

Chapter Five

Shooting in Direct Light

Taming the Beast

You might be thinking: "Scott, couldn't you have just combined this chapter with the previous one on shooting outside?" Well, yes, I guess I could have, but then you might ask: "Scott, couldn't you have combined all these chapters into one big super-chapter? Well, except maybe that window light one, that should still be its own chapter. That one and the one on lenses, and probably the one about camera settings. Those should probably both be separate chapters." Well, yeah, I guess I could have, but nobody wants some giant 100+ page chapter, right? Think about it. If you saw a chapter and it was like 100+ pages, you would think to yourself: "I can't wait to get to that super-long chapter that will take me forever to read. I wish Scott had broken it into smaller, more digestible bite-sized chapter nuggets, with your choice of sauces, like sweet and spicy sriracha, or garlic and herb ranch, or even honey mustard." See, these are the types of critical decisions we authors have to deal with every day. Well, not every day, because we don't choose how many chapters our books will have every day. In reality, we're only allowed to choose them on one particular day, and that day is determined by the publishing cartel, which is a shadowy, clandestine organization designed to crush the hopes and dreams of authors everywhere, with the noted exceptions of J.K. Rowling, James Patterson, and some guy in New Jersey named Anthony. Anyway, the important things to take away from this chapter intro are simply: (a) this chapter intro did not use any acronym jokes, (b) or any questionable Latin phrases, and (c) I didn't rap again. Though, I gotta tell ya, I feel a rap coming on! "Now what you see is not a test shot, I'm rappin' to the beat!"

The Advantages of Shooting with the Sun Behind Your Subject

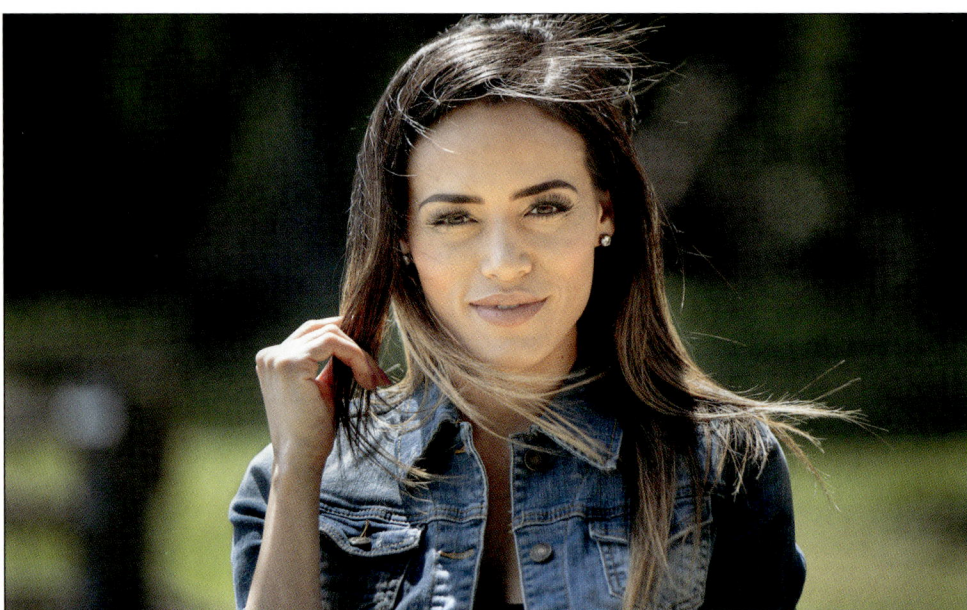

When we're outdoors, shooting with the sun behind our subject is kind of our "go-to" position, and there are a number of reasons why we prefer this setup: (1) The sun winds up becoming a hair light or a rim light behind our subject, having this second light adds a bit more separation from the background, and just generally, it makes for more interesting lighting. (2) If you shoot late in the day (and I always recommend that you do), the sun will be lower in the sky and not only will you get more of a warm look to your images, the quality of the light will be so much better—it's softer and more beautiful all the way around, and it won't be so powerful or high-angled that it blows out the edges of your subject's hair in the image. (3) When the sun is behind your subject, especially late in the day, it cuts the contrast in your image and gives it a bit of a dreamy look. (4) If you're shooting wide open, at something like f/2.8 or f/1.8, the available light that lights your subject's face is smooth, soft, even light, and that's a big plus. You won't have to overexpose or use a reflector or anything like that—you'll be able to let in enough light without either.

Watch Out for Light Spilling on Their Face

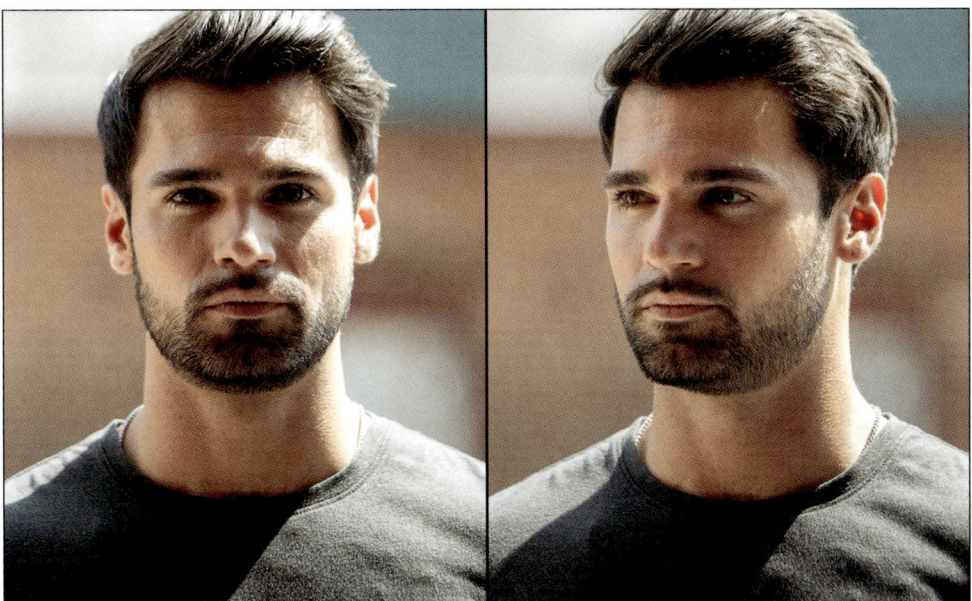

When you're out in direct light and putting your subject's back toward the sun (pretty much standard procedure unless you're shooting near sunset), make sure some of the light doesn't peek around and spill onto your subject's nose or too far over onto their face (like the shot you see above left). A little light skimming the outside edge of their face can look great, but you want your subject's face fully in shadows with nice, even light, without any harsh spots of light spilling onto their face. It's okay if light hits the back of their hair (in fact, that rim light halo around their hair can look awesome), just keep an eye out so that light doesn't hit anywhere on the front of their face. Fixing this can be as simple as having your subject move their head to the side (as seen above right), or simply repositioning your subject to get that nice, even light.

Using the Sun as a Rim Light or Hair Light

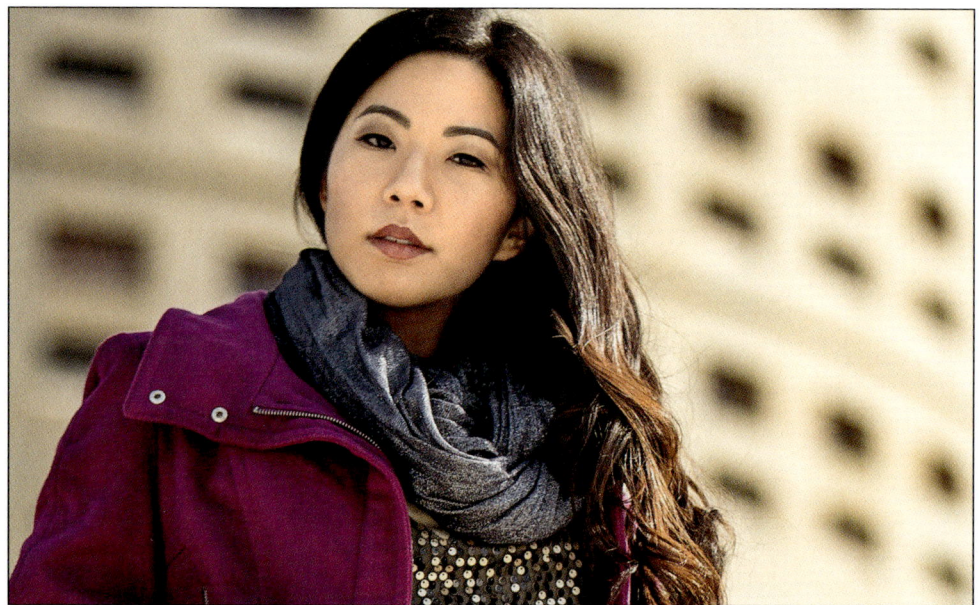

Later in the day, when the sun is lower in the sky, you can use the sun as a hair light, like the shot you see above. If we were in a photography studio, we'd call this bright light on the side "kicker light," or if it's more behind them, we'd call it a "rim light." To take advantage of the sun as your second light, turn your subject so the sun is behind them, but not directly behind them—you want it a bit to the side. Luckily, this is easy to see while you're positioning your subject, so getting them into this posi-tion where the sun is your rim light is fairly easy. It's also okay that this hair light is "hard light." Since it's not lighting the face, this hard light creates a nice contrast with the soft light on your subject's face (hard light on the hair, soft light on the face). The only thing you'll probably have to deal with is with that bright light behind your subject, your camera will automatically darken the exposure thinking the scene is too bright, so there are a few ways to deal with this: There's a great way on page 76, but another way is to (a) switch your camera to Spot Metering mode. That way, rather than evaluating the light from the entire image, it chooses your exposure from just the spot where you're aiming. Another method is to (b) move in really close to your subject—close enough so their face pretty much fills the frame and you don't see the bright areas around them. Now, look at the settings your camera would choose for a proper exposure of just their face, then switch your camera to manual mode and dial in those same settings. That way, their face will be properly exposed even though, normally, a subject like this would fool your camera's sensor, making a photo that's way too dark.

Getting Sun Flare Effects

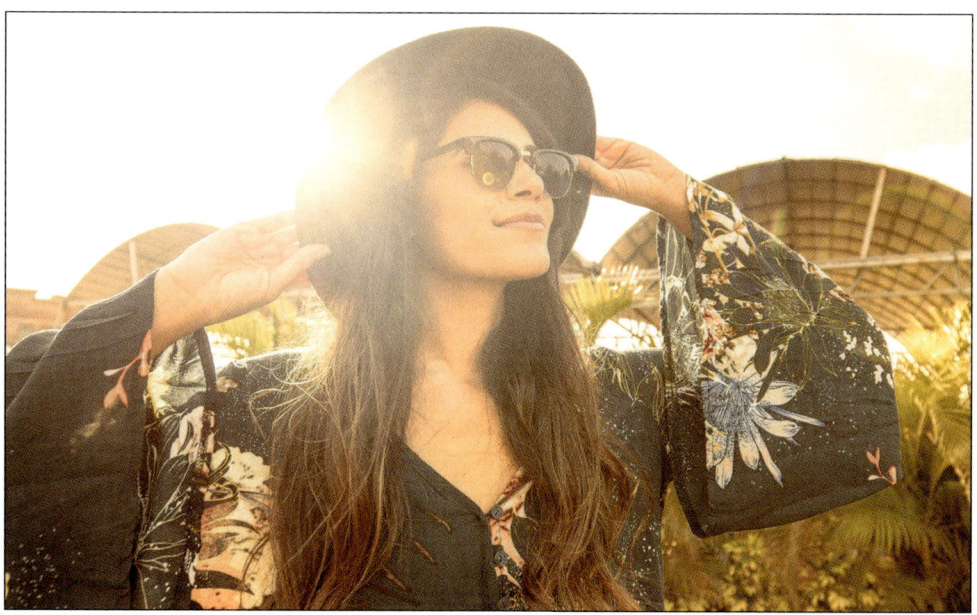

So, we spend money on lenses with special nano-coating, which helps avoid lens flare, and we walk around with the special lens hoods on our lenses to keep lens flare out, and then here I go showing you how to actually get lens flare into your photos. Why would I do that? Because this soft contrast, bright hazy look is hot right now and sooner or later (probably sooner), you're going to be asked to add this artistic effect on one of your portrait shoots. First (and this is going to sound kind of obvious), take off your lens hood. We're trying to invite lens flare into our lens. Second, use a wider-angle lens (you can use a longer lens; it's just sometimes harder to get it to flare). Third (again, this may sound kind of obvious), position your subject so you're shooting into the sun, and ideally, try to frame up your shot so you don't see the entire sun in it. I usually try to make the sun touch something (like I did here, where it's touching the edge of her hat)—you might have to get down lower to get the sun to touch your subject. Fourth, it's easier to get a lens flare later in the day when the sun is low in the sky. When it's "high noon" (between around 11:00 a.m. and 3:00 p.m.), and the sun is so high it's pretty much right above your subject, it's hard to get part of the sun at the edges or the inside of your frame. Finally, if you're struggling with how to create these effects in-camera, make sure you check out pages 132 and 134 in the Post-Processing chapter, where I show you how to add realistic lens flare effects in Lightroom or Photoshop.

The "Overexposing by a Stop or More" Trick

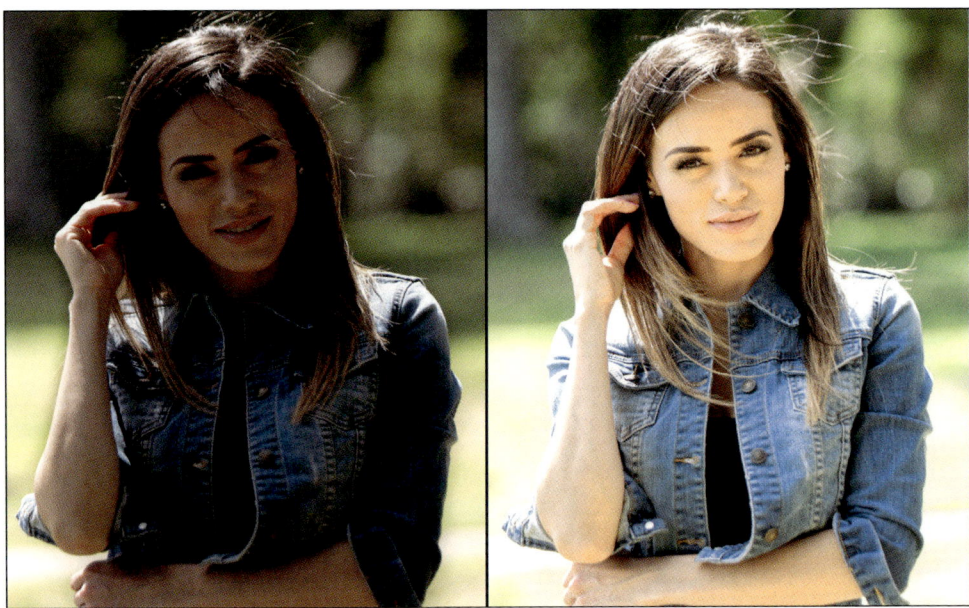

This trick works so well that it may open a whole way of shooting to you in natural light. Essentially, you want to put the sun behind your subject (as seen above left), and then you're going to overexpose the image by a stop and a half. This will make the background much brighter (which is the only downside), but it will also open up the shadows on your subject's face in a really dramatic way. An easy way to do this is to shoot in aperture priority mode, and then once you've taken a test shot (with your subject's back to the sun), use exposure compensation (the natural light photographer's best friend) to overexpose the scene by around a stop and a half. One way you can get around the downside part (the background getting too bright) is to position your subject against a somewhat dark background (like some dark trees or a dark wall, etc.), so when you overexpose the shot, it won't make the background too bright. It'll get brighter, but not too bright that it ruins the shot.

The Best Time to Shoot, Hands-Down

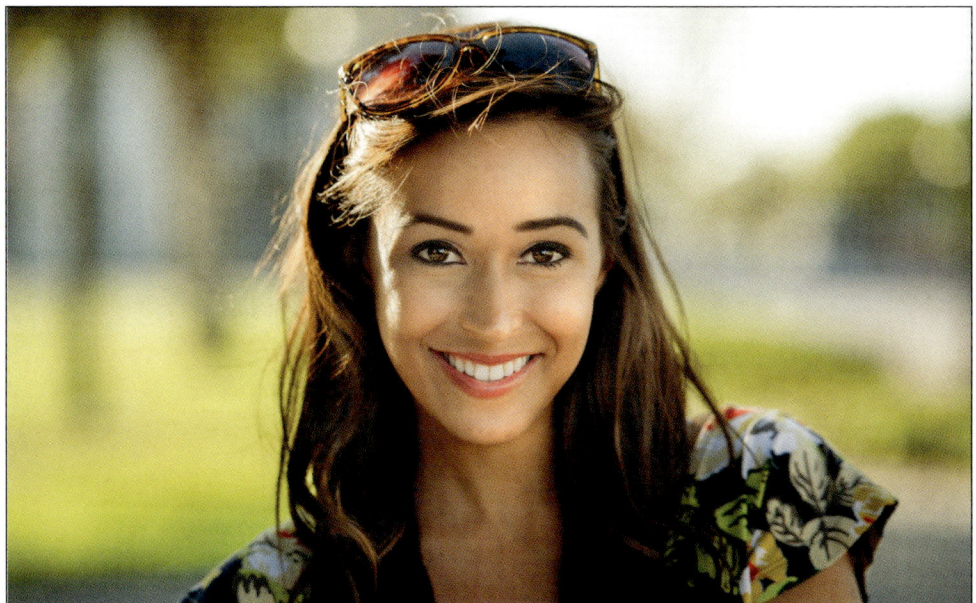

As you've seen throughout this book, there are all sorts of tricks and accessories we can use to let us shoot any time of the day. But, if you have a choice for what time to shoot, the absolute best, most flattering light outdoors is found either late in the day, around an hour before sunset, or first thing in the morning, right before dawn. Dawn is super-early, so let's just agree we'll be shooting an hour or so before sunset.

Look for Contrasting Backgrounds

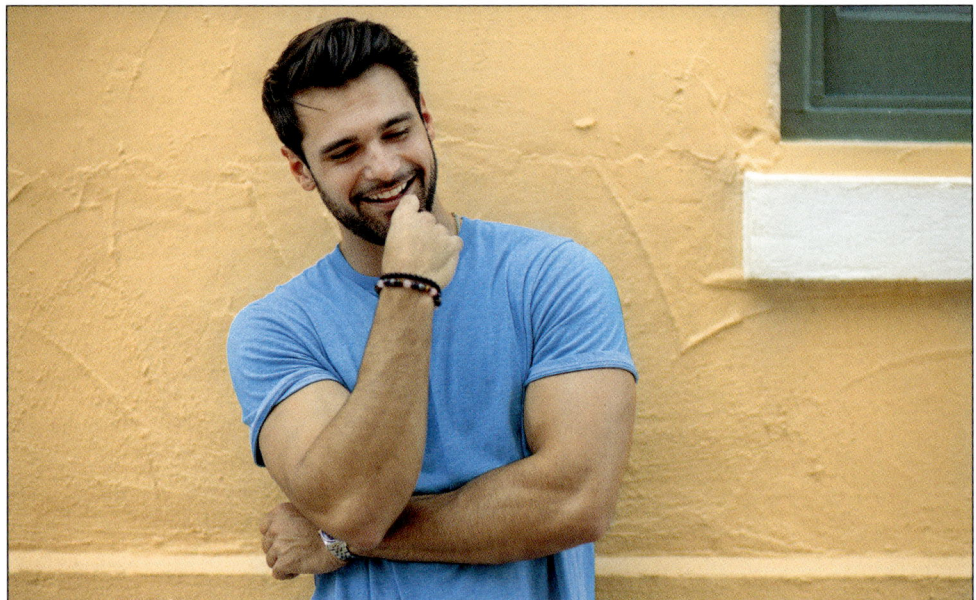

To help your subject stand out from the scene around them, look for a contrasting color to use as their background. The ideal situation is to find a background with complementary colors, so if they're wearing a blue shirt, you want to be on the lookout for a yellow wall to pose them in front of. They're wearing an orange shirt? Look for a blue wall. Of course, finding complementary color backgrounds are best-case scenarios, so if you can't find one, you can go with just a contrasting color—a bright shirt against a dark wall, and vice versa.

What to Have Your Subjects Wear

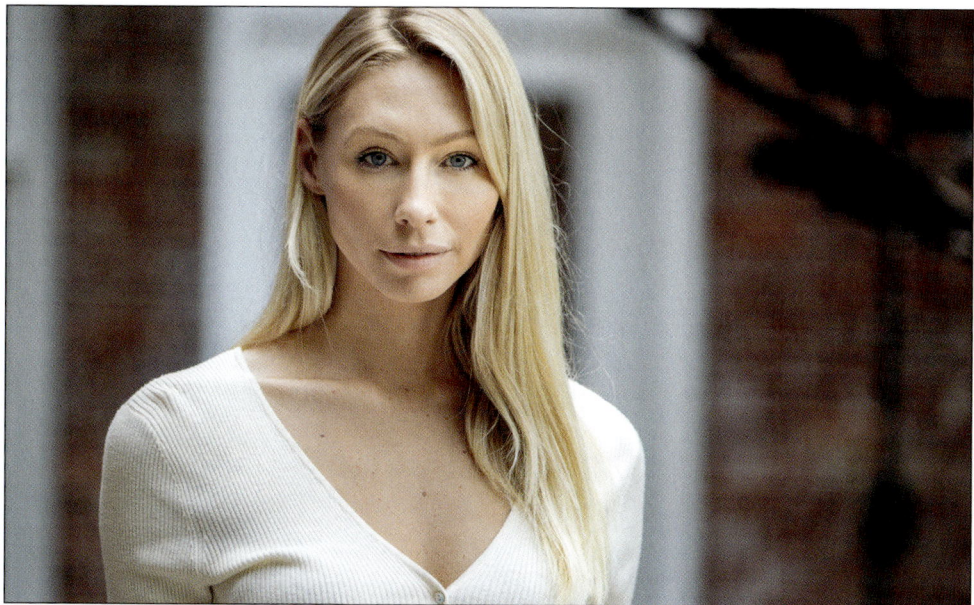

When you're working out the details of your natural light shoot, if it's going to be an outdoor shoot, one trick to help your subjects look great in natural surroundings is to have them wear lighter-colored clothing. Light colors have a fresh look that looks great outdoors. Go with light solid colors, no prints or patterns, and stay away from bright colors on these outdoor shoots. Keep the outfits simple and clean—white, tan, pastel tops and jeans look great. Stay away from dark colors or bright colors and you'll get more natural looking portraits.

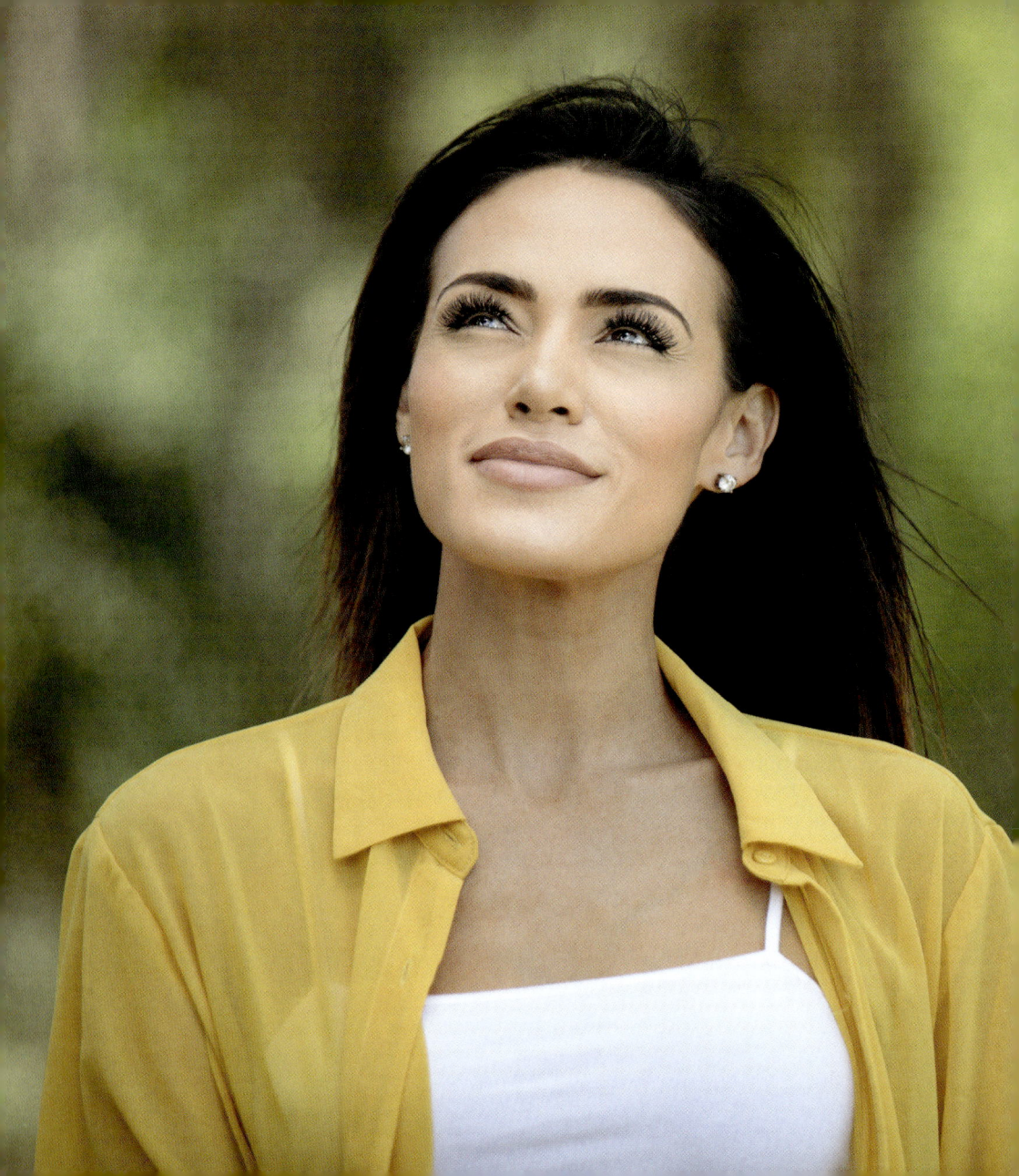

Chapter Six

Composition

Gettin' It All in the Frame

To really understand portrait composition, it helps to actually break down the word "composition." It's com-po-si-tion, so we'll start with "com," which is from the Latin word *caceus*, which means "blind." Next is "po," which is short for "poor," and if we stopped right there, we'd still be halfway to a great name for an old blues guitar player. Next is "si," which of course is Spanish for "to drink tea with jam and bread," and that brings us on to "tion," which is derived from the Latin term *talus*, which means "ankle." If you put these all together, the meaning is so crystal clear and so powerful. It's the all-important basis for everything we do when composing our images, and if you don't understand this fundamental concept of portrait photography from what you just read, you should go to eBay right now and sell all your gear. If you don't have gear yet, you should go buy some gear, and then immediately turn around and sell it all. Now, if you think I'm being hard on you, it's only because I love you. This is tough love, much like University of Alabama football coach Nick Saban gives to his players as he screams at them until a huge vein pops out in his forehead. It's that kind of screaming love I have for you, because I want you to take great portraits, and it doesn't matter if you're blind, or poor, or if you have tea to drink with jam and bread (in which case, your blues guitar name would be "Stank foot poor blind drinkin' jam Jones," which is an awesome name. I added the "Stank foot" just for effect). Anyway, I want you to compose your shots with the precision and love of an old bluesman, like the king of all fictional bluesmen, "Blind foot infected toe swamp butt Jamba Juice Jones!" Man, that guy could play. I mean compose a shot.

Composing for a More Intimate Portrait

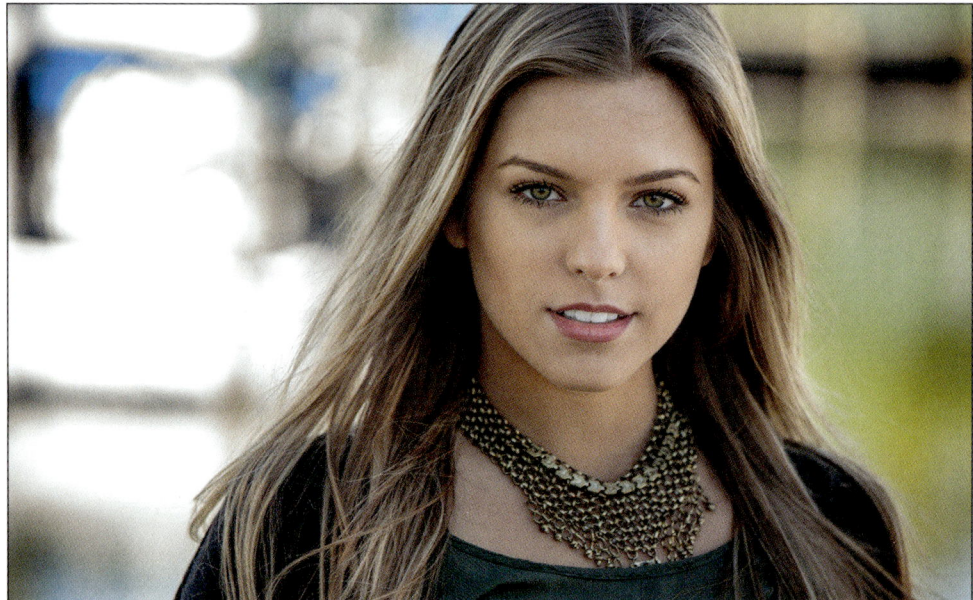

One of the easiest, yet most effective portrait techniques is to shoot in tight on your subject (using a zoom lens), so that they nearly fill the frame (as seen here). This creates a more intimate portrait by bringing your subject closer to the viewer. You can achieve this look using a longer lens (85mm or more), or by cropping the image tight, after the fact, in Photoshop or Lightroom.

Eyes Go in the Top Third of the Frame

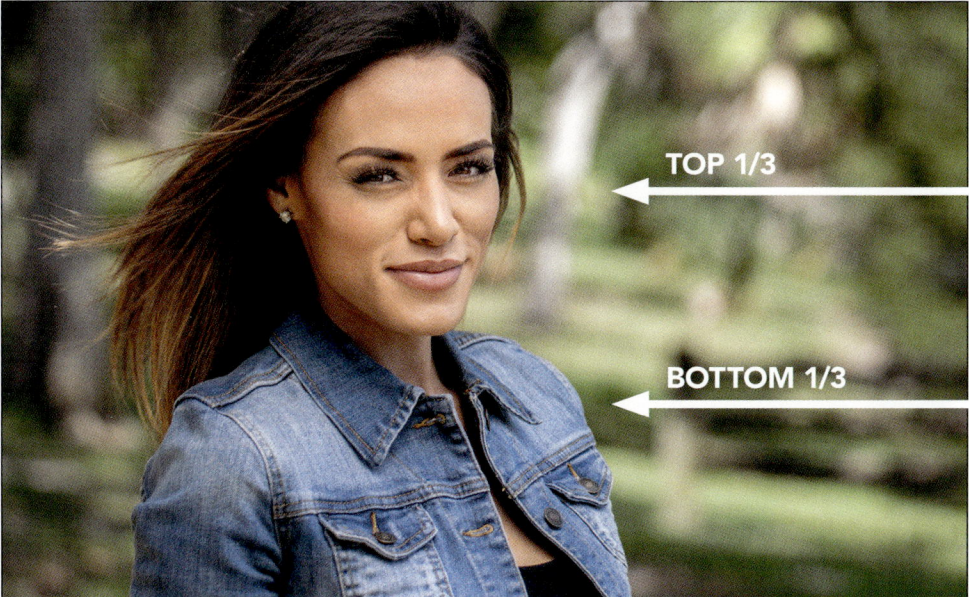

Here's an easy portrait composition rule to keep in mind: the goal is to keep your subject's eyes in the upper third of the frame. If you do that one thing, it will help you sidestep a number of compositional mistakes that you see in portraits.

Don't Center Your Subject in the Frame

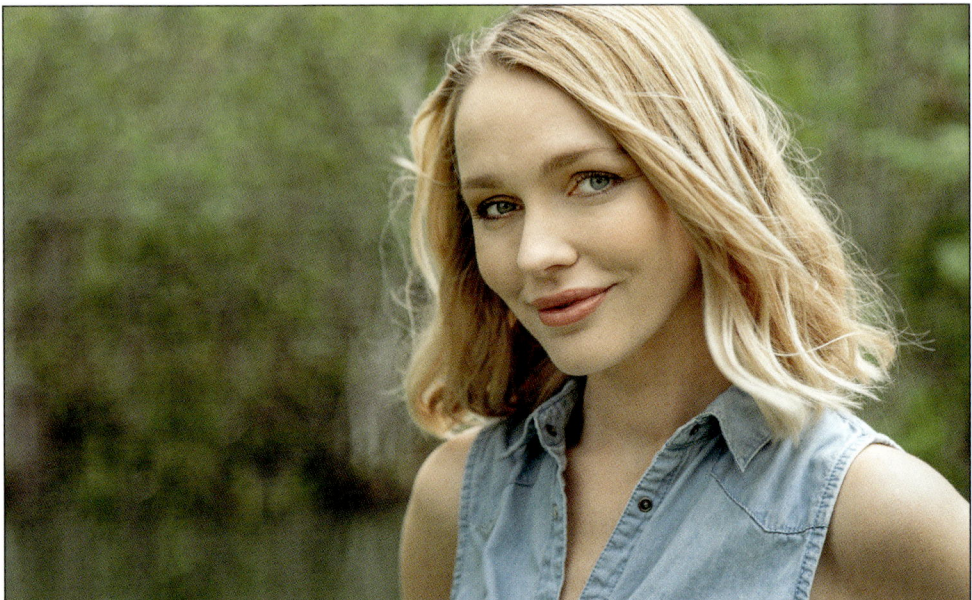

As a general rule, we don't want to put our subject in the dead center of the frame. That's what we tell our kids to do when we hand them a camera: "Look through the viewfinder and put mommy in the center." It's a direction we'd give a child because it's a simple one a child can follow, but it doesn't make a very dynamic photo. When you put your subject to one side or the other, it makes the image more interesting, more professional, and it's just a more dynamic composition.

Cut Off the Top of Their Head

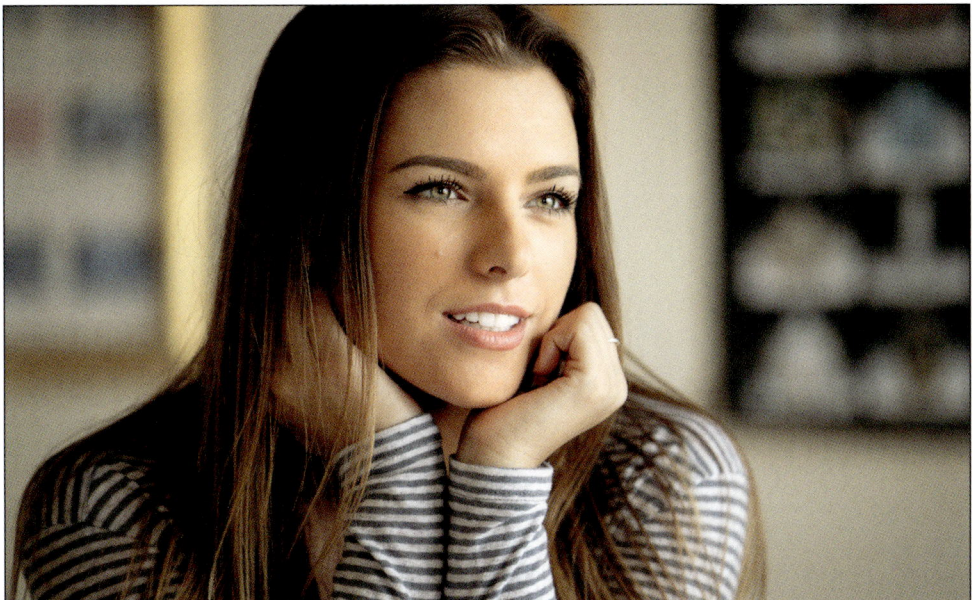

One of the most popular compositional techniques, and one that gives your portrait a more modern look, is to cut off 1/3 to 2/3 of the top of your subject's head when you compose the shot (as seen above). But, the key is to make sure you crop off enough. If you just cut off the tip of their hair, the person viewing the shot might think it was a mistake. The last thing you want to hear is: "That's a really nice shot. Too bad you cut off the top of her head." You won't hear that comment if it's obvious the shot was composed that way on purpose. Just make sure you frame it so that at least 1/3, if not 2/3, of the top of the head is cut off, so anyone can tell that was what you intended.

Don't Leave Too Much Space above Their Head

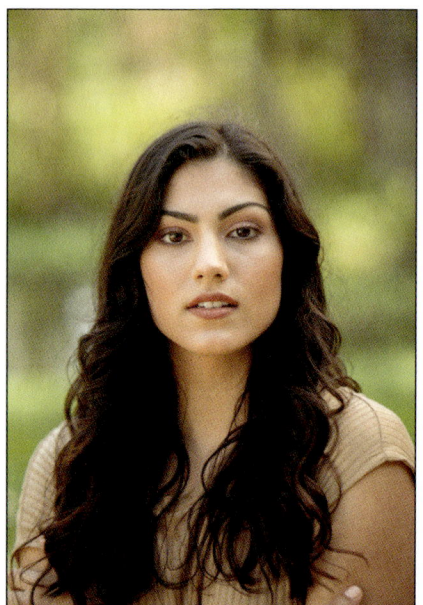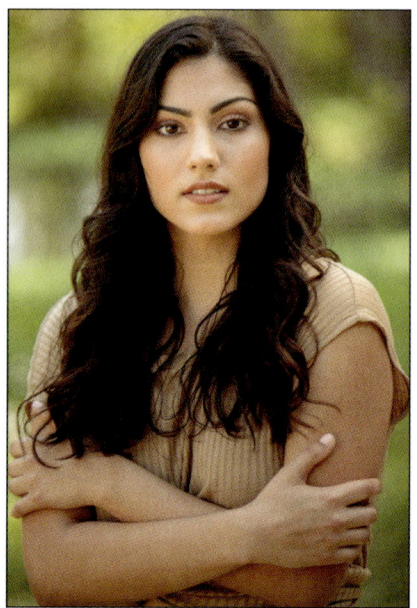

One of the most common compositional mistakes I see in portraits is leaving too much space above your subject's head. You shouldn't have a bunch of space above their head unless you are shooting it for a magazine or book cover or advertisement, and you intentionally left room for text or a logo. I think one reason people leave all this headroom is that they're trying to get the subject's eyes, or even their whole head, in the center of the frame. That's something you actually want to avoid—you want their eyes up in the top third of the frame (see page 83). Keep this little tip in mind, and your portraits will instantly have a more professional look.

Compose So There Is Space for Your Subject to Look Into

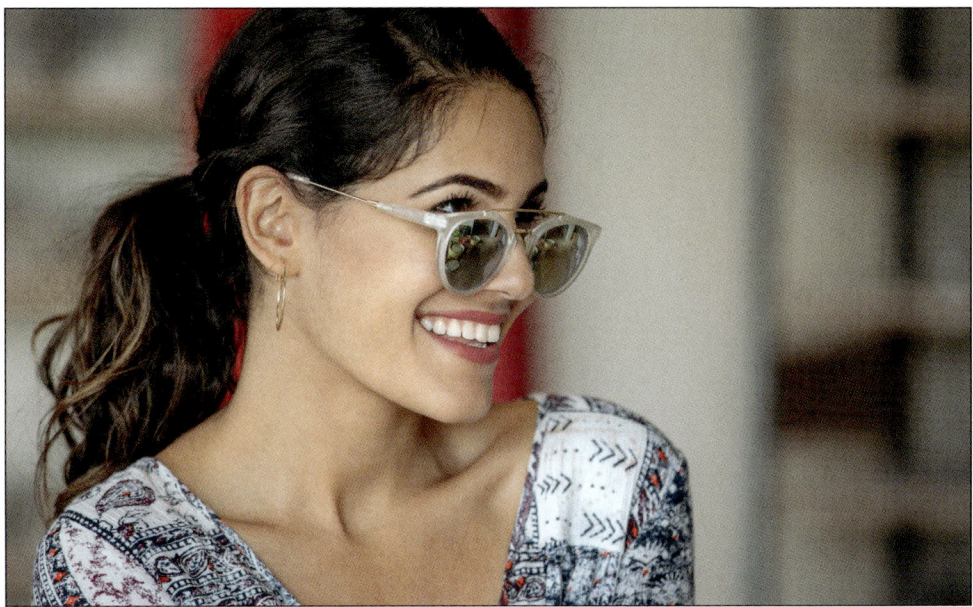

If you're going to have your subject look out of the frame, compose the shot so that they are not right up against the edge of the frame, and they've got some empty space to look into (as seen here). If you put them too close to the edge looking out, it makes the entire scene look a bit uncomfortable for the viewer. It's the same with athletes in motion or racing cars or wildlife in motion—if they're heading in a particular direction, leave some empty room in the frame for them to visually go into or you risk creating an image that subconsciously looks uncomfortable to your viewer.

You Want to See Catchlights

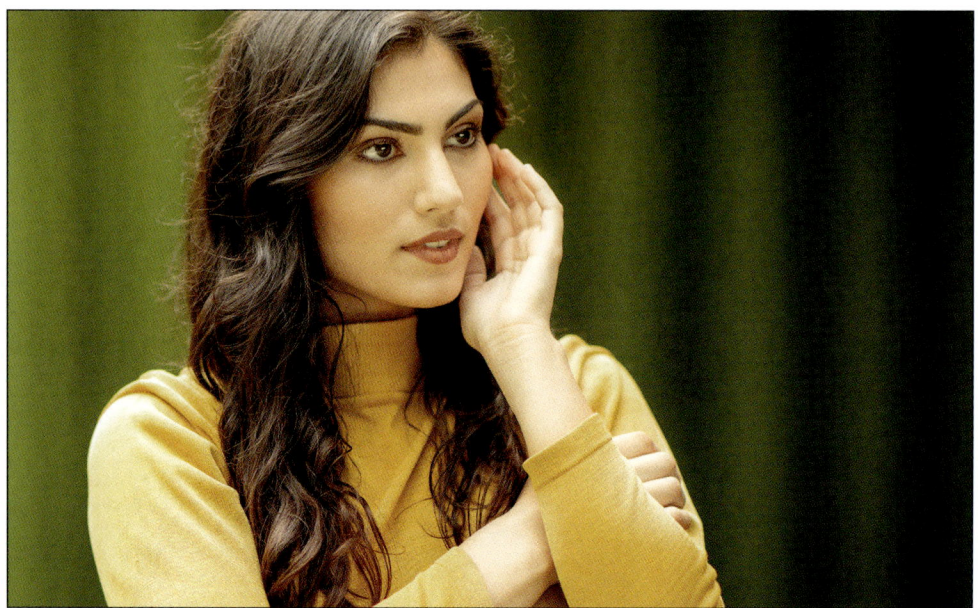

Generally, we see a reflection of the light source our subject was lit with in their eyes (as you can see here). It usually appears as a very small white circle near the center or top of their pupil when you're shooting with natural light because you're seeing either a reflection of the sun or a round reflector (if the sun is behind them). That little white dot in each eye is very important to the overall success of the portrait. That white dot of a reflection in the eyes is called a "catchlight," and if you don't see a catchlight in your subject's eyes, their eyes tend to kind of look "dead." These catchlights are so important to the overall look, sparkle, and appeal of the portrait that if I wind up with a shot where, for some reason, you can't see the catchlights in my subject's eyes, I go and add them manually in Photoshop, painting a small white dot using a small, soft-edged brush. I'm telling you all this, so (a) you'll realize the important role catchlights play in a natural light portrait; (b) you'll be on the lookout for situations where there are no catchlights, and you'll move or reposition your subject, so a catchlight appears in their eyes; and (c) you'll know that people sometimes add them in post, or even hold up reflectors just to create catchlights, even if those reflectors aren't bouncing light—they're just holding them up because it's that important to have those catchlights in the eyes.

Avoid Distracting Background Elements

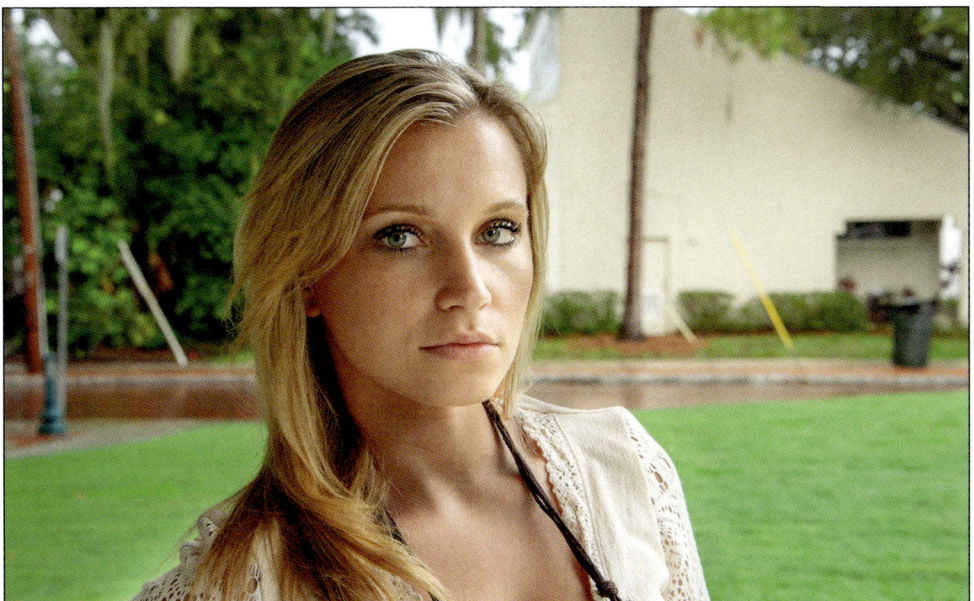

See that garbage can above on the far right, and the telephone poles, and the sign post? All of these things make for a messy, distracting background that draws your attention away from the subject. Famous painter Henri Matisse had a great saying about this, which was (I'm paraphrasing here) that if something in the image isn't helping the overall image, it only stands to reason that it's taking away from the image. He said it much more eloquently than that, but the point is spot on. That stuff in the background is taking away from our subject, and the solution would have been either to reposition the subject, so those elements don't appear clearly in the background, or zoom in tighter and use a low-numbered f-stop, so that background goes so blurry and out of focus that you don't notice those distractions. If something "kills" your image, more likely than not, it will be the background, so give that background the attention it deserves.

Keep the Scene Simple

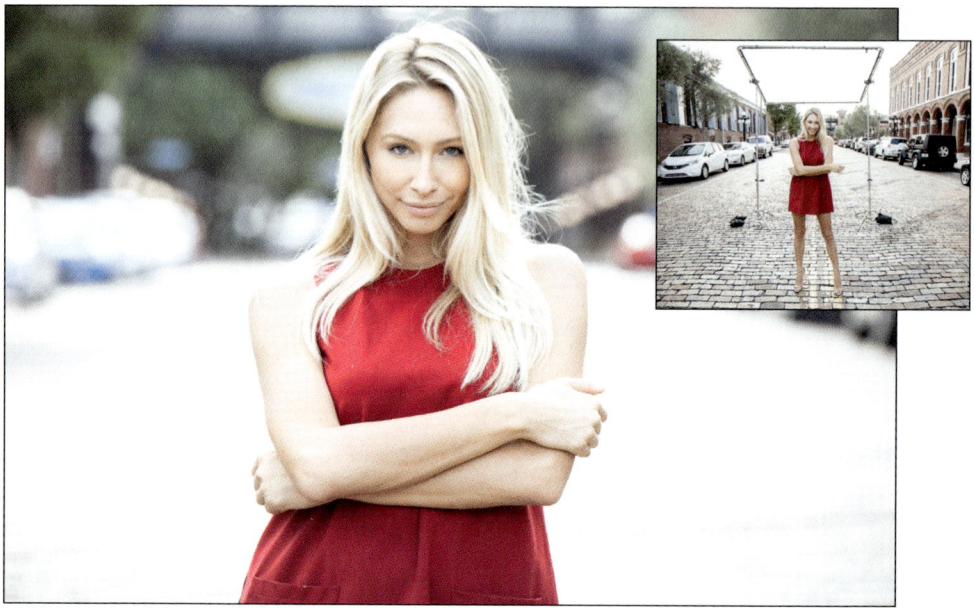

When it comes to portraits, for the most part, "less is more" and simplifying the scene is one of the easiest things you can do to have more powerful portraits. I know I've said it before, but it bears repeating: your background is more likely to ruin your shot than your subject, so do your best to either put the background way out of focus, or compose your shot to avoid anything that would pull the viewer's eye from your subject. This simplification is one of the reasons we shoot at those wide-open f-stops, like f/2.8 or f/1.8 or lower, because when we put the background out of focus, we remove distractions and simplify the scene. It's not what you add to the portrait that will make it stronger; it's what you take away. *Note:* You can see in the behind-the-scenes shot (in the inset above) that this was taken in a very busy area with cars and buildings and signs and so on. That's why I chose to shoot at f/2.8 with a long lens to put the background out of focus—all that stuff gets blurred away (you can see how we made the light soft and beautiful on page 63 where we talk about scrims).

Avoid Bright Spots in the Background

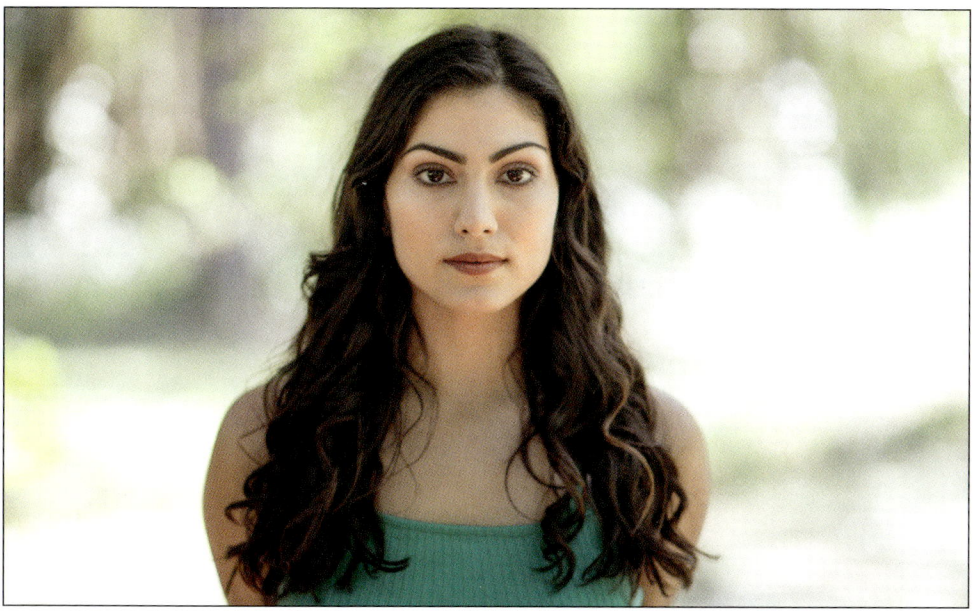

One mistake we often see is when there's something really bright in the background. Since our eyes are drawn to the brightest thing in the image, they are dawn to this bright spot in the background first, before they are drawn to the subject, and that's the last thing you want.

Get Low for Full-Length Shots

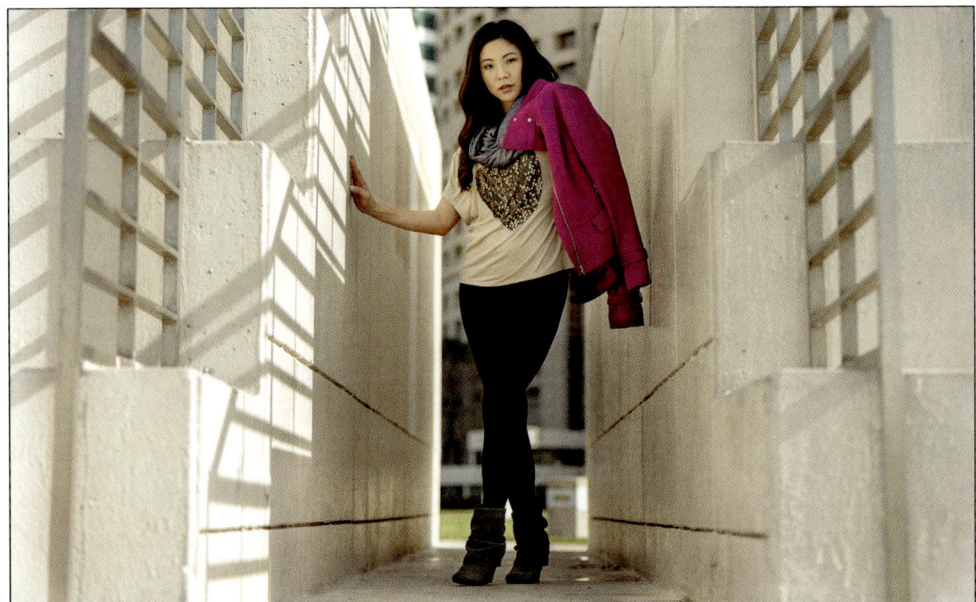

To get the right perspective for full-length photos (and to make your subject look their best), it makes a huge difference to get down low and shoot from that angle. This is one of those times where you're either kneeling or literally sitting cross-legged on the ground. I've even seen photographers lie on their stomachs when shooting full length— it makes that big a difference.

Shoot from a Slightly Higher Angle

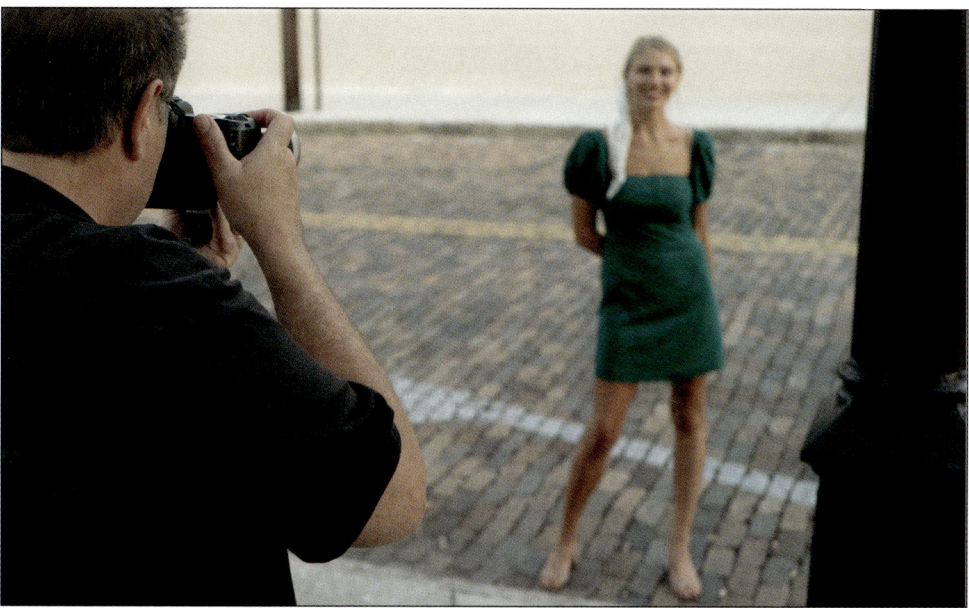

Have you ever noticed that people who are really good at selfies always hold their phone up a few inches higher than their head, and then they look up at their phone when they take the selfie? The reason why is simple: it makes them look better. That slightly higher point of view, above eye level, is more flattering to the face as it accentuates the jawline. By looking up at the camera it tightens the skin in the face and neck, as well. It makes a bigger difference than you'd think, and it's why many pro portrait photographers will shoot from a slightly higher angle, as well—it's a more flattering angle. In fact, if their subject is standing, they'll sometimes stand on top of something to put themselves up a little higher, so they can shoot from that angle. Matthews, a studio accessories maker, makes wooden boxes in a variety of different heights, called "Apple Boxes," which are sturdy as anything, and I use them if I have a tall subject and I need to get up a little higher than them to get that slightly higher angle. In the shot shown above, I'm standing on the sidewalk curb, to get a higher angle on my very tall subject, who is also wearing very high heels.

Avoid This Framing Mistake

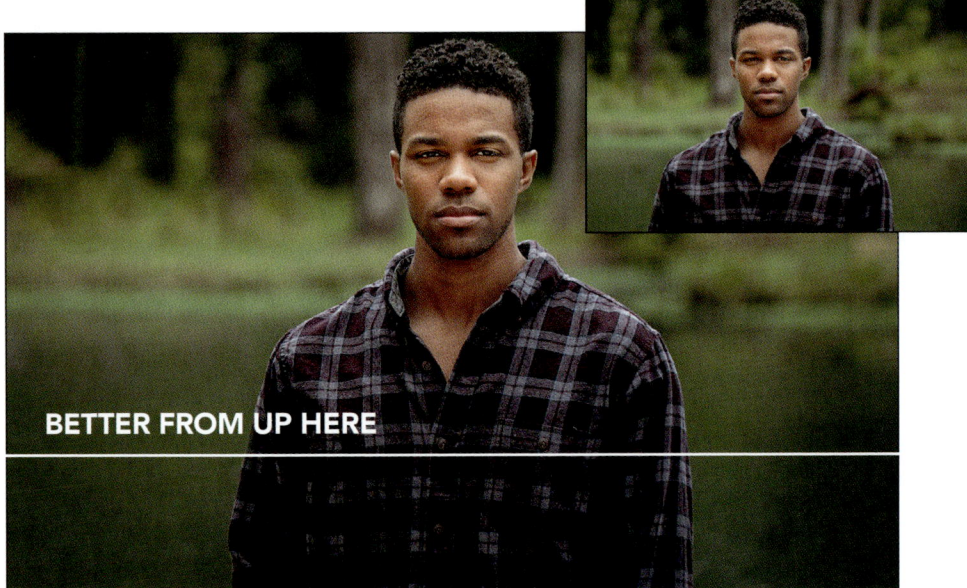

BETTER FROM UP HERE

One thing we want to make sure to avoid when composing our shots is framing them where we cut our subject off at any of their joints—we're talking elbows, wrists, or knees. It's another one of those things that makes the viewer feel uncomfortable when they're looking at the shot, even if they don't know why. Of course, unless you're shooting full-length, you're going to have to cut them off at some point, so our goal is to choose a place that's not uncomfortable to do so, and as long as you stay away from the joints, you'll be okay. Take a look at the image above. It's cut off too low—right at his elbows—and it makes for an uncomfortable composition. The white line is where a much better crop point would be (you can see the inset above has the proper framing).

Don't Cut Off Their Feet

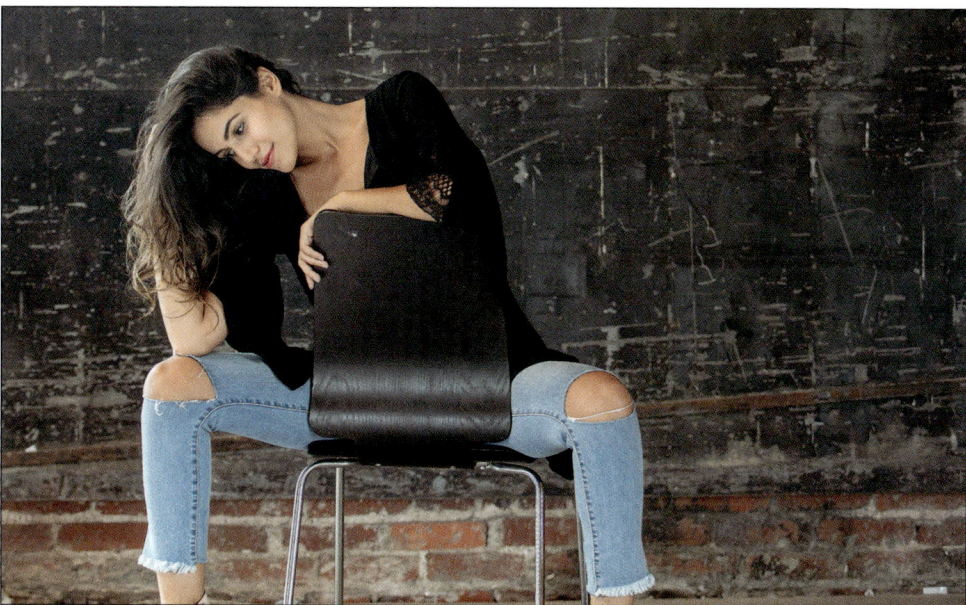

There is another part of the body you want to avoid cutting off when you're framing a shot: your subject's feet. Again, it's one of those things that your viewers will find uncomfortable—so much so, they might even call you out on it: "Oh, that's too bad you cut off her feet." The double-amputee look is probably not what you were going for, so pay attention to these critical areas when you're composing the shot—either keep them all the way in, or frame it so they're well out of the way.

Environmental Portraits

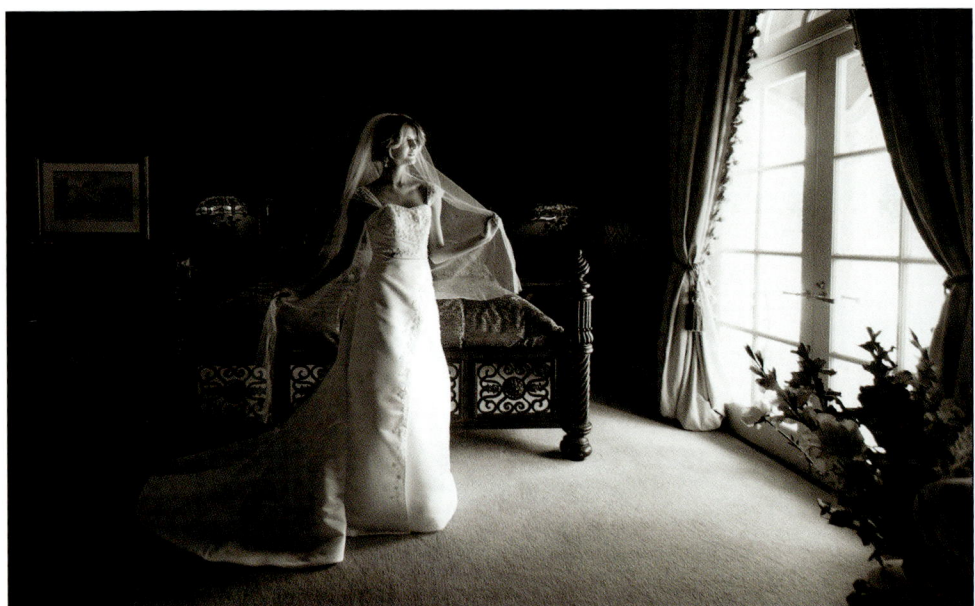

For the most part, when we're making portraits, we're shooting nice and tight in, making as flattering a portrait as we can, using lenses that flatter our subject. But there's another type of portraiture, the environmental portrait, where we're telling a bigger story, and the place where you're taking the portrait is part of the story of the person whose portrait you're making. You see this a lot in magazine articles, where the story is about the person and what they do. For example, if the article is about a mechanic, the environmental portrait might be taken in his or her garage, and the tools and work area and cars in the background are critical to the story. In this case, we're generally not trying to separate the subject from the background; we're not trying to create a soft, blurry background because that background is very important to the story we're trying to tell. It also affects our lens choice, as you'll probably want to use a wide-angle lens, like a 24–70mm to capture your subject and this larger scene. We're trying to make a captivating, storytelling image—not just a beautiful portrait.

Photographing Kids

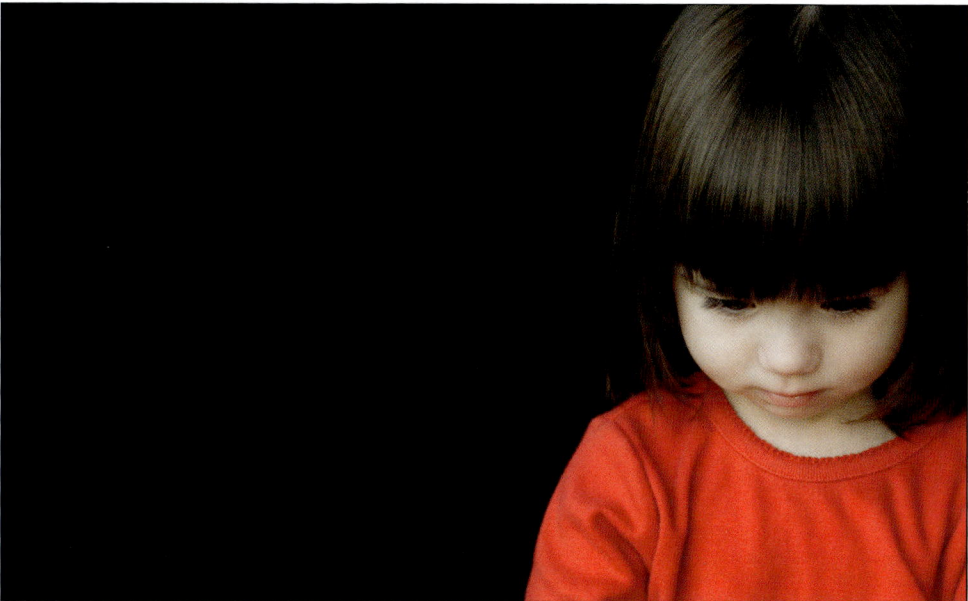

There's a simple compositional trick for photographing kids that makes a huge difference, and that's to not shoot down on them from a standing position. We generally see children in our daily lives from a standing position, looking down at them, and while that's the reality because of our height differences, it doesn't make for a very engaging portrait. You're seeing them as we usually see them. But, if you want to make really engaging portraits of kids, ones that are more personal, with a real connection, get down and shoot at their height level. This might mean shooting down on your knees, or even sitting on the ground to get down low enough to be at their height, but the difference it makes in your portraits of children will be worth it.

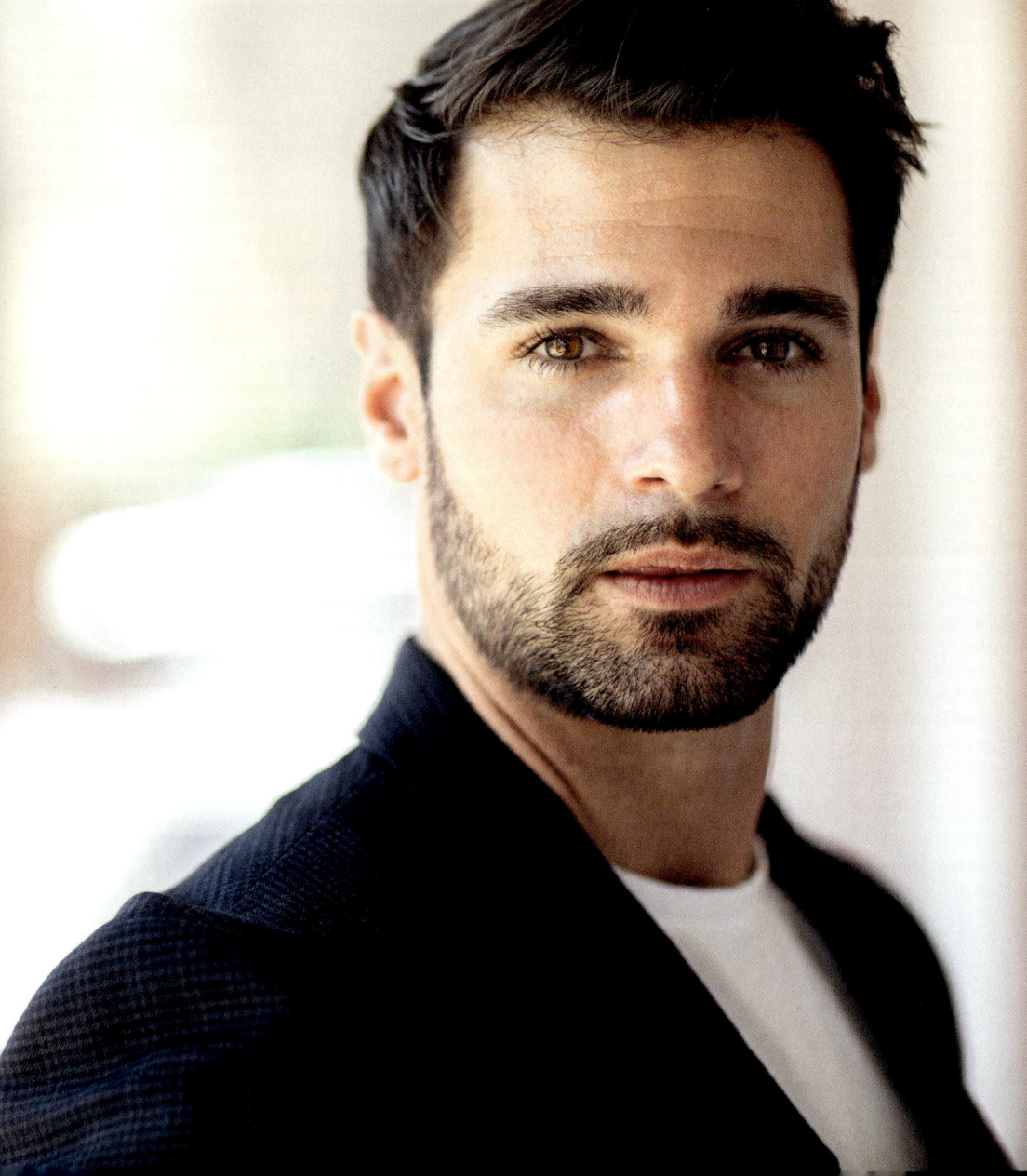

Chapter Seven

Posing
How to Be a Poser

Reading that subhead above, "How to Be a Poser," you might think, at first, that it's a negative subhead. But, look at it again. Just a quick glance. If you glanced fast enough, you might have read it as "How to Be a Loser." It's just one letter off, so it's an easy mistake. But, if you don't know how to pose your subject, well…I think you can see where I'm going with this. Now, you might be thinking: "Scott, is this more of that tough love that you were talking about in the previous chapter?" No, this is just me being mean, which is a lot of fun (for me anyway). This being mean stuff; this is what we became authors for in the first place. Sure, the private jets are fun, and the all-night raves, and hanging out with Hollywood celebrities at those star-studded photography book author parties. Did I mention the private jets? Well, we all get one the day we sign our book contracts. Some of us get two. That way, one can be used as a decoy when Russian Su-35 fighter jets intercept us out in international waters on our way to (you guessed it) one of those star-studded photography book author parties. Look, who am I kidding? There are no jets, or parties, or Hollywood celebrities, so our only perk is yelling at our readers while they're reading the book. This is it. Making them feel bad, so we can feel better about ourselves. It's invigorating. Intoxicating even. This is what we get for all the blood, sweat, and tears we put into our books (that and spinning wheels, which got to go round). Anyway, back to the yelling. Listen, the truth is there are poses that are flattering and make people look awesome, and if you don't know those, it's likely your subjects will all look like Jabba the Hutt in their pictures. Have you ever seen a tight close-up shot of Jabba? Well, there's a reason for that. Don't let your subjects down. Learn to be a poser, and then becoming an Instagram influencer can't be far behind.

What Makes a Truly Memorable Portrait?

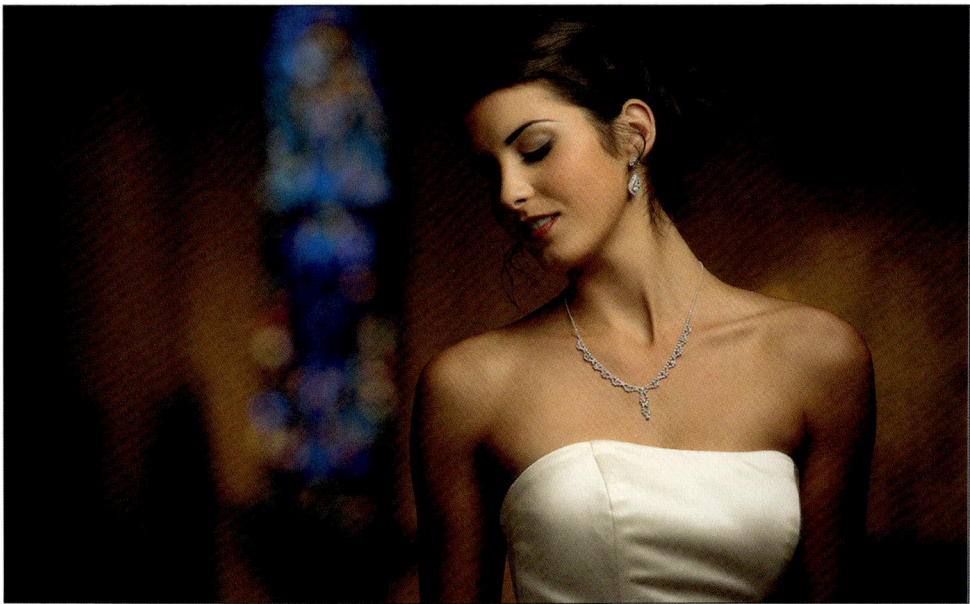

One of the greatest photographers of our time, Paul Caponigro, once said, "It's one thing to make a picture of what a person looks like, it's another thing to make a portrait of who they are." That nailed it plain and simple. You can have great lighting, a wonderful pose, and you can be shooting in a great location and still create a really average portrait. One that's more of "here's who was there that day" rather than "here's who this person really is." Capturing their spirit, their character, and a genuine look into who they are, not just what they look like, is what makes a truly great portrait that connects with the viewer in a meaningful way. This is why many top professionals often do research on their portrait subjects before the shoot, learning as much about them as possible and building a connection to them before they even meet. Thanks to Facebook, the process of researching someone (getting to know a bit about them digitally before meeting them in person) is easier than ever. But, at the end of the day, spending time with your subject one on one, and learning about who they are and what they are like, gives you a much better chance of bringing that side of them out in your portraits. One thing that helps is building enough time into your portrait shoots so that you're not rushing through them—rushing to get set up, rushing through different poses, and rushing to get done. If you build enough time into the shoot to have time to connect with your subject and learn about them, you'll have a better chance of making a portrait that truly speaks to who they are.

Photographing Photogenic People

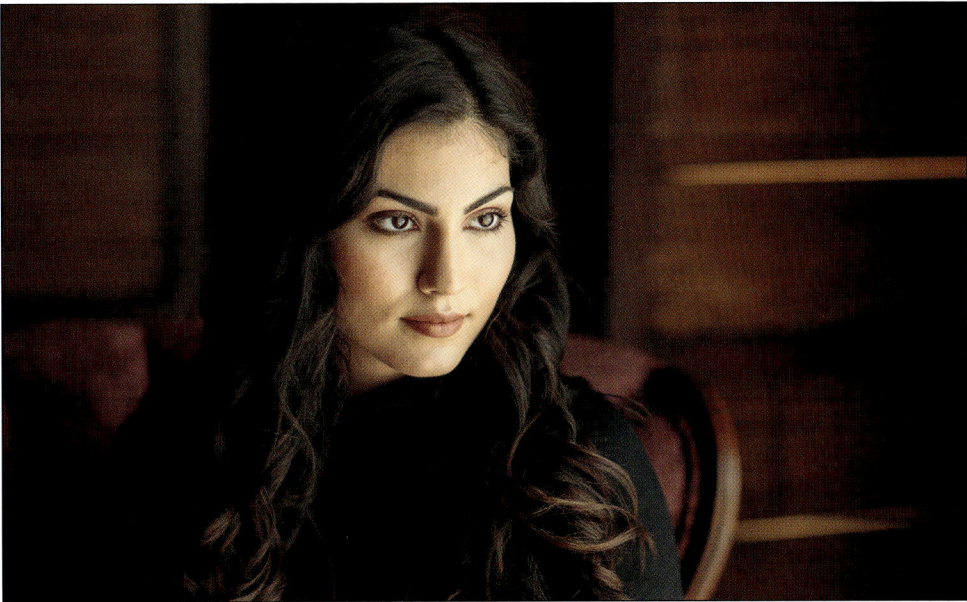

There are people who have a particular facial bone structure that the camera just loves, light just loves, and they're so photogenic that you can't take a bad picture of them. We've all known people like this—even when they're goofing off for the camera, they still look great. If you're lucky enough to get one of those people in front of your camera, it's a lock that you're going to get a great image, and you're going to think, "Hey, I'm getting pretty good at this." At the same time, there are also people who, in real life, look very attractive, but for some reason they don't look nearly as good in pictures as they do in real life. If you get one of those people in front of your camera, you're going to think, "This is a good-looking person, but I'm making a lot of 'meh' pictures of them. I guess I just don't have a feel for this." I'm telling you this up front, so you'll understand what a difference photographing someone who is truly photogenic makes to your success as a photographer. It's also important to understand that it's not just "pretty" people who make awesome portraits; interesting people can have that wonderful bone structure, too. I'm telling you this so you don't get frustrated while you're practicing portrait photography. If you've been practicing by shooting your cousin Earl and you're not happy with how it's going, it might be that Earl is just not photogenic. His bone structure may be one the camera just doesn't like. Seek out a friend, or a cousin, or a neighbor who looks great in snapshots. Now, get that person in front of your camera, with these techniques, and you'll crush it. This is more important than anyone else will tell you.

Build a Posing List

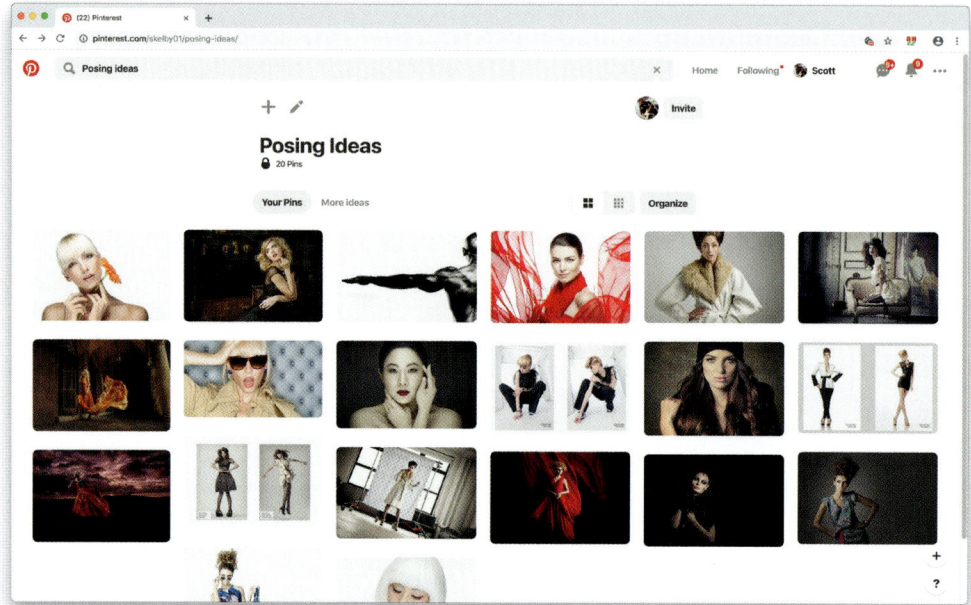

One of the best features of the free Pinterest website is that you can create private boards of pictures you find on the web that can't be seen by the public. I have a number that I created just for posing ideas, and that's what I would recommend you do. When you're browsing the web and you see an awesome pose, just save that image to your Pinterest Posing Ideas board. What's nice about these boards is that you can then use the free Pinterest app on your phone to view your posing inspiration board while you're out on a shoot. You can create as many different boards as you'd like, so you can have one for outdoor fashion, one for outdoor headshots, another for poses for family portraits, another for couples, etc. It's incredibly helpful to have these right on your phone, so you can refer to them during your shoot.

Build Rapport

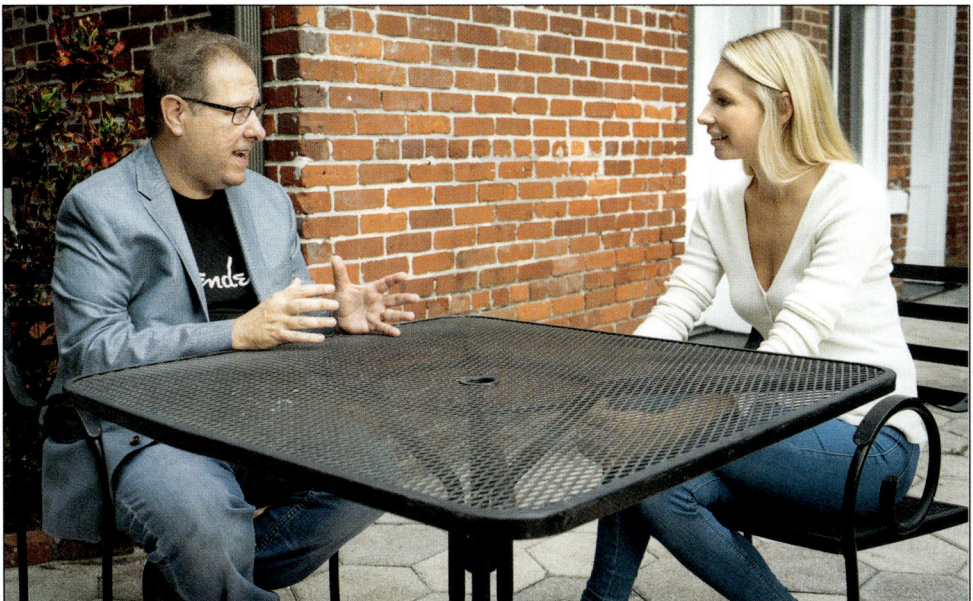

Before you start your shoot, one of the best things you can do for the success of your shoot is not to pick up the camera right away, but spend a few minutes chatting with your subject and getting to know them. This is when you want to find out what topics they're passionate about (their kids? Sports? Volunteering? Their job? Their pets? Their favorite types of music? Favorite movies? These are things people love to talk about and that put them at ease. Coffee is always a great topic because everybody can talk about coffee. I'd stay away from politics and religion— you might find out you don't like or you disagree with their views, and that's going to affect your connection with them). This time you spend before the shoot, getting to know your subject, is actually a real investment in its success. If you can make your subject feel comfortable, if you can build a rapport now, and if you can connect with them, it will show in the final images. Don't underestimate the power of this time you spend with them before the shoot.

Which Outfit Should They Wear First?

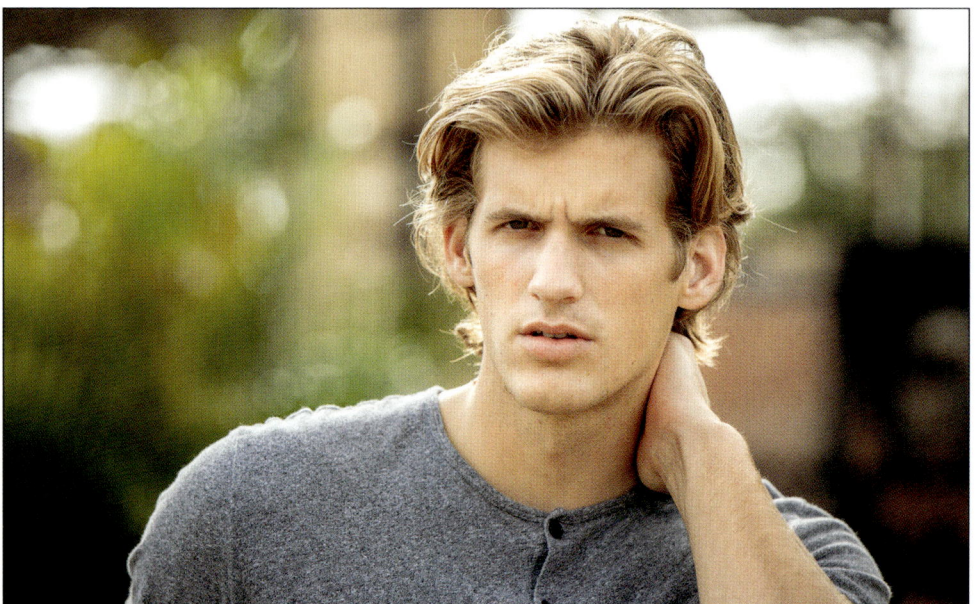

This is another trick I've been using for years, and it works like a charm. Very often, my subject for the shoot will show up with a number of different outfits (if they're a professional model, they'll sometimes show up with an entire wardrobe), and I have a great tip for picking the first outfit for the shoot: I always pick the outfit I like the least to shoot first, or choose the outfit that they brought that they like the least. Why? It's because at the beginning of the shoot, both my subject and I are "ice cold." Neither of us is warmed up yet, we're not "in the zone," and usually the subject is still a bit uncomfortable and awkward. All of this will go away 15 or 20 minutes into the shoot. You'll have warmed up and gotten into your groove, you've already spent some time with your subject, they're feeling more comfortable, and you're starting to connect with them. Once you feel you're both in the zone, it's time to move on to outfits you like and the results will be much better. Don't shoot that great outfit while you're both ice cold—wait till everybody has warmed up before you bring out their best look.

Stop and Review Five Minutes into the Shoot

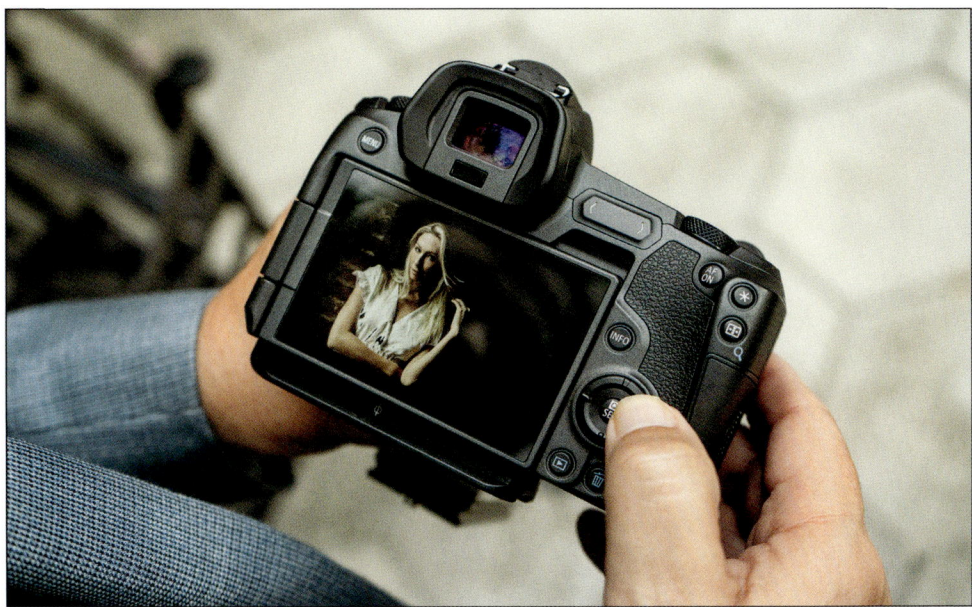

Here's a trick I learned (the hard way) that has helped me get more "keepers" in any portrait shoot: About five minutes into the shoot, I stop and take a quick break and look through the first batch of shots we've taken. What I'm looking for is any particularly unflattering look that my subject is giving me that they don't realize they're doing. For example, let's say instead of smiling, my subject gives a smirk (I've seen this a lot). Or, they give me a really big smile that shows a lot of their gums, but they would look better with a small, less gummy smile. So, when do you want to learn about this gummy smile issue? When the shoot is over and you see 150 gummy smile shots, or five minutes into the shoot when you have a chance to subtly direct your subject to give you just a "little smile" instead? By doing this, you only have those really gummy shots in the first five minutes of the shoot, not throughout the whole shoot, and you'll wind up with a lot more keepers. Also, of course, don't mention to your subject that they have a "gummy smile"—you don't want to make them upset or self-conscious. You just want to direct them toward the kind of look they'll love in pictures, giving you both more keepers to choose from at the end of the shoot.

The Shots between Poses

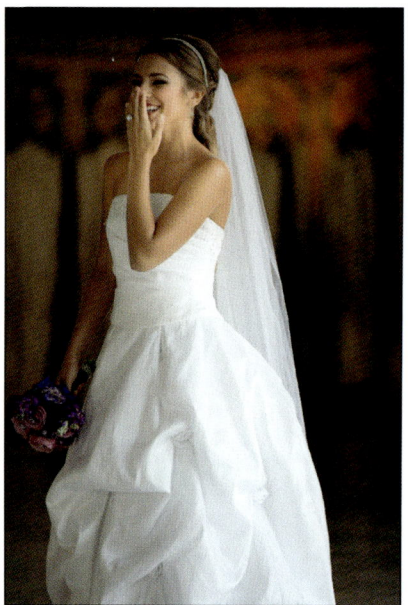 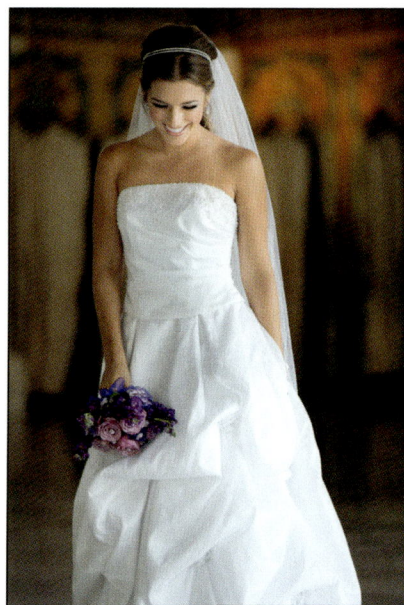

This whole chapter is about posing, and it can really help a lot in making people look their best. But, if you ask almost anybody which kind of portraits they like, they'll probably tell you they like portraits that look real and unposed the best. Here's a trick I use for getting real expressions that works well: I let them go ahead and do a pose first (thanks to Instagram, most people these days have some default pose they're comfortable with). The key is to let them do that pose, and then try to capture the real moments between poses that happen while you're just chatting. I try to find something that they're passionate about before the shoot (see page 103), and then we start chatting about that during the shoot, between the poses. You have to get used to chatting with the camera up to your eye because you have to be ready to fire those shots between the poses, if you really want to capture those real emotions. The real expressions. It's those moments in between where you'll come away with your best shots from the shoot.

Directing Your Subject during the Shoot

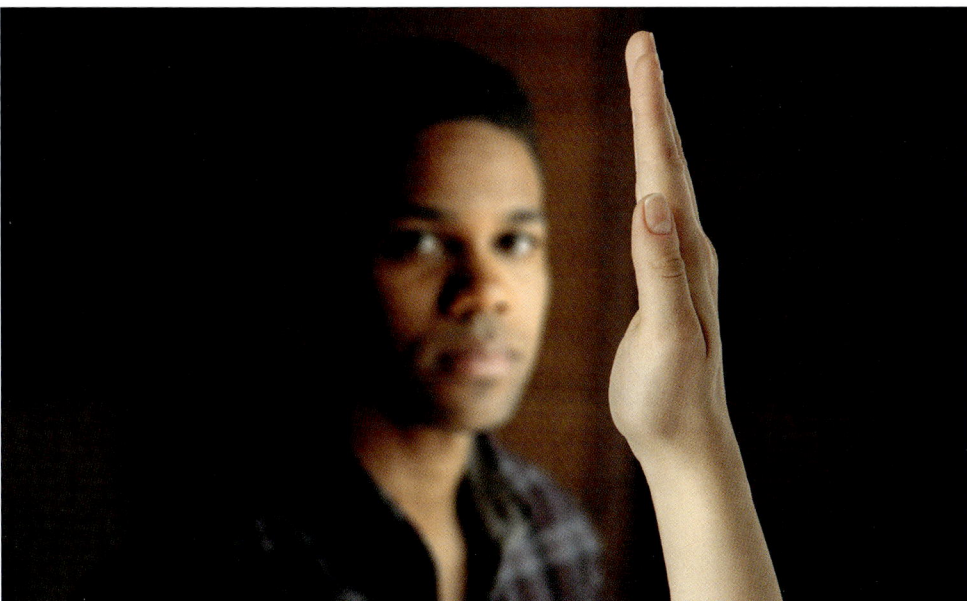

When you're standing in front of your subject with your camera, it's like you're shooting into a mirror. Everything is reversed—their right is your left, your left is their right—and if you tell your subject to "move about a foot to the left," there's a pretty good chance they're going to move to their left, not your left. Then you have to correct them and have them move the other way. You feel silly, they feel stupid—it's not an awesome situation. That's why I recommend not using "lefts or rights" at all during a shoot. Instead, hold your hand up vertically in front of you and direct them with it. Move your hand in the direction you want them to go and say, "Can you move a little this way?" You can also move them forward, backward, and have them tilt their head or chin, etc., all by having them follow your hand. Now, if you move your hand to the left, and you ask them, "Can you move a little this way," and they move in the opposite direction, you might have an entirely different problem—one you won't be able to fix on a photo shoot. But I digress. Anyway, this directing-by-hand-movement is a great thing to get used to using, and it's especially helpful when photographing younger children, since they probably don't know their left from their right yet anyway. Get used to this method, and you'll sidestep some potentially awkward situations.

Looking Directly Toward the Camera

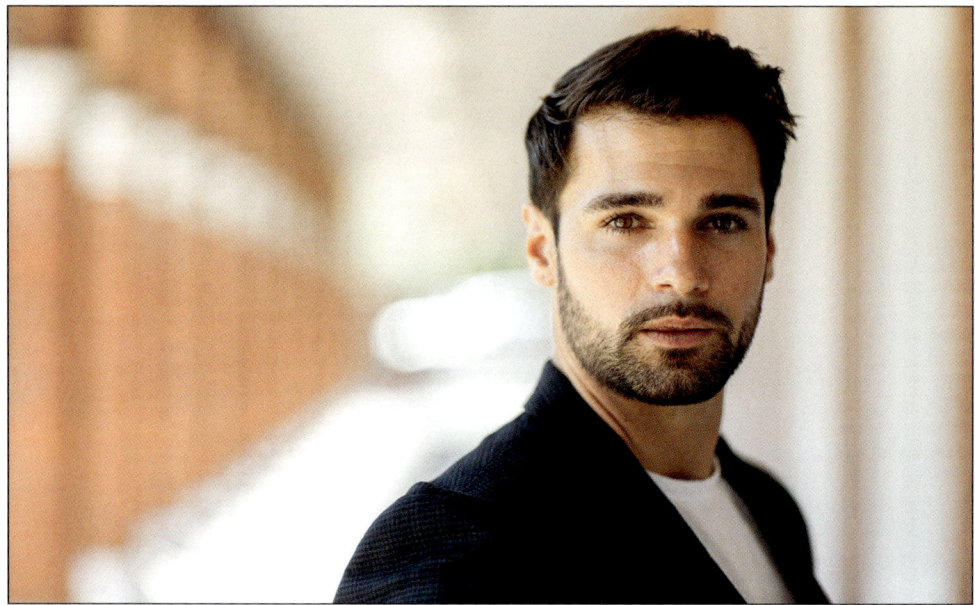

There are two main positions for your subject, and each has a different impact on the overall look and feel of the portrait. They are: looking directly into the camera or looking off and away from the camera. The most commonly used pose is for your subject to look directly at the camera, and by doing so, they make direct eye contact with the viewer and immediately engage them. It can be a very intimate type of look where you feel the connection to the subject. Also, when your subject looks directly at the camera like this, it's clear they are aware they're being photographed. Of course, depending on their facial expression, this direct engagement can be solemn, sad, happy, confrontational, intimate, intense, and so on, so this direct-at-the-camera pose generally offers more possibilities for expression and connection.

Looking Off-Camera

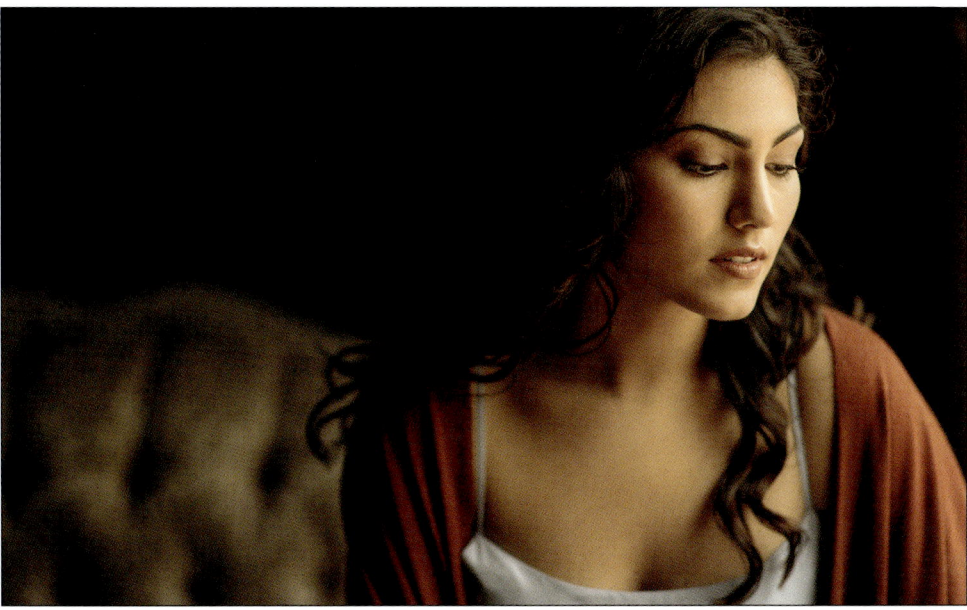

When you have your subject look off-camera (away from your shooting position), you're telling an entirely different story. In fact, it can be a better storytelling device because it makes you wonder what the subject is looking at. Are they just lost in thought, or is something happening off in the distance that they're looking at? It makes you wonder what the story is. Looking away from the camera like this is a less intimate look than looking straight toward the camera, but at the same time, it's a very casual look and feels more unposed and candid. Looking off-camera like this is also a very popular look in fashion photography, so if you want your portrait to have a more fashiony look (not sure fashiony is even a word), have your subject look away from the camera.

The Eyes Have It

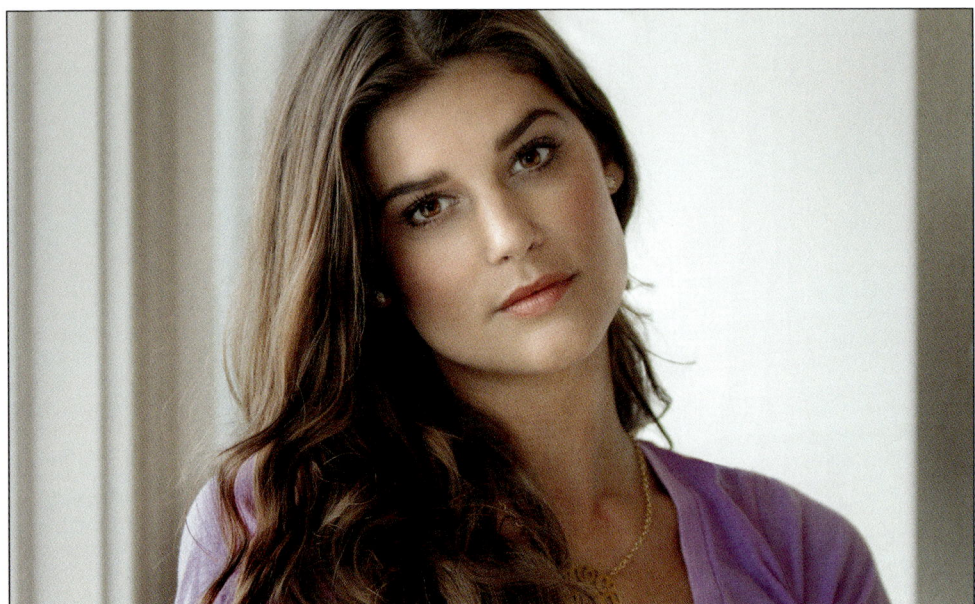

When we talk about expression and emotion in our portraits, it's important to realize that most of that will come from your subject's eyes. The eyebrows help, the lips can help, too, but in the end, it's the eyes that will have the greatest impact on the emotion and expression in your shot. It's one of the reasons we try to make sure the eyes are well-lit and why it's so important that they're in focus. The eyes will be the most striking feature of your subject, so make sure you nail the focus (see Chapter 2), as it's the eyes that will likely make or break your portrait.

Avoid Seeing Too Much Whites In the Eyes

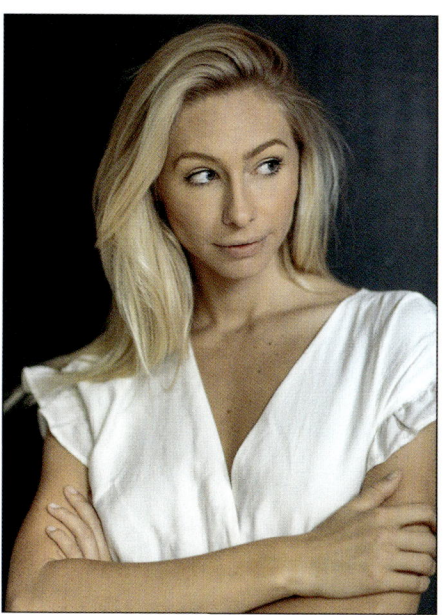 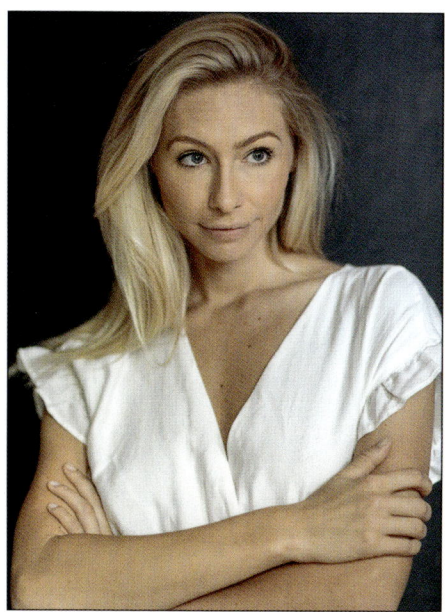

When your subject is looking away from the camera, you want to be careful to not have them look too far to the side or you'll see too much of the whites of their eyes. We want to see lots of their iris and pupil and only a little of the whites. One technique I use when I'm at my camera position is to hold my hand out straight away from my body, and I tell them to look at my hand. That way, they don't look too far away from the camera, and that keeps them from looking too far way. This keeps their irises where you want them, and avoids you seeing too much of the whites of their eyes.

If They Have a Roundish Face, Do This

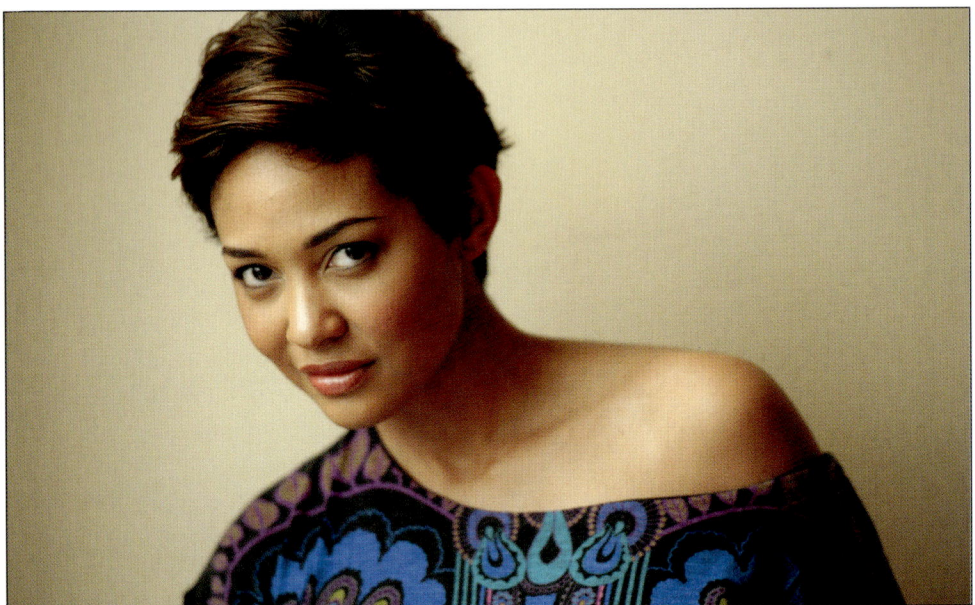

Most people have more of a round face, and there's a way we can pose them that slims their face and gives them an overall more flattering look. It's called "short lighting," and all you have to do to short light somebody is to shoot into the shadow side of their face (so the lit side of their face is the farthest side from you). Take a look at the shot above. The light is coming from the window on the left side of the frame, so that side of her face is the side that is well-lit. The side closest to the camera (seen here on the right) is the side in shadows, and shooting into this side of her face makes her face look longer and thinner, and is more flattering. Generally, I short light everybody, because I think pretty much everybody looks better this way, and I think shadows are just awesome, so I love seeing more of them. That being said, there are situations where you realize you need to light their face, so it looks rounder, or more broad. That's when we use broad lighting (see the next page).

If They Have a Thin Face, Do This Instead

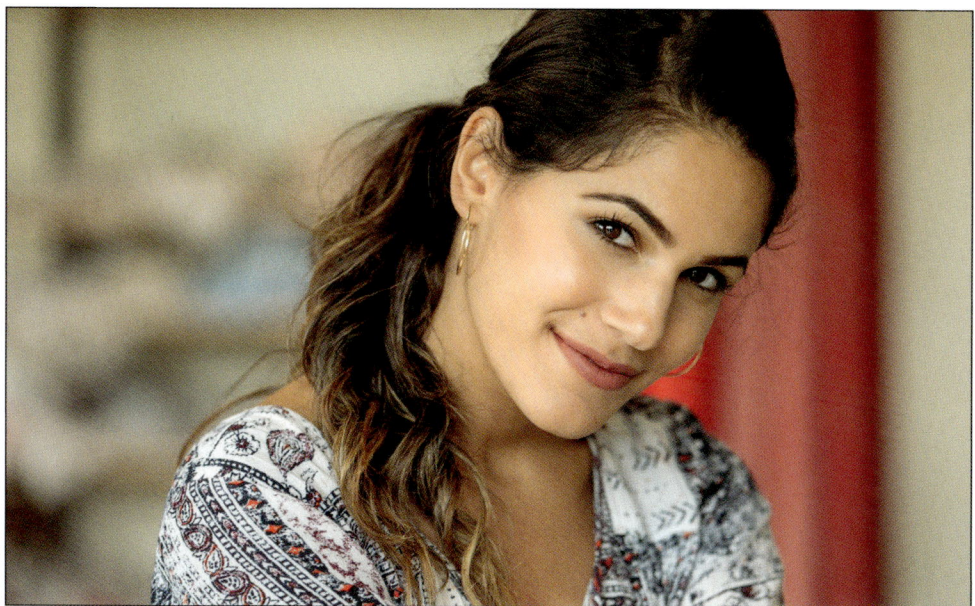

If your subject has a long, thin face, and you want to make it look fuller and rounder, then you would shoot into the lit side of their face. In the shot above, the window light is on the left and she's turned away from the window, so the part of her face that is closest to the camera is the one that has the most light. Shooting into this side of her face, with the lit side closest to the camera, is called "broad lighting" and it makes your subject's face appear rounder and fuller. If you look at the shot above, the shadows are on the far side of her face (the part farthest away from the camera). That's broad lighting.

Peter Hurley's Famous Jawline Trick

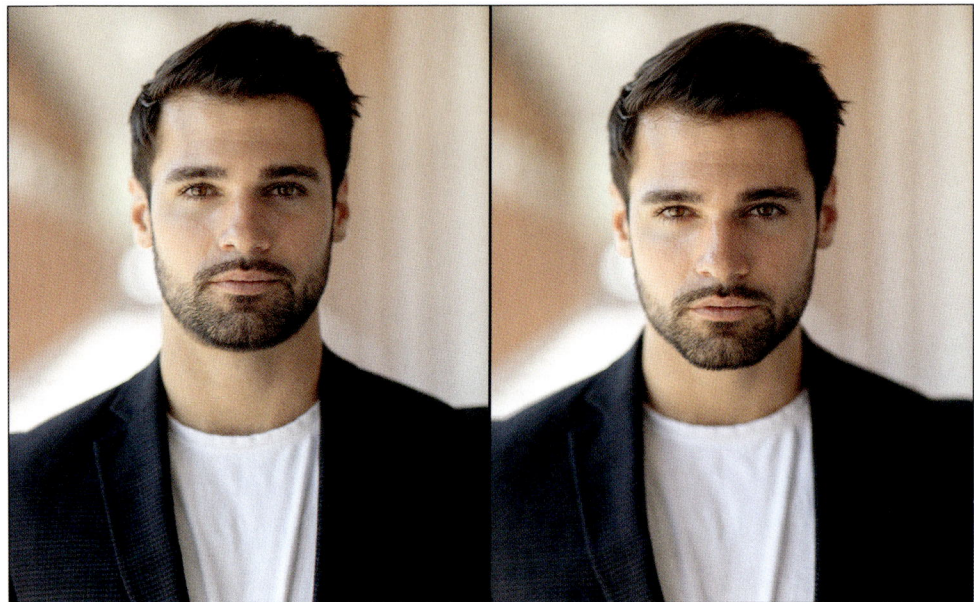

Famous New York City-based headshot photographer Peter Hurley did a video back in 2012 that debuted on my daily photography blog (scottkelby.com). The video was called "It's All About the Jaw!," and it showed a posing technique that does wonders for faces by stretching the skin, strengthening the jawline, and reducing any type of double-chin. The video went viral overnight, getting millions of views and landing Peter on the *Today Show*, teaching people this jawline technique so anyone could look better in photos. I teach Peter's technique to people I'm photographing because it really makes such a huge difference and it's so easy to do. Essentially, you have them push their forehead out and chin down (kind of like a turtle). They feel a little silly doing this at first, so I show them the same shot with and without the jawline trick. Once they see the difference, they have no problem doing it from that point on because they immediately see how much better it looks. In fact, it works so well, chances are they will be doing this jawline trick any time they have their picture taken. Thanks to Peter Hurley for turning us all on to this amazingly effective technique.

Chin Down for Better Eyes and Much More

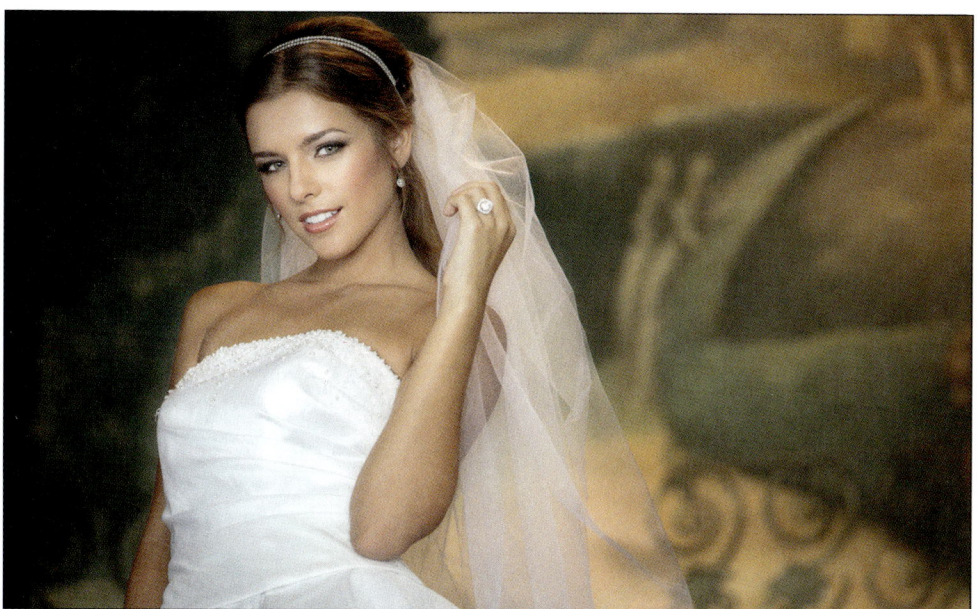

When your subject tilts their chin down, it does a couple of important things: First, it tends to make their eyes look bigger, wider, and just plain better. That's enough right there to make you want to direct your subject to "tilt their chin down just a bit." However, there's another benefit, and that is if their chin is up a bit, it accentuates their nostrils, often giving them unwanted attention (seeing directly into two dark holes on a face probably isn't the most flattering view). So, tilting the chin down keeps from having "nostril face," which I'm not sure is even a term, but, well…I guess it is now. While we're tilting the chin down, also have your subject push their chin forward a bit (like we did on the previous page), which stretches the skin, reducing any double-chin and strengthening the jawline. It's all good, so get that chin down and out to take care of a bunch of things at once.

Thinning the Nose

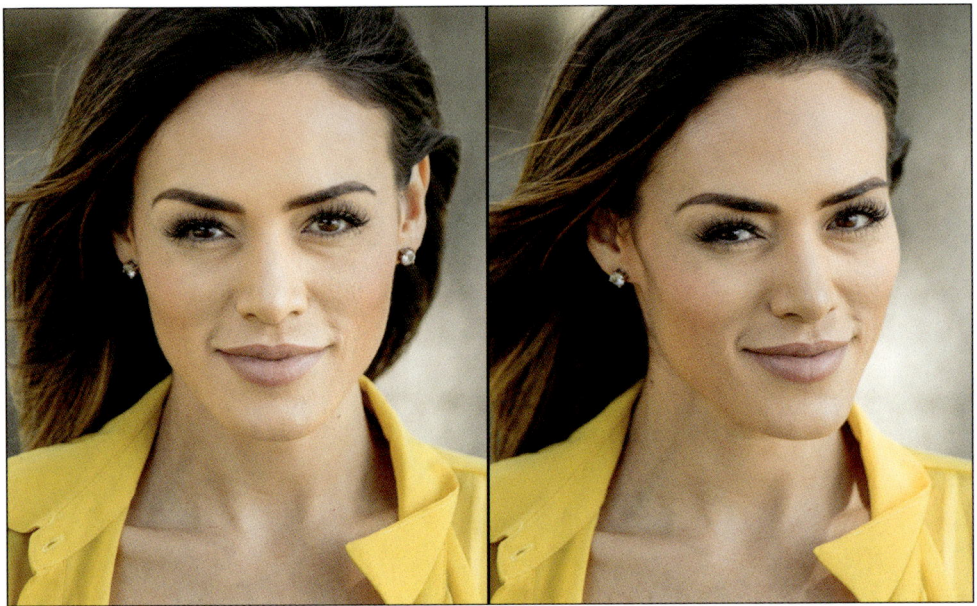

If your subject has a large nose...wait, that doesn't sound great. Let's restate that: If your subject would prefer that their nose doesn't appear as large in photos. Look, there's no good way to say this. If your subject has a "schnoz," then turn their honker slightly away from the camera, so it's not facing straight on to the camera. When it's turned away like you see above on the right, their nose doesn't look quite as wide. It fact, it might not look like a schnoz at all. Doubtful, but it does help.

Tilt Their Face Up toward the Light

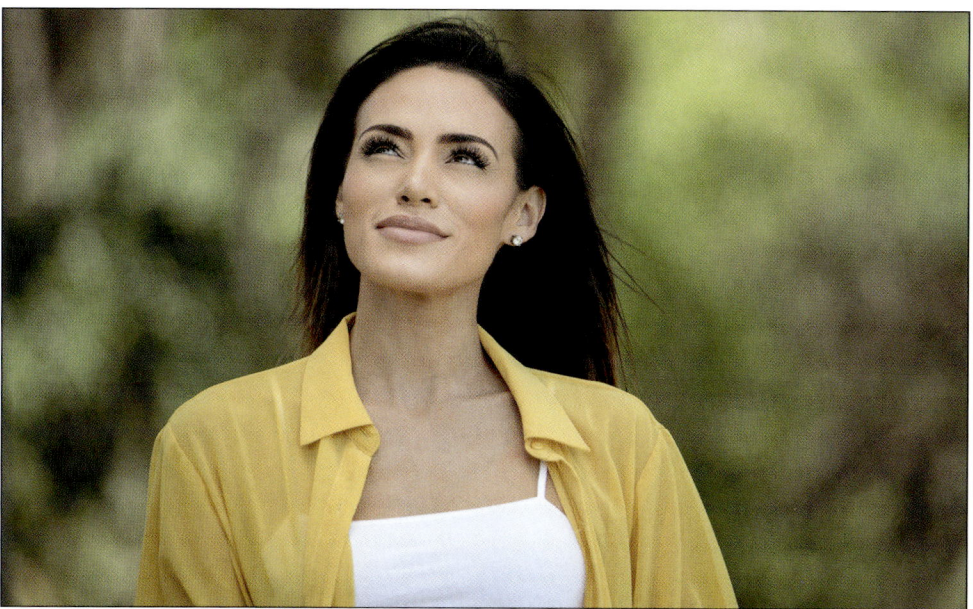

Here's a pose that gives your subject a fresh look, as it fills their face with light: have your subject look up toward the sky. Even though we won't be shooting in direct sunlight (hopefully) and they won't actually be looking into the sun, since they are looking up into the sky, the light will fill their face, making their eyes look bright, their face look fresh, and giving them a very flattering overall look. Put this one in your posing bag of tricks.

Don't Let Their Expression Go Blank

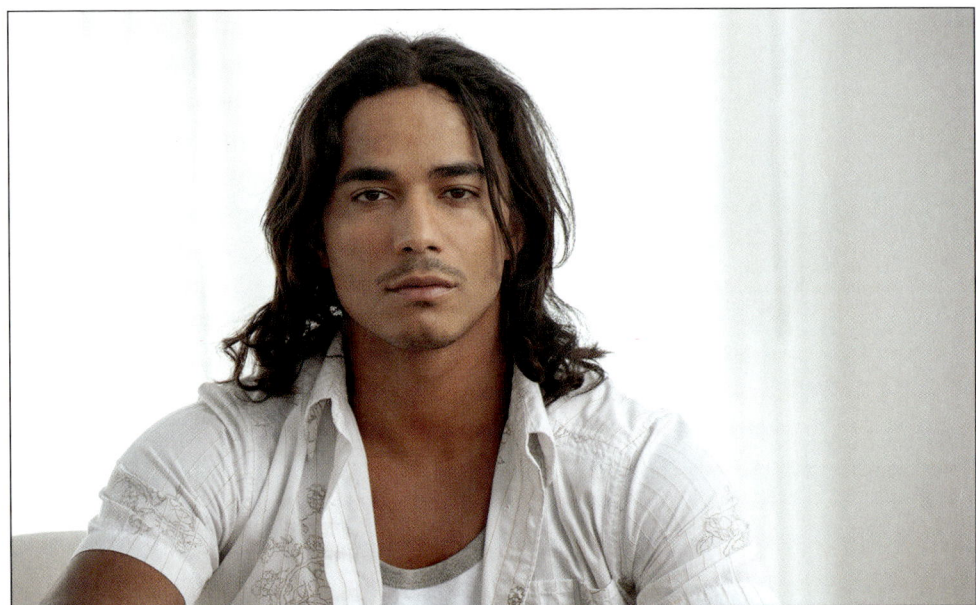

If you're looking through the lens and you see your subject isn't giving you anything (they're looking kind of blank), pause and re-engage with your subject. Sometimes they're not sure what they should be doing (which is on you) and sometimes, during a long shoot, they just kind of zone out and start thinking about what they're going to watch later on TV and what to have for dinner. So, when you see a blank look on your subject's face, know that you're about to take a picture that will never see the light of day (you're not going to like it and neither will your subject). You might want to take a quick break at that point, so both you and your subject can come back re-engaged.

Add Volume and Movement to Hair

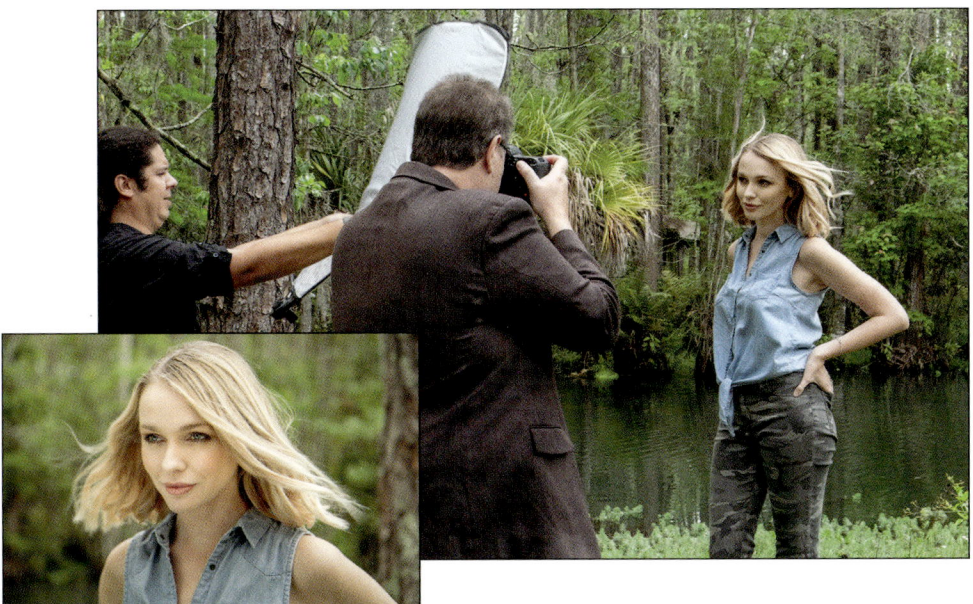

A very popular accessory in a photo studio is a fan, which we use to add volume and movement to our subject's hair, but it's not practical to bring one outside, set up a generator to power it, etc. So, instead, we take one of our reflectors and we use it to create a self-powered fan by waving it up and down (like you see my assistant Julio doing in the shot above). It gives that same type of volume and movement—it's just not consistent like the studio fan, so you have to time your shooting to right after you see (or feel) the "whoosh" of air. Getting the timing down is easier than you'd think, and it sure beats hauling a generator and fan out on location.

Turn Their Shoulders for a More Flattering Look

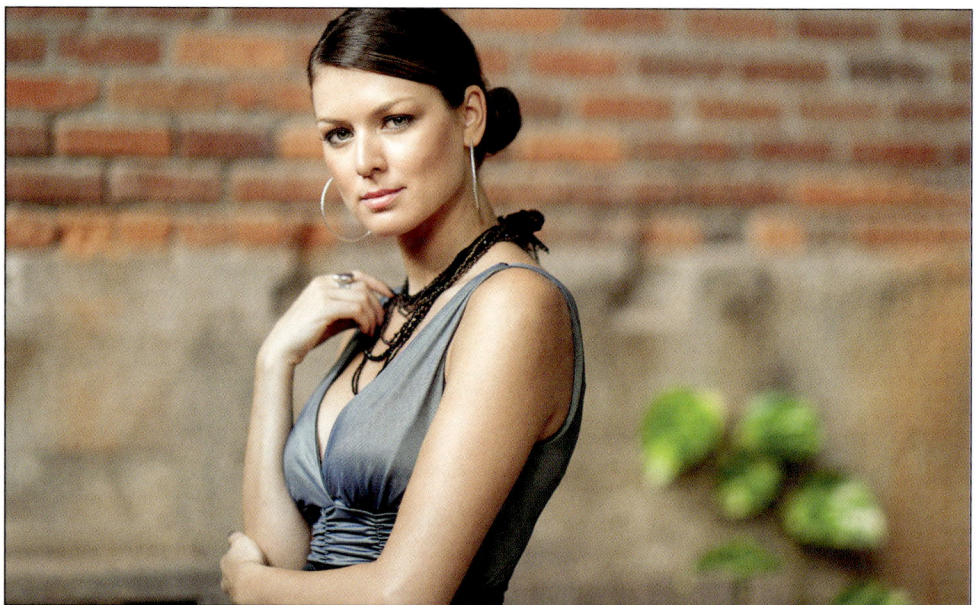

When you're photographing women, avoid having your subject face straight toward the camera. This straight-on look takes up a lot more space in the frame, and that gives them the appearance of being wider. Nobody wants to be wider. A much more flattering and slimming pose is to have your subject turn their shoulders sideways a bit (as seen above). This works like magic for making your subject look slimmer and trimmer.

Don't Shoot Flat-Footed with Straight Legs

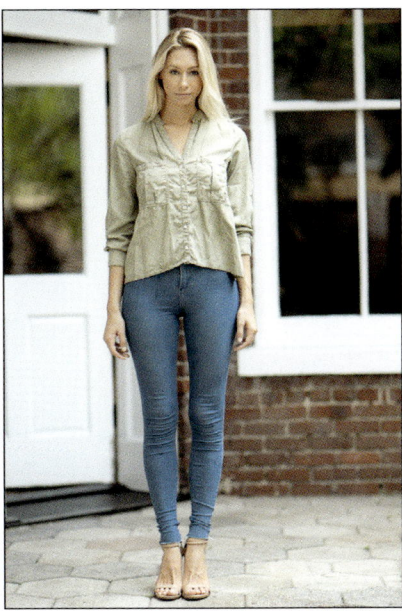 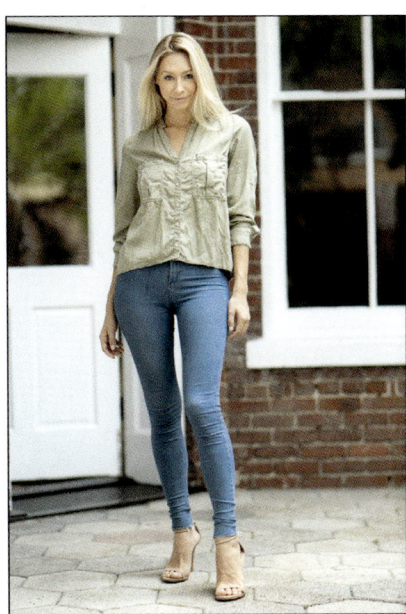

If you're shooting full-length or three-quarter-length shots, particularly of women, you don't want your subject to stand flat-footed or with their legs straight together. It tends to create kind of a "dumpy" look (for lack of a better term). One thing that will help is to have your subject wear high heels—high enough that they arch their feet. This arch helps make their legs look more toned and thinner, and it deals with the flat-footed issue as well. Next, have your subject put one leg out in front and slightly bend their knee. Then, have them shift their weight to their back leg. This helps elongate the body and gives a more slender look. Here's another trick: Remember the apple box I mentioned back on page 93 to get a higher shooting angle toward your subject? Well, they make those boxes in all different heights, and a very popular use is to have your subject put one leg up on a short apple box. It helps add a bend to that one leg, which adds more angles and gives an overall better look. You can do this if they're sitting as well, by putting one foot up on a small apple box. If you don't have a box, try having them cross their legs in front of them to give a more flattering look.

Another Trick for Thinner Waistlines

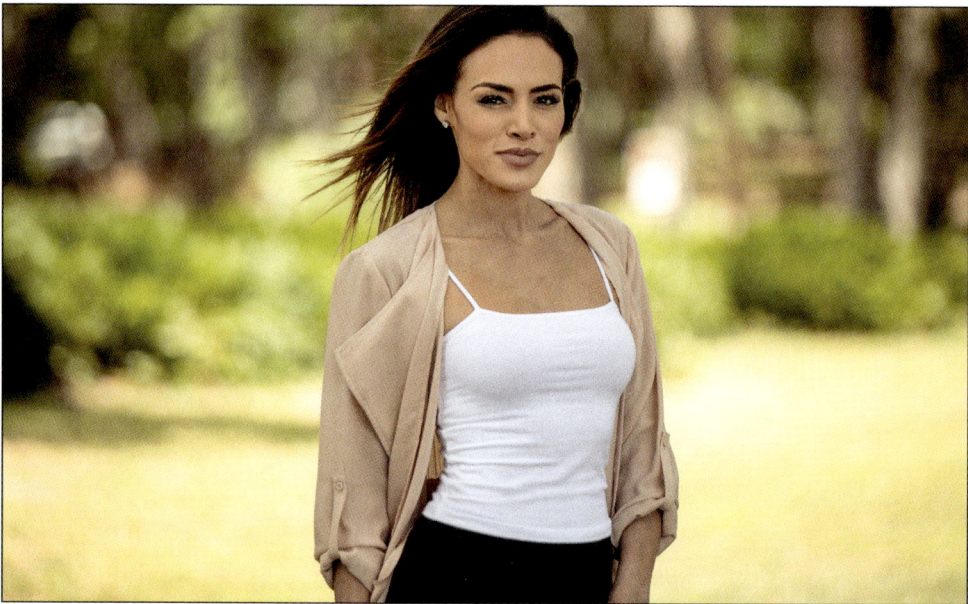

To give your subjects a thinner-looking waist, have them use one of those Hollywood tricks and have them rotate their upper body, twisting at the waist, and they'll thank you for it. For a more flattering overall look, have your subject shift their weight to the back leg. Another posing trick to try is to have your subject lean forward a bit. This is based on the idea that whatever is closest to the camera will appear largest, and whatever is farthest away will seem smaller. By leaning forward a bit, into the camera, it helps put your subject's waist farther back. This is easier to do with your subject sitting, as it looks perfectly natural to lean forward while seated.

Making Legs Look Thinner

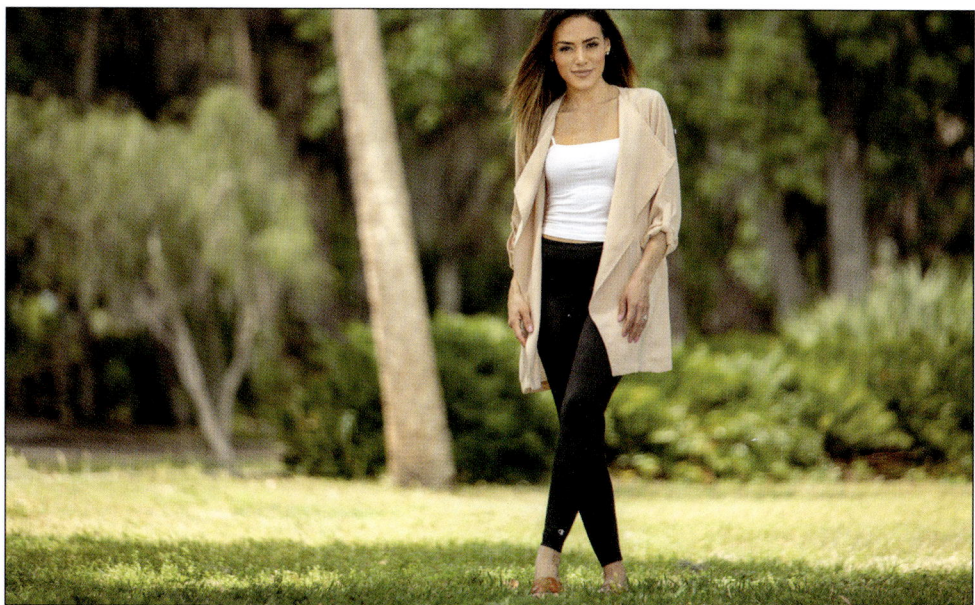

If you're shooting full-length or three-quarter-length shots, you don't want your subject's legs to look big, and luckily there are some easy ways to create thinner-looking legs. Simply have your subject cross their legs, one in front of the other (as seen here), for an overall slimmer look to the legs. You can also have them cross one ankle in front of the other for a similar look. There's another trick that celebrities sometimes use to make their legs look thinner in photos: They turn their bodies sideways, so they're in a profile position. The leg closest to the camera is straight, and the leg that's farthest from the camera is bent slightly (like they're squashing a bug with their heel), and then they turn their head back to face the camera. Boom. Drop the mic.

Keep Their Arms Away from Their Sides

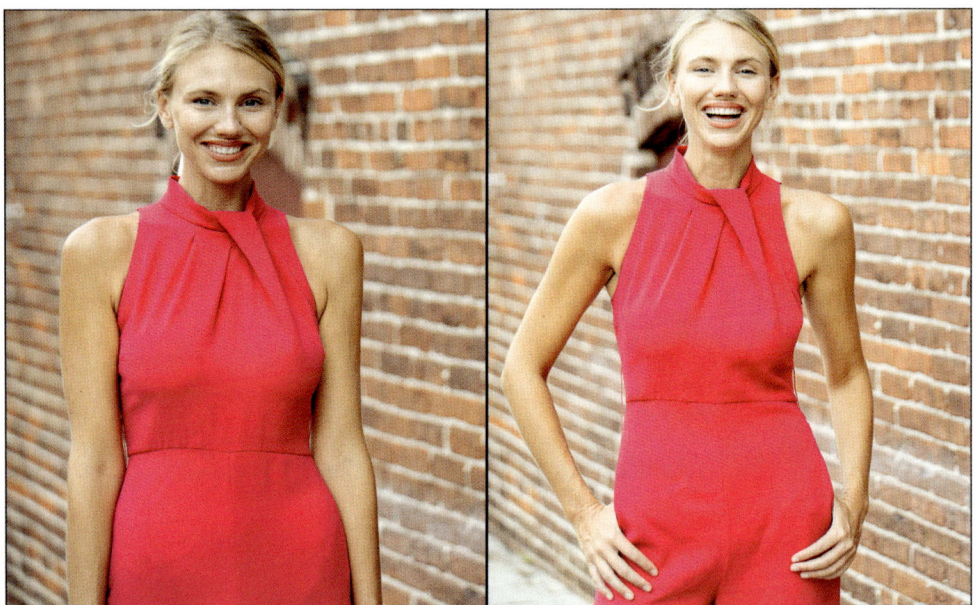

There are any number of poses that can work against us and make our subject's waist look thicker than it really is. I guess that's why we have so many techniques to make sure it doesn't look too thick in photos. When your subject's arms are up against their sides, it tends to add mass to your subject's body, making them look thicker. An old trick we use to reduce this mass is to put some space between their sides and their arms. Basically, we just have them bend their arms out and away from their waist (think of the ol' hands-on-hips pose, which accomplishes this task rather nicely—say that last part with a British accent). Creating that gap between the waist and the arms shows where the waist ends, so it doesn't look thicker than it really is.

Sitting? Put Them on the Edge

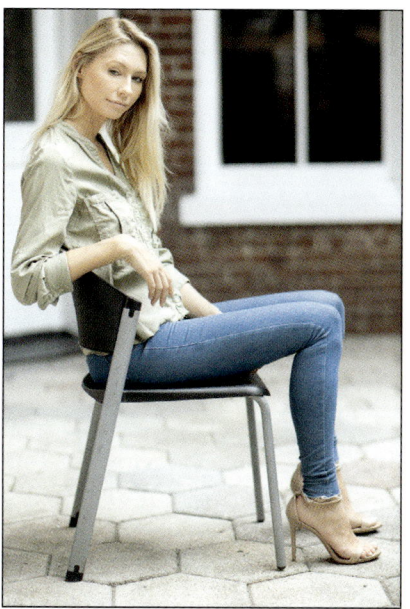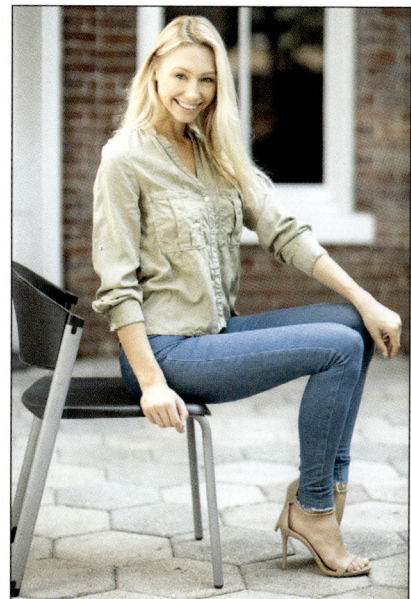

If you're having your subject sit during the shoot (maybe they're sitting on a wall, or on a park bench, etc.), don't let them lean back and get cozy. To keep them looking trim and fresh, have them sit on the edge of the seat. This really cleans up their posture quite a bit and makes their body look longer and leaner.

Keep Arms, Legs, Fingers, Everything Bent

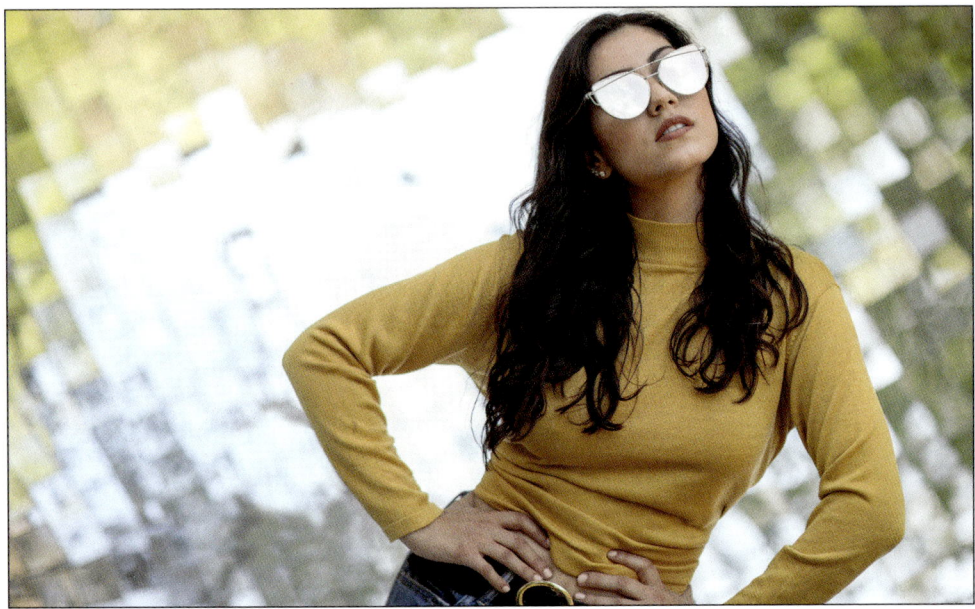

There's a basic rule for posing body parts: arms, legs, elbows—bend 'em. In fact, I've heard the phrase, "If it bends, bend it." It makes for more interesting, and more flattering poses. Essentially, you don't want straight arms (don't let them just hang there) or legs (bend those legs!) because they make your subject look stiff. When their arms are straight against their body, it can also make their body look thicker. And, there is one simple rule to watch out for about bending: don't bend their arms at 90° angles. Just a little bend will do it.

Avoid Showing an Open Palm

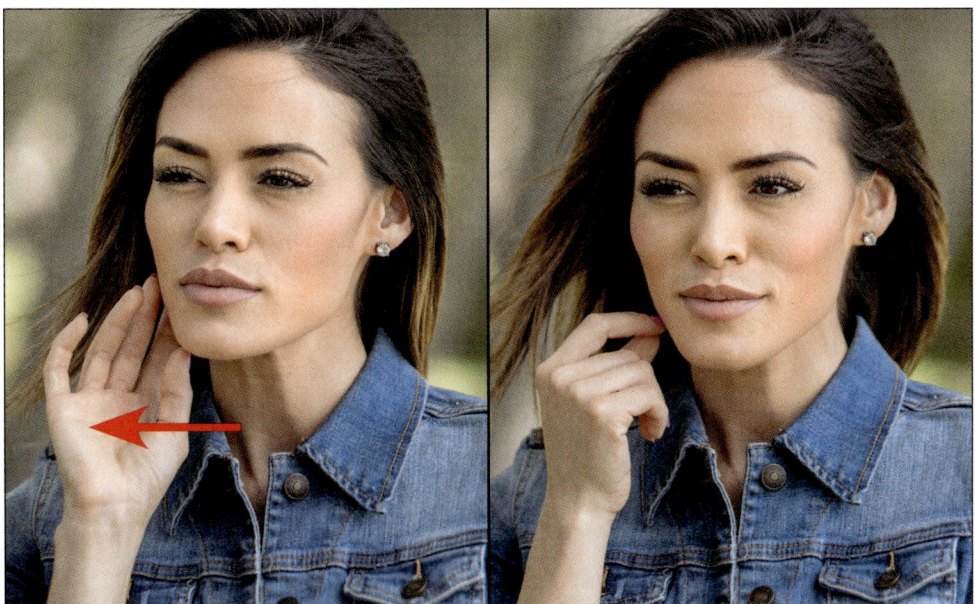

When it comes to showing your subject's hands in the shot, there's a simple rule to go by and that is to make sure your subject doesn't show the inside (palms) of their hands. The outsides of the hands are fine, and can look very graceful and beautiful, but by and large, the insides of our hands are…well…let's just say they're not as beautiful, and they can become a distraction. So, keep an eye out to make sure your subjects are only showing the outsides or sides of their hands.

Keep Fingers Closed, Not Open

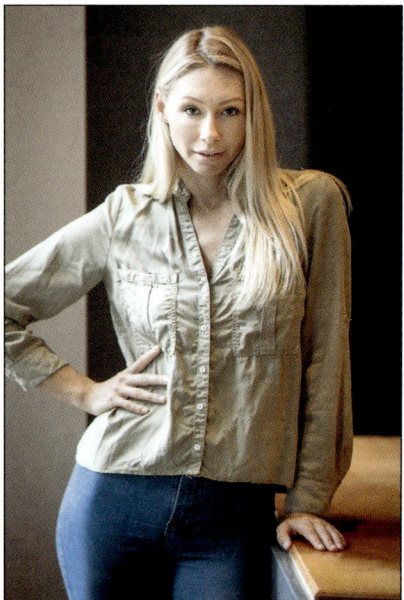 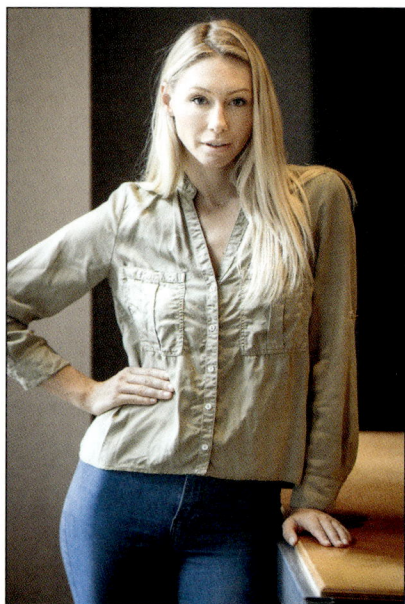

Just like we don't like to see the open palm of our subject's hand, another thing to keep an eye out for are open fingers. Hands look much more graceful when the fingers are closed (touching). Also, if your subject touches their face with their hand, make sure it's a light touch—don't let their hand press against their face, and you'll get a better, more graceful look.

Add Simple Props

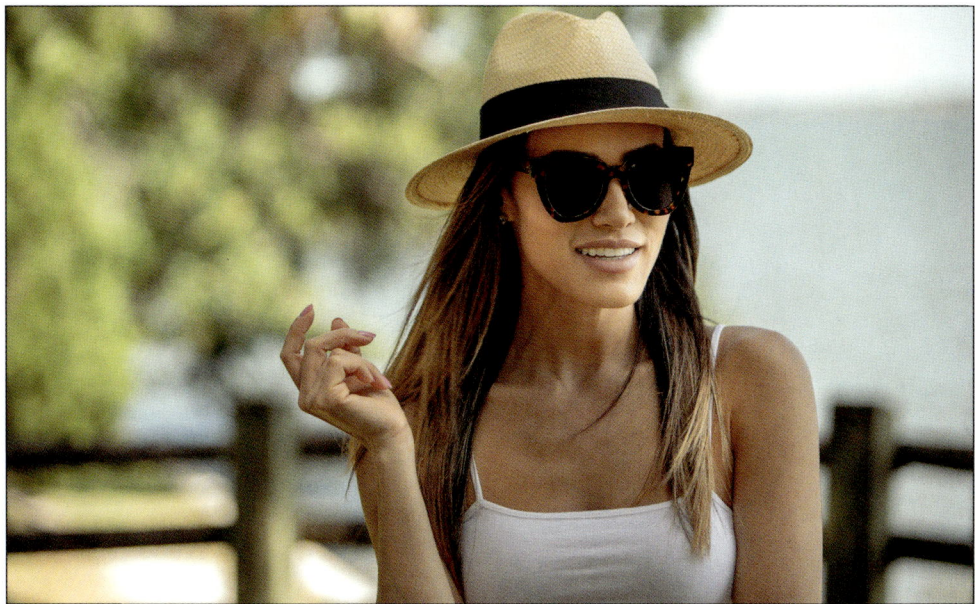

If you want to give a portrait some fashion flair, simply add a prop or accessory— anything from a hat, to sunglasses, a long silk scarf, an umbrella, etc. I've worked with subjects who were very stiff and uneasy at first, but once I had them slip on a pair of sunglasses, all of a sudden it was like they came alive. It's like once they have sunglasses on, they're actors in a play. It's really something to see when someone's personality at a shoot transforms like that. Stick with simple stuff like this, and stay away from the goofy props (unless, of course, that's the type of shoot you have planned, and if that's the case, the sky's the limit). Also, if you have a subject that doesn't know what to do with their hands (this is more of a problem when you're photographing guys, who tend to either cross their arms or put their hands in their pockets because they don't know what to do with them), hand them some kind of prop and that will usually help them feel more at ease, even if you wind up removing the prop at some point— it will have already done its job.

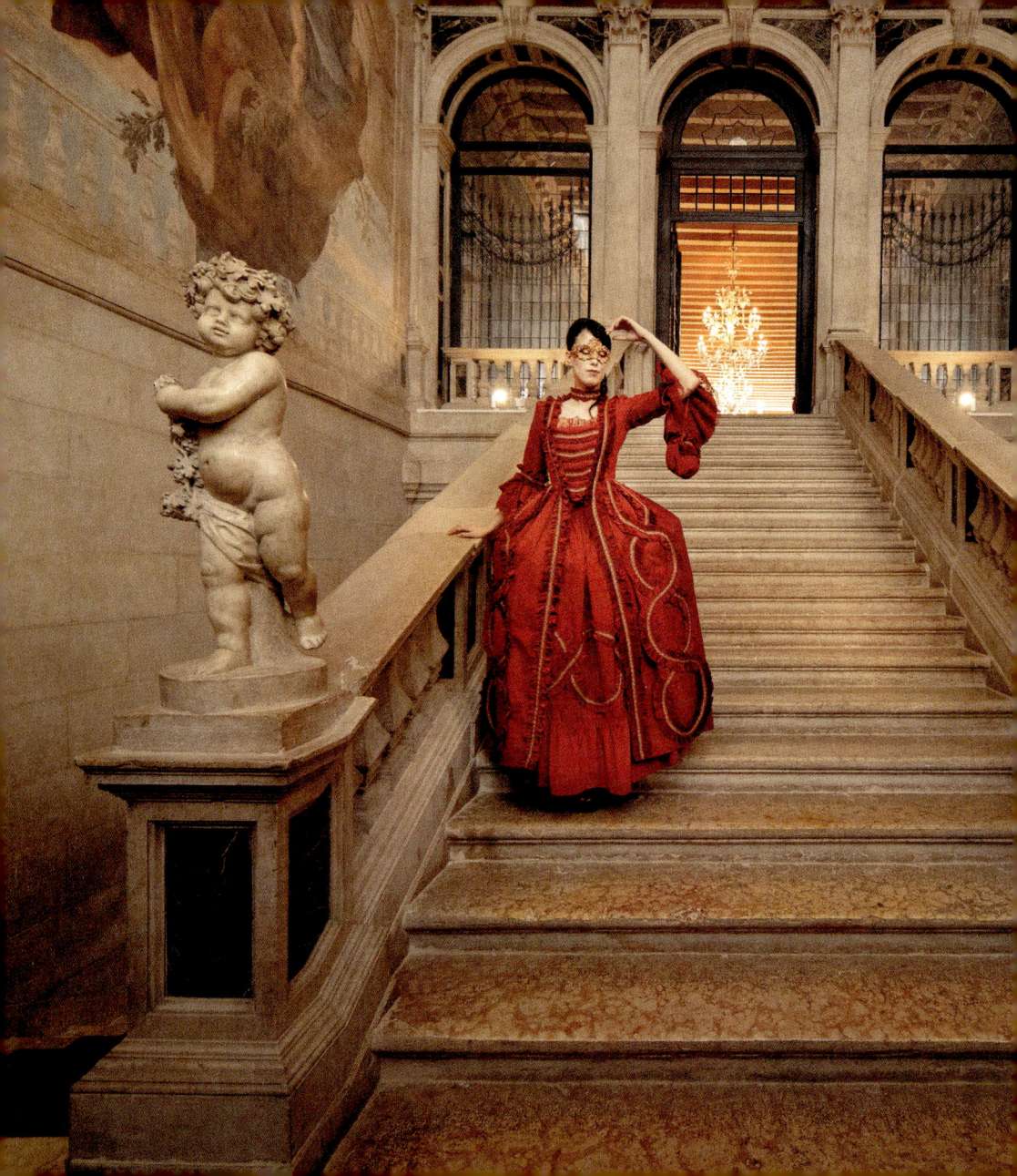

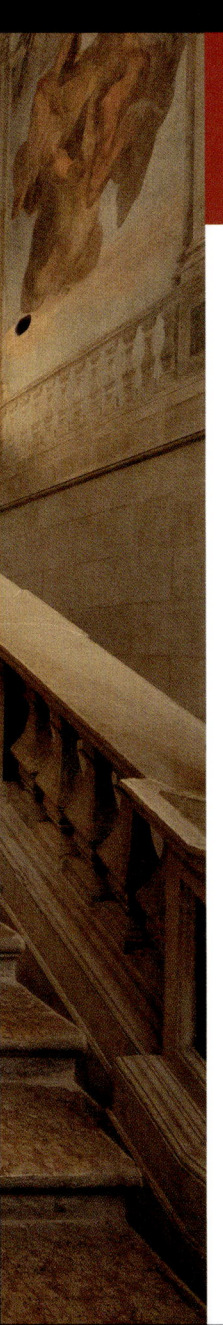

Chapter Eight

Post-Processing
The Important Lightroom & Photoshop Stuff

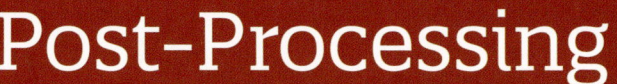

When you think about the term "post-processing" for even two seconds, you know something is not right. We all know that "pre" means "before" and "post" means "after" and "processing" means…well…"processing." So, putting them together would actually mean "after processing," but what we do in Lightroom and Photoshop isn't *after* the processing. It *is* the processing. So, this led me to do some research on the topic, and I was able to uncover some pretty mind-blowing facts about how this phrase even came to be. According to research conducted by the French National Center for Scientific Research (Centre National de la Recherche Scientifique, or CNRS), early photographers were actually rural farmers and one of the challenges they sometimes faced was keeping their livestock from wandering off. Today, farmers use woven wire, high-tensile electric netting and other types of fence to keep their cattle safe. But, back in the day, they used very simple types of fencing, from wood panels to stringing barbed wire from post to post, or even fences made of stone. Stone fences were the most rugged, but were expensive and time-consuming to build, so many went the barbed wire route, but the cattle would rub up against the posts and often accidentally knock them over, breaking the posts. To be able to file an insurance claim, these farmers would photograph the fallen posts, and then make a black-and-white print to give to their Ferme d'État agent. This act of going into the darkroom to create prints of these broken posts was referred to as "post-processing," and that's why, today, anytime I hear a cow mooing, I feel an uncontrollable urge to run into a darkroom and call my Ferme d'État agent. True story.

Adding a Sunburst Effect

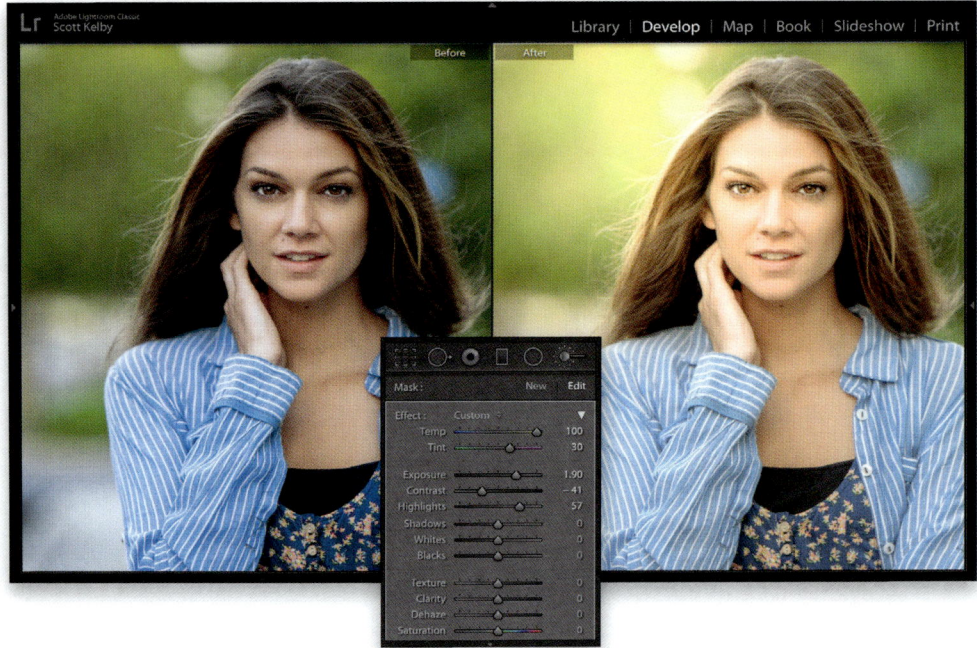

Adding a low-contrast lens flare look kinda goes against what we've been trying to avoid for years (lens flare), but if you haven't been asked to apply this effect to your portraits yet, you probably will be, so it's worth knowing. Essentially, we're going to add a giant orange ball of soft light to our image.

In Lightroom: In the Develop module, choose the Adjustment Brush **(K)** from the toolbox near the top of the right side Panels area. Then, in the panel of adjustments that appears, double-click on the word "Effect" to reset all the sliders to zero. Now, drag the Temp slider all the way to the right (toward yellow) and the Tint slider to the right to 30 to give our "sun" a lot of warmth. Increase the Exposure slider to around 2.00 to brighten our sun ball, lower the Contrast to –41 to simulate how a real lens flare would wash out the contrast, and then crank up the Highlights to around 57 to help make it glow a bit by blowing out the highlights a bunch. Now, make your brush size really huge, using the **Right Bracket key (])** on your keyboard, and click it once where you want your warm sunburst to appear. If it needs to be more intense, go to the top of the Adjustment Brush panel, click on New, and then click the huge brush again right over where you clicked the first time. This has kind of a doubling effect. Well, not kinda. It is a doubling effect.

In Photoshop: This works the same in Photoshop's Camera Raw, so open the image in Camera Raw (or go under the Filter menu and choose **Camera Raw Filter**), and then follow the Lightroom steps above.

Adding a Soft Glow Effect

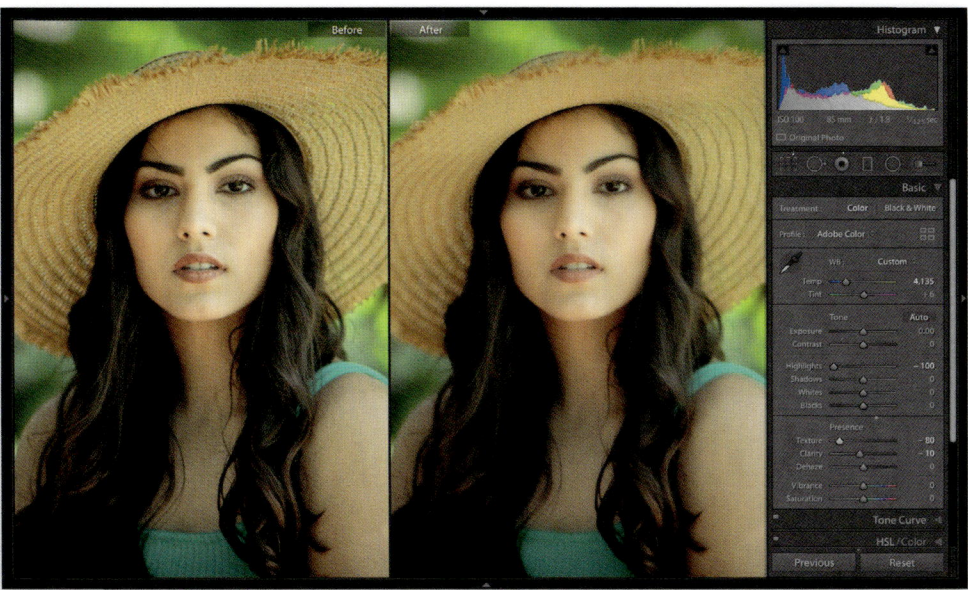

This creates kind of a dreamy effect over your portrait, and it's so easy to do.

In Lightroom: In the Develop module's Basic panel, drag the Texture slider nearly all the way to the left (here I dragged it to –80) to create the initial glow. Then, lower the Clarity amount to –10 to add a bit of fog to the scene, adding the soft glow effect to your portrait.

In Photoshop: Open your image, then duplicate the Background layer by pressing **Command-J (PC: Ctrl-J)**. Go under the Filter menu, under Blur, and choose **Gaussian Blur**. When the dialog appears, enter a Radius of 50 pixels and click OK. Your image looks totally blurry at this point, but you're going to lower the Opacity amount for this layer to 20% (at the top right of the Layers panel). When you do this, the image is clearly visible again, but it has this soft haze over it that completes the effect.

Adding a Sun Flare Effect

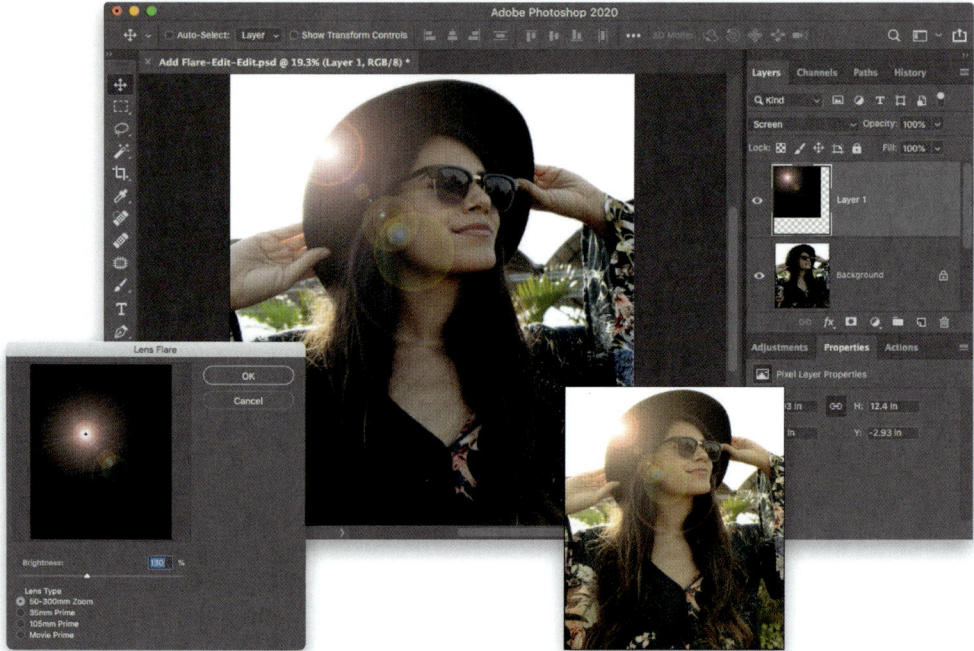

Open the image in Photoshop, then go to the bottom of the Layers panel and click on the Create a New Layer icon (it's the second icon from the right). Press **D** to set your Foreground color to black, then press **Option-Delete (PC: Alt-Backspace)** to fill this layer with black. Next, go under the Filter menu, under Render, and choose **Lens Flare**. When the dialog appears, increase the Brightness to 130%, click OK, and it applies a lens flare to the black layer. Now, to get that lens flare to blend in to your image, go to the top of the Layers panel and change this black layer's blend mode from Normal to **Screen**. You can reposition your lens flare using the Move tool **(V)**, as I did here, but depending on how you reposition it, you might see a hard edge along one or more sides. If that happens, click on the Add Layer Mask icon (it's the third icon from the left) at the bottom of the Layers panel, get the Brush tool **(B)**, choose a large soft-edged brush from the Brush Picker up in the Options Bar, and then paint over the hard edge to hide it and blend it in. Now, press **Command-E (PC: Ctrl-E)** to merge this black lens flare layer down with the layer below it, so there's only one layer—the Background layer. Finally, go under the Filter menu and choose **Camera Raw Filter**. When the window appears, drag the White Balance Temperature slider to the right toward yellow to give the image a warmer look. Then, drag the Contrast slider to the left to lower the overall contrast in the image, as would happen with actual lens flare. If the image isn't bright enough at this point, you can either increase the Highlights slider or the Exposure slider until it looks overexposed a bit. Then, click OK to finish the effect. You can see the final in the inset above.

Desaturating Skin

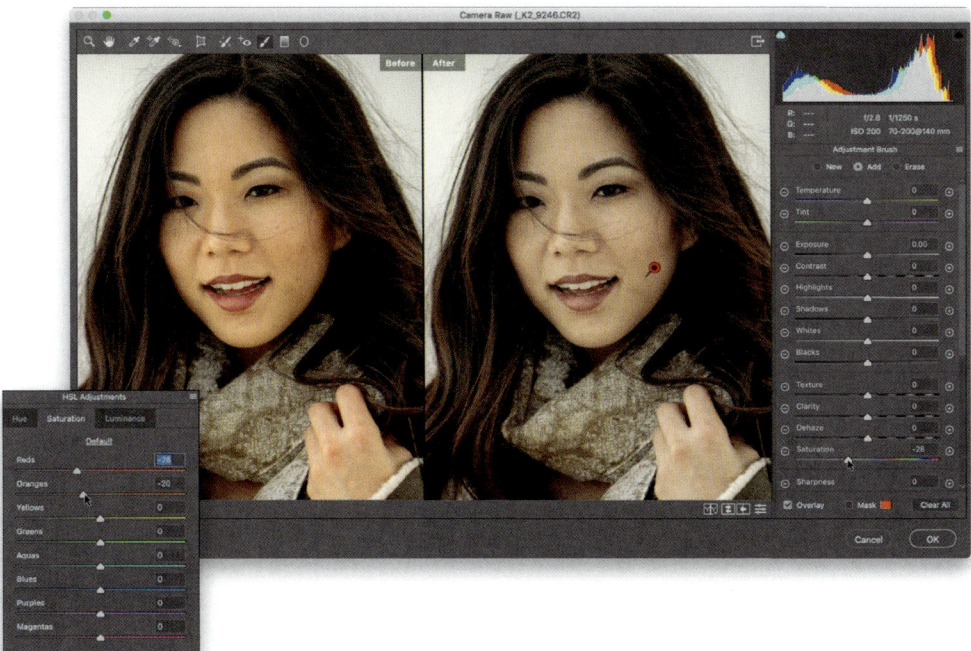

This is an incredibly popular effect in portraits these days. You're essentially going to remove some of the color from your subject's skin, so it doesn't look so warm, and you get this really trendy desaturated look.

In Lightroom: In the Develop module, choose the Adjustment Brush **(K)** from the toolbox near the top of the right side Panels area, and then double-click on the word "Effect" in the panel of adjustments that appears to reset all the sliders to zero. Now, decrease the Saturation amount to around –28 and paint over any visible skin areas to desaturate them. Another method you can try doesn't use the brush at all: go to the HSL/Color panel, click on the Saturation tab at the top, then drag the Red and Orange sliders to the left to desaturate the skin tones.

In Photoshop: Open the image in Camera Raw (or go under the Filter menu and choose **Camera Raw Filter**) and choose the Adjustment Brush **(K)** from the toolbar at the top of the window. In the panel of adjustments on the right, click on the – (minus sign) button to the left of Saturation, which resets all the sliders to zero and decreases the Saturation amount to –25. Now, lower the Saturation amount to around –28 and paint over any visible skin areas to desaturate them (as seen above). Another method is to go to the HSL Adjustments panel (it's the fourth icon from the left at the top of the Panel area), click on the Saturation tab at the top, then drag the Reds and Oranges sliders to the left to desaturate the skin tones.

Removing Blemishes

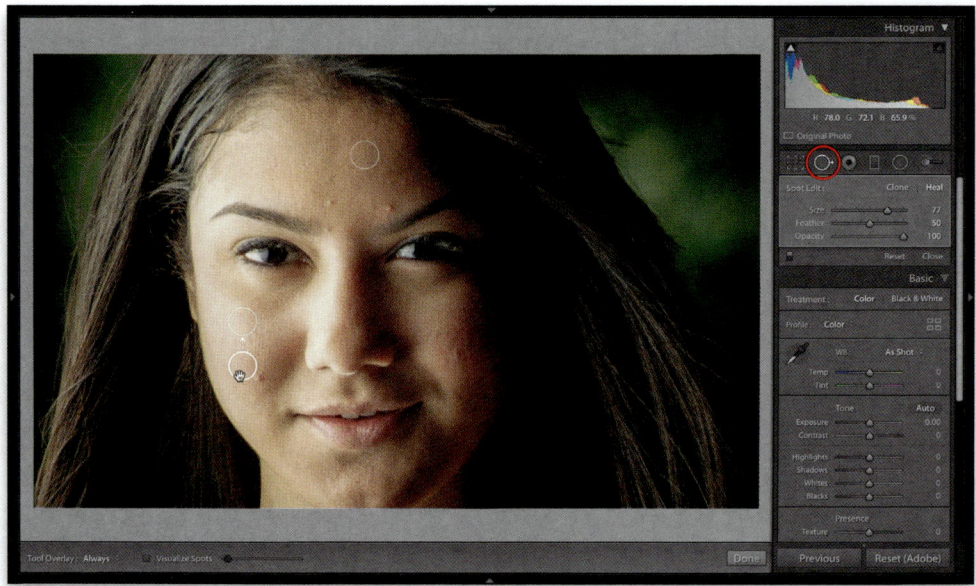

This is a quick and easy fix. The Spot Removal tool in Lightroom does a decent job, and the Healing Brush tool in Photoshop is pretty incredible. Here's how to use both:

In Lightroom: In the Develop module, choose the Spot Removal tool **(Q)** from the toolbox near the top of the right side Panels area. Move the tool over a blemish you want to remove, resize the brush so it's a little bit bigger than the blemish (you can resize it using the **Left** and **Right Bracket keys** on your keyboard), and click once. Lightroom will automatically choose a nearby area to sample texture and tone from, and then remove the blemish (you'll see a second circle that shows the area where Lightroom sampled from to make that retouch). If the result doesn't look good, you can move that second circle to a different nearby location (as shown above) or have Lightroom choose a different area to sample from by pressing the **Forward Slash key [/]** on your keyboard.

In Photoshop: Open your image, and then get the Healing Brush tool from the Toolbar on the left (or press **Shift-J** until you have it). Take the tool and move it over a clear area right near a blemish, then press-and-hold the Option (PC: Alt) key and click once to sample that area to use for the retouch. Now, move the Healing Brush tool over the blemish you want to remove, resize the brush so it's a little bit bigger than the blemish (you can resize the brush using the Left and Right Bracket keys), and then click once to remove the blemish.

Reducing Wrinkles or Moles

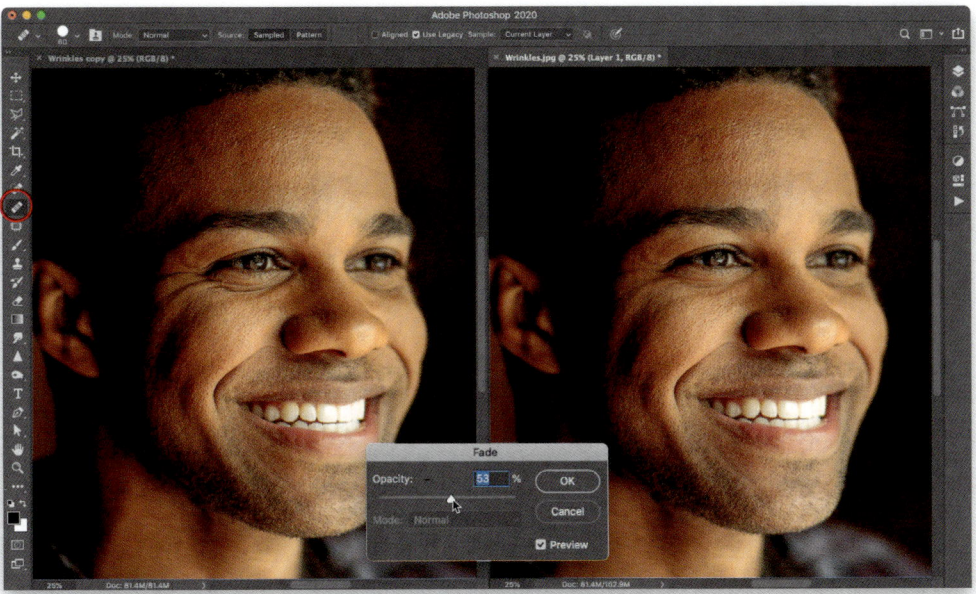

When it come to wrinkles, for the best, most realistic results, we want to reduce their intensity; we don't want to remove them altogether, or it will be an obvious retouch. It's the same with moles (which we usually just want to reduce, not remove). Here, my subject is very young, but when he smiles, he gets crow's feet and wrinkles under his eyes that normally aren't there.

In Lightroom: In the Develop module, choose the Spot Removal tool **(Q)** from the toolbox near the top of the right side Panels area, and paint a stroke over a wrinkle (or mole) you want to reduce. If the result doesn't look good, have Lightroom choose a different area to sample from by pressing the **Forward Slash key [/]** on your keyboard. Once you're happy with how it looks, go to the tool's adjustments panel on the right and drag the Opacity slider to the left until some of the wrinkle reappears. You want to reduce the wrinkles (or moles), not remove them, or you'll have a very unrealistic retouch.

In Photoshop: Open your image, and then get the Healing Brush tool from the Toolbar on the left (or press **Shift-J** until you have it). Take the tool and move it over a clean area right near a wrinkle, then press-and-hold the Option (PC: Alt) key and click once to sample that area to use for the retouch. Now, paint over the wrinkle (or mole) you want to remove. It'll remove it completely, so we need to bring some of it back. Go under the Edit menu and choose **Fade Healing Brush**. When the dialog appears, drag the Opacity slider to the left (as shown above) to bring back some of the original until it looks realistic (reducing the problems, not removing them altogether).

Reducing Shiny Spots on the Skin

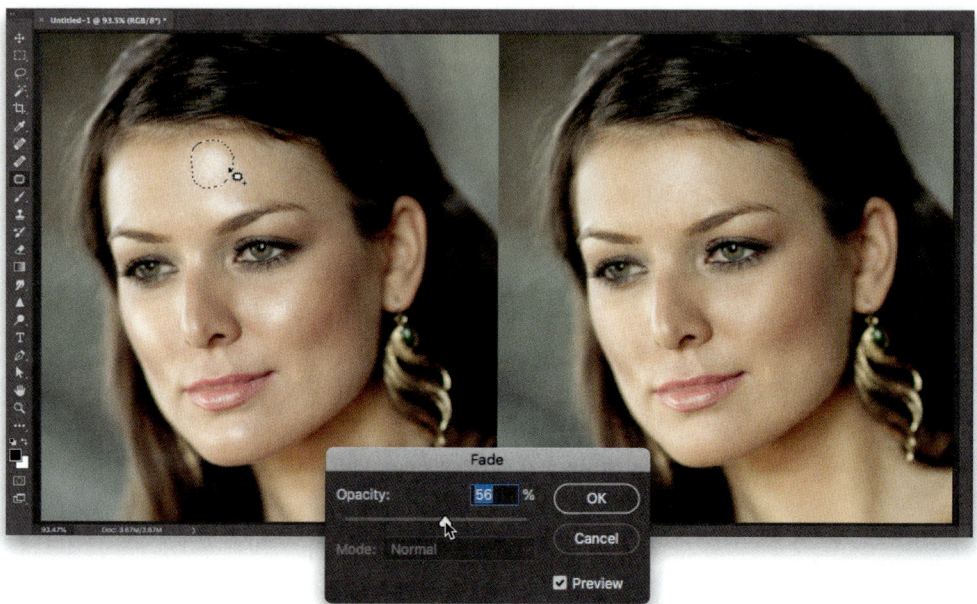

These shiny areas make your subject's skin looks sweaty or oily or both. Here's how to quickly reduce them, while leaving the highlights intact:

In Lightroom: In the Develop module, choose the Spot Removal tool **(Q)** from the toolbox near the top of the right side Panels area. Make the brush size a little larger than the shiny area you want to remove and click once on it, or paint a stroke over it, to remove it completely. If Lightroom picks a weird area to sample from, click-and-drag the second circle to a new location to choose a different area to sample from. The shine is now fully gone, but so are the highlights. We'll bring them back by lowering the Opacity slider, in the tool's adjustment panel, until they come back. This slider kind of works like "undo on a slider."

In Photoshop: Open your image, then get the Patch tool from the Toolbar on the left (or press **Shift-J** until you have it. You can use the Healing Brush tool instead [see the previous page], if it's a really small shiny area) and make a loose selection around a shiny area (like you would with the Lasso tool). Now, move your cursor inside the selection, click-and-drag it to a clean nearby area, and you'll see a preview of what the removal will look like inside your originally selected area. When it looks good, release your mouse button and the selection snaps back into place, removing the shine completely. To bring back some of the lost highlights, go under the Edit menu and choose **Fade Patch Tool** to bring up the Fade dialog (seen in the inset above), and then drag the Opacity slider to the left to bring back some of the highlights (it works like "undo on a slider," so don't drag too far left or the shine will come back).

Enhancing the Irises

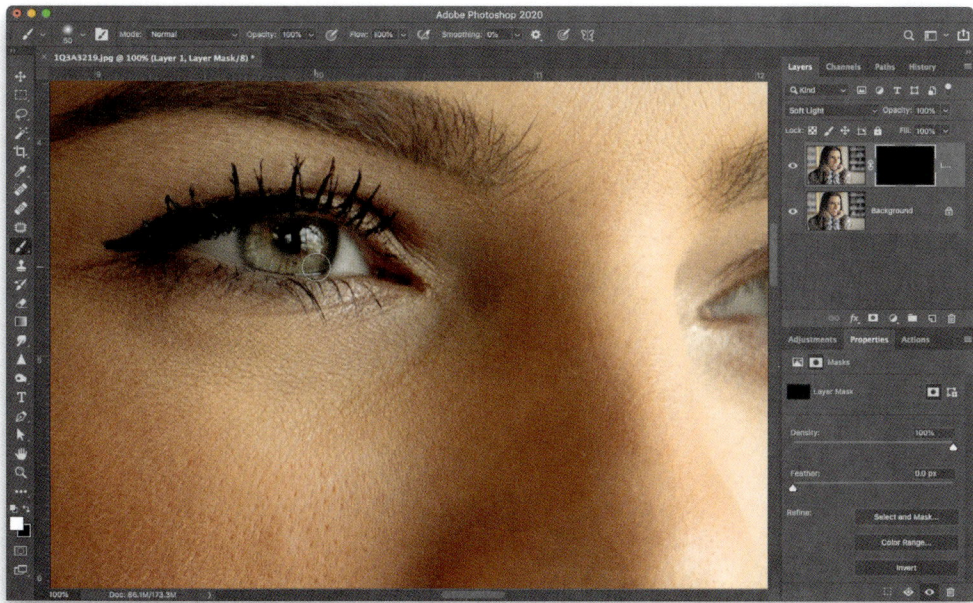

Adding contrast to the irises really makes a big difference, especially since the eyes are such an important focal point of most portraits.

In Lightroom: In the Develop module, choose the Adjustment Brush **(K)** from the toolbox near the top of the right side Panels area. Then, in the panel of adjustments that appears, double-click on the word "Effect" to reset all the sliders to zero. Now, increase the Contrast amount to 50, zoom in on the eyes, and paint over both irises to increase their contrast. If they get too dark, drag the Exposure slider to the right to lighten them a bit.

In Photoshop: Open your image, and then duplicate the Background layer by pressing **Command-J (PC: Ctrl-J)**. At the top of the Layers panel, change the duplicate layer's blend mode from Normal to **Soft Light** (as seen above) to add a lot of contrast to the image (or you can choose Overlay, instead, if you want a more intense effect). Now, press-and-hold the Option (PC: Alt) key and click on the Add Layer Mask icon (it's the third icon from the left) at the bottom of the Layers panel to hide this contrasty layer behind a black layer mask. Get the Brush tool **(B)** from the Toolbar, choose a small soft-edged brush from the Options Bar up top, zoom in on the eyes, and with your Foreground color set to white, paint over just the irises to add lots of contrast and enhance the eyes.

Sharpening Portraits

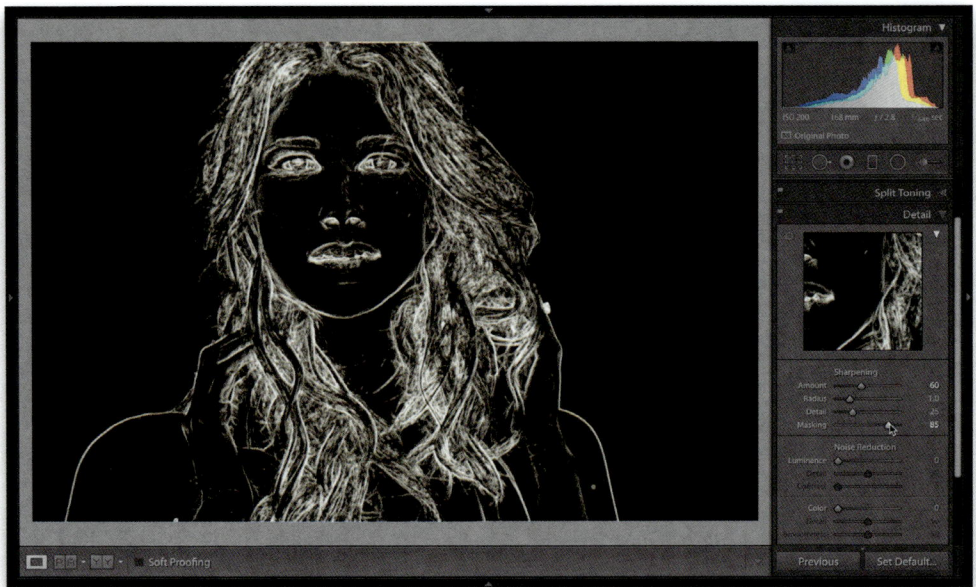

When it comes to men, sharpening is easy. We go to the Detail panel, crank up the Amount slider and boom. Done. Why? Because nobody cares about men. But with women and children, we go a step a further. We want their detail areas (eyes, eyebrows, nostrils, lips, teeth, hair, and the outside edges of their face and hands) to be sharp, but we don't really want their skin sharpened or to look rugged like we would with men. Here's how to apply sharpening to portraits of women and/or children:

In Lightroom: Go to the Develop module's Detail panel, and in the Sharpening section, increase the Amount to around 60. Leave the Radius and Detail sliders set at their defaults of 1.0 and 25. It's the last slider at the bottom of this section, the Masking slider, where the magic happens. To see it work, press-and-hold the Option (PC: Alt) key, then click-and-hold on the Masking slider, and the image will turn solid white. That's Lightroom telling you the entire image is being sharpened. Keep holding the Option key down, and as you drag the Masking slider to the right, parts of the image will turn black (as seen here). The parts that turn black are no longer being sharpened— only the areas that still appear in white will be—and if you drag far enough, those will be the detail areas (eyes, eyebrows, nostrils, lips, teeth, hair, and so on).

In Photoshop: This works the same in Photoshop's Camera Raw, so open the image in Camera Raw (or go under the Filter menu and choose **Camera Raw Filter**), and then follow the Lightroom steps above.

Brightening the Eyes

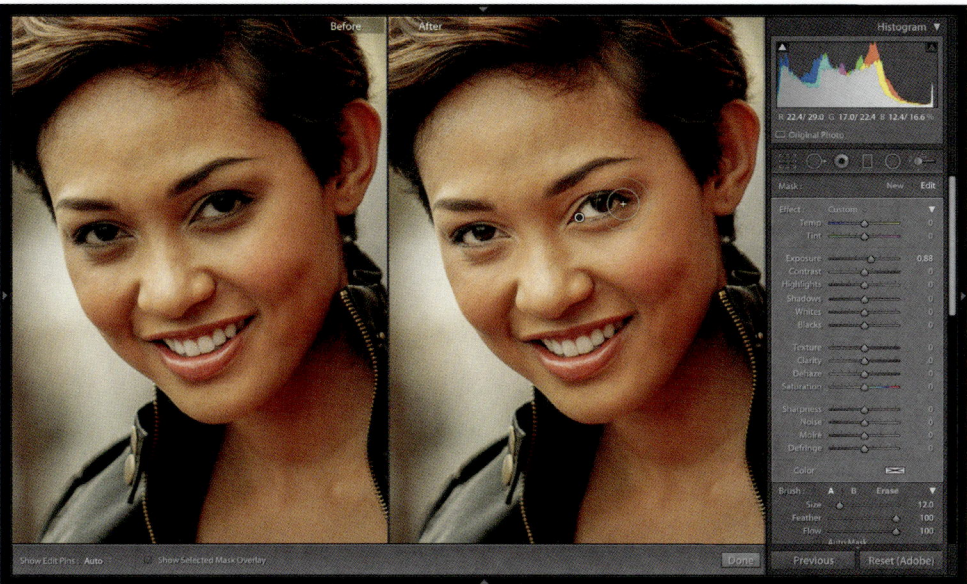

This is a very easy one to overdo, by brightening the eyes too much, so be careful or the retouch will look artificial. You're trying to use an amount that will match the eyes and the areas around them with the brightness of the rest of the face, so we'll start with one setting, and then adjust the amount up or down until it looks natural.

In Lightroom: In the Develop module, choose the Adjustment Brush **(K)** from the toolbox near the top of the right side Panels area. Then, in the panel of adjustments that appears, double-click on the word "Effect" to reset all the sliders to zero. Now, increase the Exposure amount to 0.50 for starters, zoom in, and then paint over an entire eye—eye socket and all (as shown in the After image above). Then, just tweak the amount of brightness by adjusting the Exposure slider until it matches the brightness of the rest of the face. Here, I increased it to 0.88.

In Photoshop: Open the image in Camera Raw (or go under the Filter menu and choose **Camera Raw Filter**) and choose the Adjustment Brush **(K)** from the toolbar at the top of the window. In the panel of adjustments on the right, click on the + (plus sign) button to the right of Exposure, which resets all the sliders to zero and increases the Exposure amount to +0.50. Now, paint over an entire eye—eye socket and all—and then tweak the amount of brightness by adjusting the Exposure slider until it matches the brightness of the rest of the face.

The Perfectly Clear Retouching Plug-In

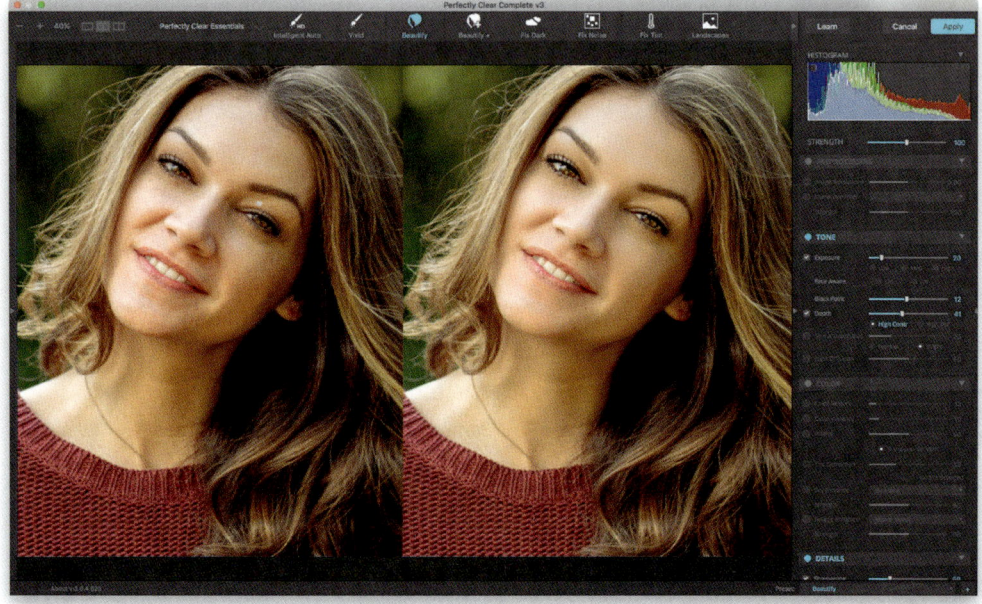

Besides doing all of these individual retouches, which I do for important images, I also use a third-party plug-in that I have to admit does a pretty darn good job at portrait retouching tasks when I don't want to take the time to do it all manually. It uses facial recognition and some one-click presets to deal with the common everyday things we need to retouch, like smoothing skin, that are much more complicated to do in Photoshop, especially if you're new at it. The plug-in is from EyeQ (you can use it in both Lightroom and Photoshop) and is called "Perfectly Clear Complete v3" (they constantly update it, though, so by the time you read this, it could be v4, v5, etc.). When you open a portrait in Perfectly Clear, by default, it analyzes the photo and applies an "Intelligent Auto HD" retouch to the photo, which usually does a pretty good simple retouch and brightening. If you need a more thorough retouching, you can choose one of the Beautify or Beautify+ presets, and you'll instantly see the changes onscreen. A couple things I think it retouches best are the eyes and the skin—it softens the skin without obliterating the pores and details, so the result doesn't look plastic (as it does with some retouching plug-ins). Of course, you can manually adjust all different sorts of areas using the sliders and panels along the right side of its window. But, if you're going to mess with a bunch of sliders, you might as well do it yourself in Lightroom or Photoshop, so I mostly stick with the presets (there are more presets that deal with specific areas of the face). You can download a free, fully functional, 21-day trial version at https://eyeq.photos/perfectlyclear.

Cinematic Color Grading for Portraits

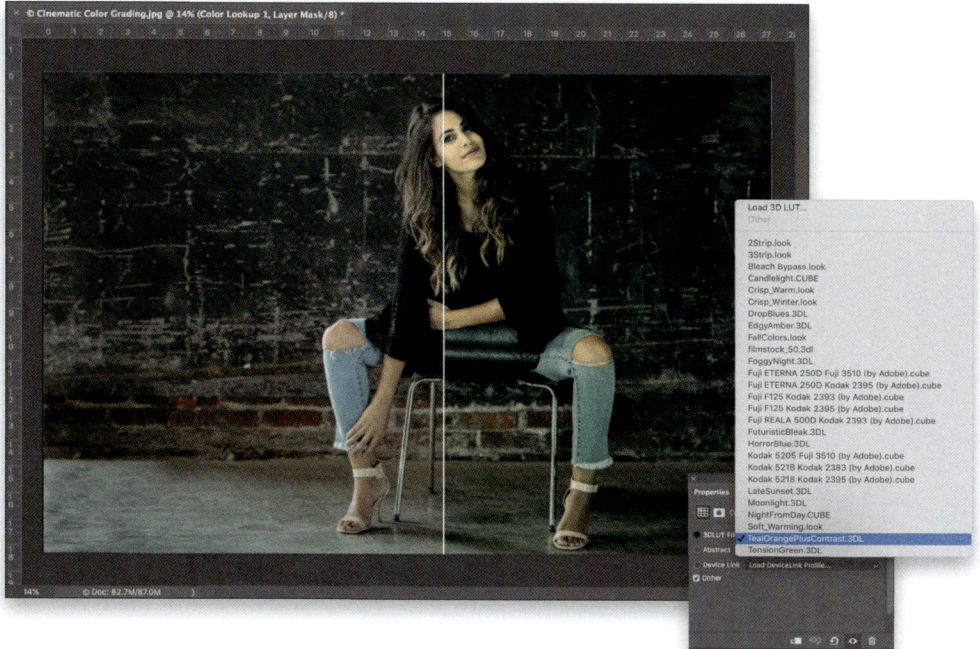

You can hardly find a major motion picture that doesn't use some sort of color grading throughout the movie to help give it an overall tone or feel. It spread to TV (check out *The Handmaid's Tale*, *The Walking Dead*, *Breaking Bad*, and a ton more), and well, now it has spread to stills, as it's super-popular to add a cinematic-style color grade to your images. Luckily, it's also super-easy to do in Photoshop. Open your image, then click on the Create New Adjustment Layer icon (it's the fourth icon from the left) at the bottom of the Layers panel and choose **Color Lookup**. What you're about to do is apply a LUT (short for lookup table) to your image, which is pretty much like applying a bi-color tint over it. In the Properties panel, you'll see three pop-up menus of choices. Click-and-hold on the 3DLUT File pop-up menu and a list of preset LUTs appears (as seen above). Start by choosing one of my favorites, TealOrangePlusContrast.3DL (it's right near the bottom of the menu), and it applies a tint to your image—kind of like a cross-processing effect (this particular color combination is really popular today). While you're there, try a few of my other favorites, most of which are traditional film simulations that give you that old-school film look that's so popular on Instagram: Kodak 5218 Kodak 2383 (by Adobe).cube; Soft_Warming.look; and then lastly, Fuji REALA 500D Kodak 2393 (by Adobe).cube When you apply these LUTs, the amount of tint is pretty heavy, so I find I usually have to go to the Layers panel and lower the Opacity amount of the Color Lookup adjustment layer to lower the intensity of the tint until it looks right for my image.

Using Liquify's Face-Aware Feature

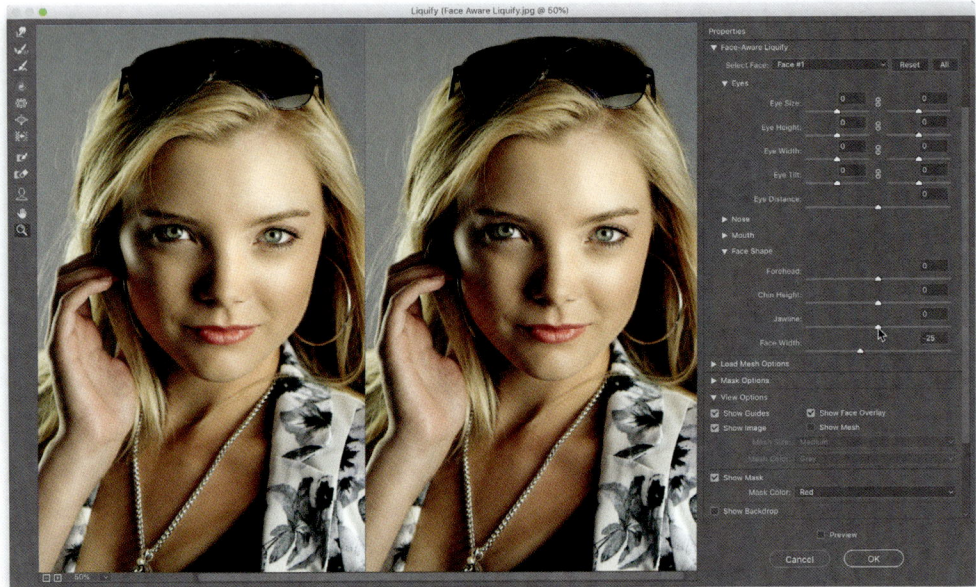

This is the king of Photoshop retouching tools because it uses its own built-in facial recognition to assign sliders to different parts of the face, and you can pretty much adjust any facial feature using those sliders. You can adjust anything from the width of the face, the amount of smile (or frown), size and position of the nose, eyes, jawline, and so on. Here's how it works: Go under the Filter menu, choose **Liquify**, and it opens in its own separate window (shown above). To make facial adjustments, all you have to do is drag the appropriate sliders—dragging to the left reduces an effect and dragging to the right increases it (i.e., dragging the Face Width slider to the left makes the face thinner, as seen above on the right, and dragging it to the right makes it wider). That's all there is to it. Also, if you have more than one person in the photo, it will recognize each face, so you can choose which person you want to work on from the Select Face pop-up menu at the top of the Face-Aware Liquify section.

Removing Fly-Away Hairs along the Outside

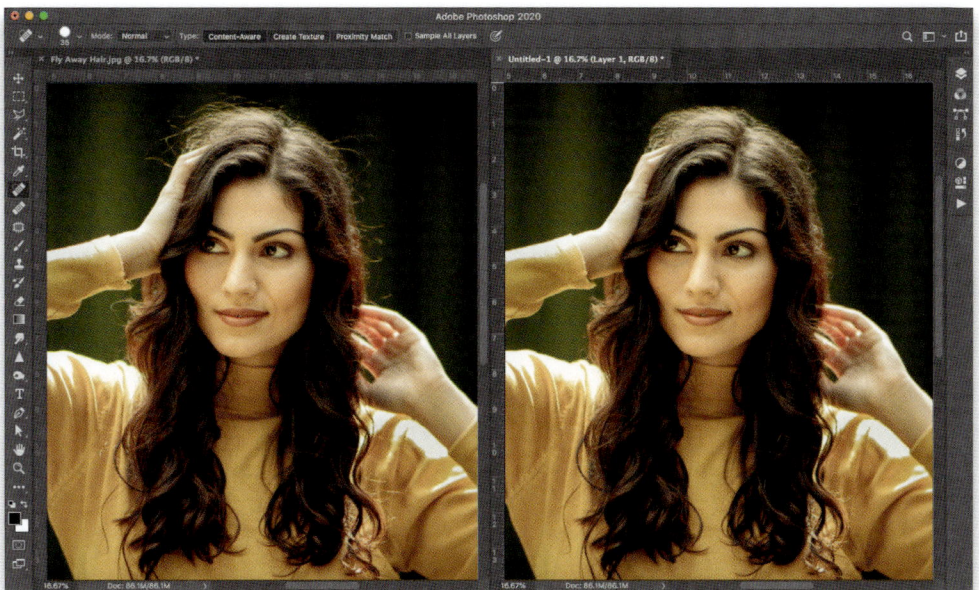

This one's kind of tough to do in Lightroom because, generally, its Spot Removal tool doesn't work well for removing fly-away hair, so I recommend using Photoshop instead, which makes it quick and easy. You're going to use two tools: (1) The Spot Healing Brush tool, found over in the Toolbar on the left (**J**; its icon looks like a Band-Aid, with a half circle on its left). Make your brush size a little bit larger than the fly-away hair you want to remove (using the **Left** and **Right Bracket keys** on your keyboard), then start at the end of the fly-away hair and paint a stroke going back, toward the head, but stop right before you reach the main hair on the head. The reason we stop is because the Spot Healing Brush tends to smudge things when it reaches that main part of the hair. So, at that point we switch to (2) the Clone Stamp tool (**S**; its icon looks like a rubber stamp) because it doesn't smudge at all. So, get that tool, choose a small soft-edged brush from the Brush Picker up in the Options Bar, press-and-hold the Option (PC: Alt) key, and then click in a clean nearby area of the background right near where you stopped with the Spot Healing Brush. Now, move your cursor over the stray hair, make your brush size just a little larger than it, then paint over that last little bit of leftover fly-away hair and the background area you sampled is cloned over it. You'll probably wind up switching back and forth between these two tools until all the fly-away hairs are gone (as seen above on the right). By the way, you'll find times where, for some reason, the Spot Healing Brush doesn't smudge, so when it doesn't, just consider that a bonus.

Brightening the Face, So It's the Focal Point

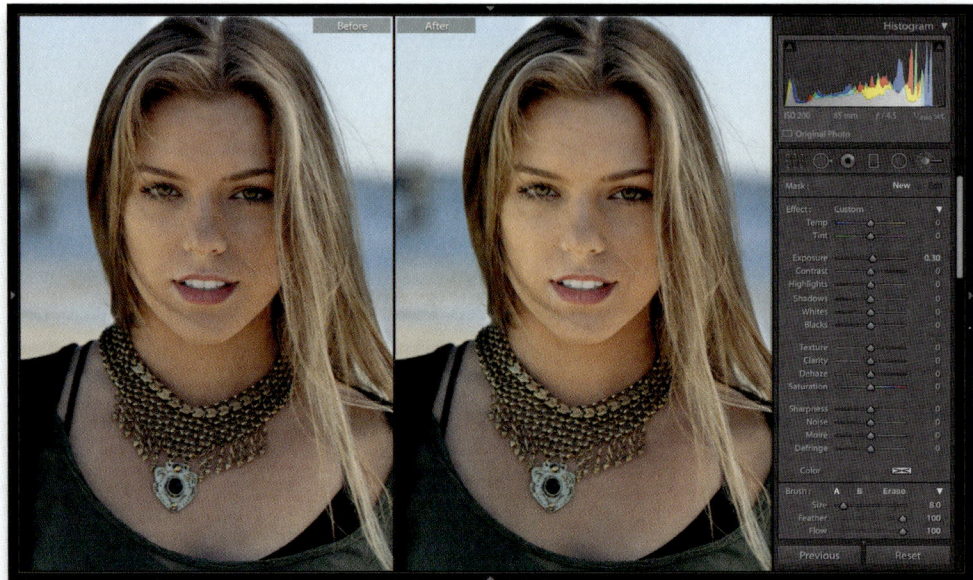

Our eyes are drawn to the brightest part of an image, and in portraits, that should be your subject's face. To help with that, there's something I do to almost every portrait I take, and that's to brighten the face by around 1/3 of a stop. Here's how:

In Lightroom: In the Develop module, choose the Adjustment Brush **(K)** from the toolbox near the top of the right side Panels area. Then, in the panel of adjustments that appears, double-click on the word "Effect" to reset all the sliders to zero. Now, increase the Exposure amount to 0.30 and paint over your subject's face to brighten it up a bit. After brightening, if you see a big difference between the face and neck, you can spill over a bit and paint the top of the neck, as well. The whole retouch is supposed to be kind of subtle, but if you feel it's still too dark, you can crank up the Exposure as high as 0.50.

In Photoshop: Open the image in Camera Raw (or go under the Filter menu and choose **Camera Raw Filter**) and choose the Adjustment Brush **(K)** from the toolbar at the top of the window. In the panel of adjustments on the right, click on the + (plus sign) button to the right of Exposure, which resets all the sliders to zero and increases the Exposure amount to +0.50. Now, drag the Exposure slider to the left to +0.30 (1/3 of a stop), and paint over your subject's face to brighten it up a bit. It's supposed to be kind of subtle, but if it's still too dark, you can crank up the Exposure as high as +0.50.

Adding a Subtle Vignette

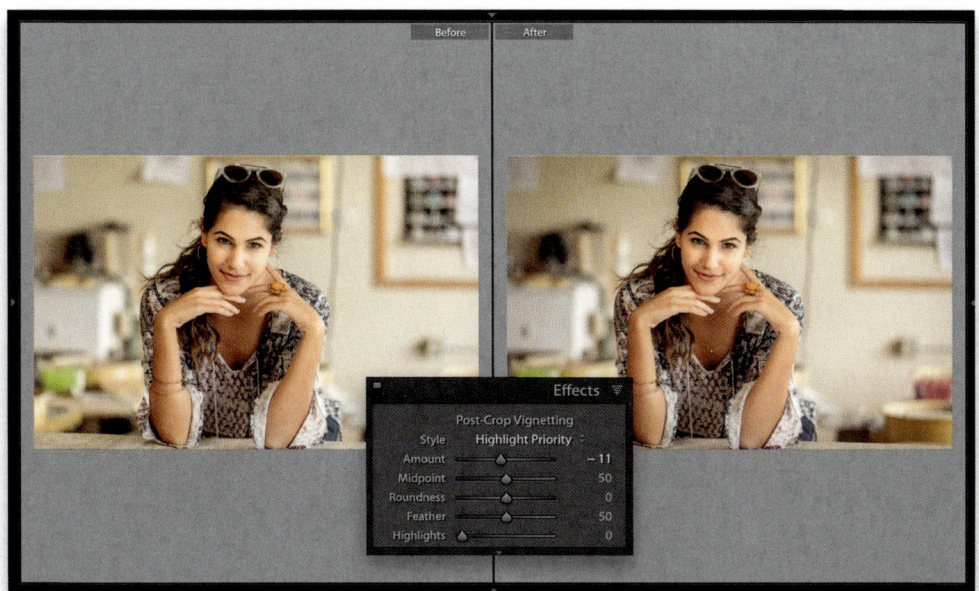

This is one of those finishing moves you do after everything else. It darkens the outside edges all the way around your entire image, which helps to focus the viewer's attention toward your subject and away from the edges. It's going to seem like a really subtle effect (especially with the low amount I use, and I always pretty much use the same amount), but once you toggle the effect on/off, you'll see it really does make a difference. Here's how to apply this edge darkening vignette:

In Lightroom: In the Develop module, scroll down to the Effects panel in the right side Panels area. Then, in the Post-Crop Vignetting section, drag the Amount slider over to the left to –11 (as seen above). That's all there is to it. To toggle the effect on/off, so you can see the difference this little change makes, click on the little switch in the top left of the panel header.

In Photoshop: Open the image in Camera Raw (or go under the Filter menu and choose **Camera Raw Filter**), and then click on the Effects icon (it's the third icon from the right) at the top of the Panel area. In the Post Crop Vignetting section, drag the Amount slider over to the left to –11. That's all there is to it. To toggle the effect on/off, so you can see the difference this little change makes, click on the icon that looks like three little sliders below the bottom-right corner of your image.

Adding a Spotlight Effect

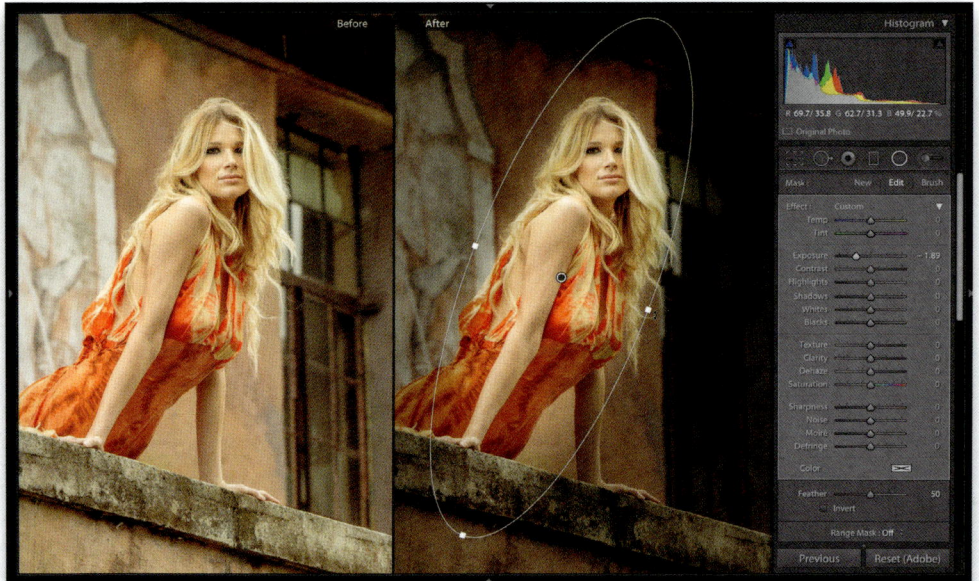

I love this technique because it lets you add a soft spotlight. You can rotate this spotlight, resize it, or stretch it, so it creates a beam of light effect, too. It's pretty awesome.

In Lightroom: In the Develop module, choose the Radial Filter tool **(Shift-M)** from the toolbox near the top of the right side Panels area. Then, in the panel of adjustments that appears, double-click on the word "Effect" to reset all the sliders to zero. Now, jump down to the paragraph below the Photoshop directions.

In Photoshop: Open the image in Camera Raw (or go under the Filter menu and choose **Camera Raw Filter**) and choose the Radial Filter tool **(J)** from the toolbar at the top of the window. In the panel of adjustments on the right, click on the – (minus sign) button to the left of Exposure, which resets all the sliders to zero and decreases the Exposure amount to –0.50.

Next, drag the Exposure slider to the left to –1.00 or –1.50, or more if you want a more dramatic effect (here, I dragged it to –1.89). At the bottom of the panel in Camera Raw, to the right of Effect, click on the Outside radio button, so the changes you make only affect what's outside the oval you're going to make. At the bottom of Lightroom's panel, make sure the Invert checkbox is turned off. Now, click-and-drag an oval out over the area where you want your spotlight to appear. To move the oval, click in its center and drag it. To rotate it, move your cursor just outside the oval and your cursor will turn into a two-headed arrow, click-and-drag up or down to rotate. To resize the oval, click on a side, top, or bottom point and drag.

Adding Texture to Solid Backgrounds

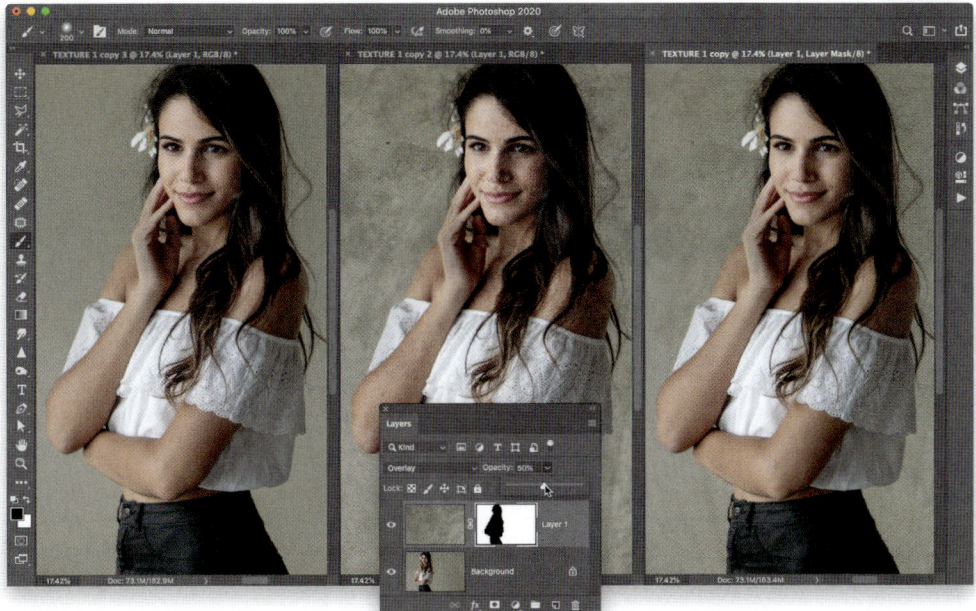

Here, on the left, is a window light shot taken with a solid-color wall as the background, and we're going to add some texture to it, simply to make it more interesting. You can either buy a royalty-free stock background (which is what I did here, from Adobe Stock), or you can find a free textured background online (just make sure you get a Creative Commons image that's free for commercial use), or you can simply keep your camera with you, so the next time you're downtown, you can shoot a few old textured walls.

In Photoshop: Open both your portrait image and your textured background image. Press **Command-A (PC: Ctrl-A)** to select your textured image, then **Command-C (PC: Ctrl-C)** to Copy it, click on your portrait image, and then press **Command-V (PC: Ctrl-V)** to Paste it. It'll appear on its own separate layer, covering your portrait image, which is on the layer below it. To get it to blend in with your portrait image, go to the top of the Layers panel and change its layer blend mode to **Overlay** (as seen in the Layers panel above). Now it blends in, but this texture also covers your subject (as seen in the middle image), giving her a pretty serious case of psoriasis. To fix that problem, click on the Add Layer Mask icon (it's the third icon from the left) at the bottom of the Layers panel to add a layer mask to your texture layer. That way, if you make a mistake in this next step, you can undo it. Get the Brush tool **(B)**, choose a soft-edged brush from the Brush Picker up in the Options Bar, and with your Foreground color set to black, paint over your subject. As you paint, it removes the texture from them. Lastly, at the top of the Layers panel, lower the Opacity of this layer until the texture looks realistic (here, I lowered it to 50%).

Brightening Skin

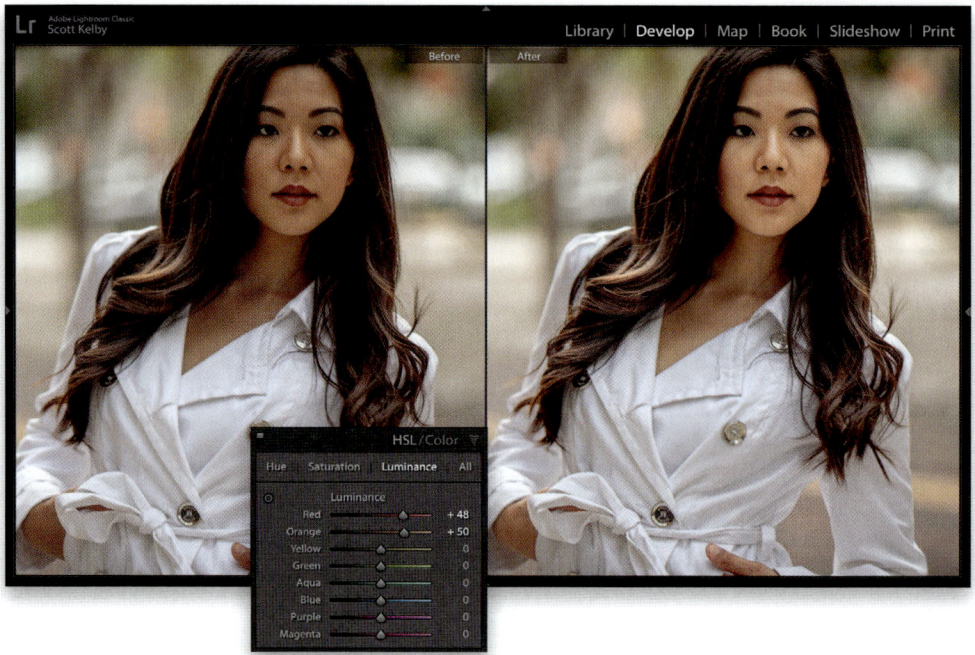

If you've got everything looking good, but you want to brighten just your subject's skin, here's a trick that allows you to easily brighten the skin without messing a bunch with the rest of the image.

In Lightroom: In the Develop module, scroll down to the HSL/Color panel in the right side Panels area, click on the Luminance tab at the top, and then drag the Red and Orange sliders to the right to brighten the skin (the skin tones are mostly found in those two sliders). Notice it's not just brightening her face, but all of her skin—her neck, hands, etc. You might see a small bit of brightening in other areas in your image that have red and orange as well, but they should be pretty minor in most cases.

In Photoshop: Open the image in Camera Raw (or go under the Filter menu and choose **Camera Raw Filter**), and then click on the HSL Adjustments icon (it's the fourth icon from the left) at the top of the Panel area. Click on the Luminance tab at the top of the panel, and then drag the Reds and Oranges sliders to the right to brighten the skin (the skin tones are mostly found in those two sliders). Notice it's not just brightening her face, but all of her skin—her neck, hands, etc. You might see a small bit of brightening in other areas in your image that have red and orange as well, but they should be pretty minor in most cases.

Smoothing Skin

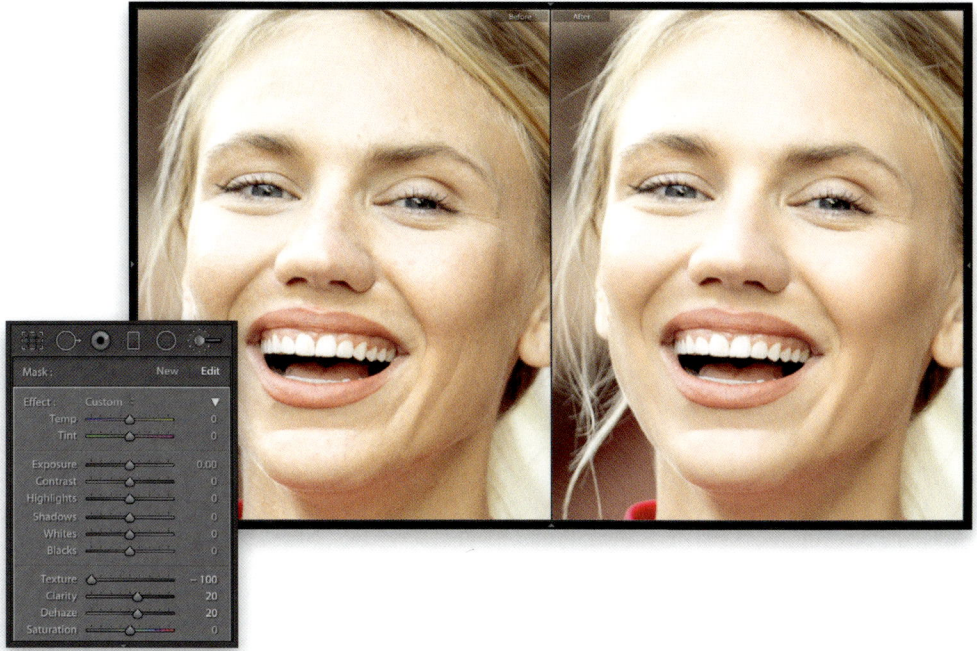

For years, I didn't recommend anyone do skin softening or smoothing in Lightroom. You could do it, and it was "okay," but it wasn't great. Now, with the Texture slider, it's a lot better (but still not as good as Photoshop's Frequency Separation technique, which is beyond the scope of this book. I did make a step-by-step video for you on how to do it, though. Why? Because I totally dig you, my esteemed reader and BFF. You can find it, along with a few other videos showing you some of the techniques from this chapter, on the book's companion webpage mentioned in the book's introduction). I want to give a nod to my dear friend and colleague, fashion and glamour photographer Frank Doorhof, who turned me on to this method for skin smoothing. Here's what he does: Start by getting the Adjustment Brush **(K)** from the toolbox near the top of the Develop module's right side Panels area. Then, in the panel of adjustments that appears, double-click on the word "Effect" to reset all the sliders to zero. Next, lower the Texture amount a lot (between –80 and –100), then increase the Clarity amount to bring back a little detail and texture, and then paint over the skin, being careful to avoid detail areas like the eyes, lips, eyebrows, hair, etc. You'll probably have to shrink your brush size (use the **Left Bracket key** on your keyboard). Finally, once you've painted over the skin, use the Dehaze slider, dragging it to the right to around 20, to control the amount of highlights and shadows in the face. It works pretty darn well! (Thanks, Frank.)

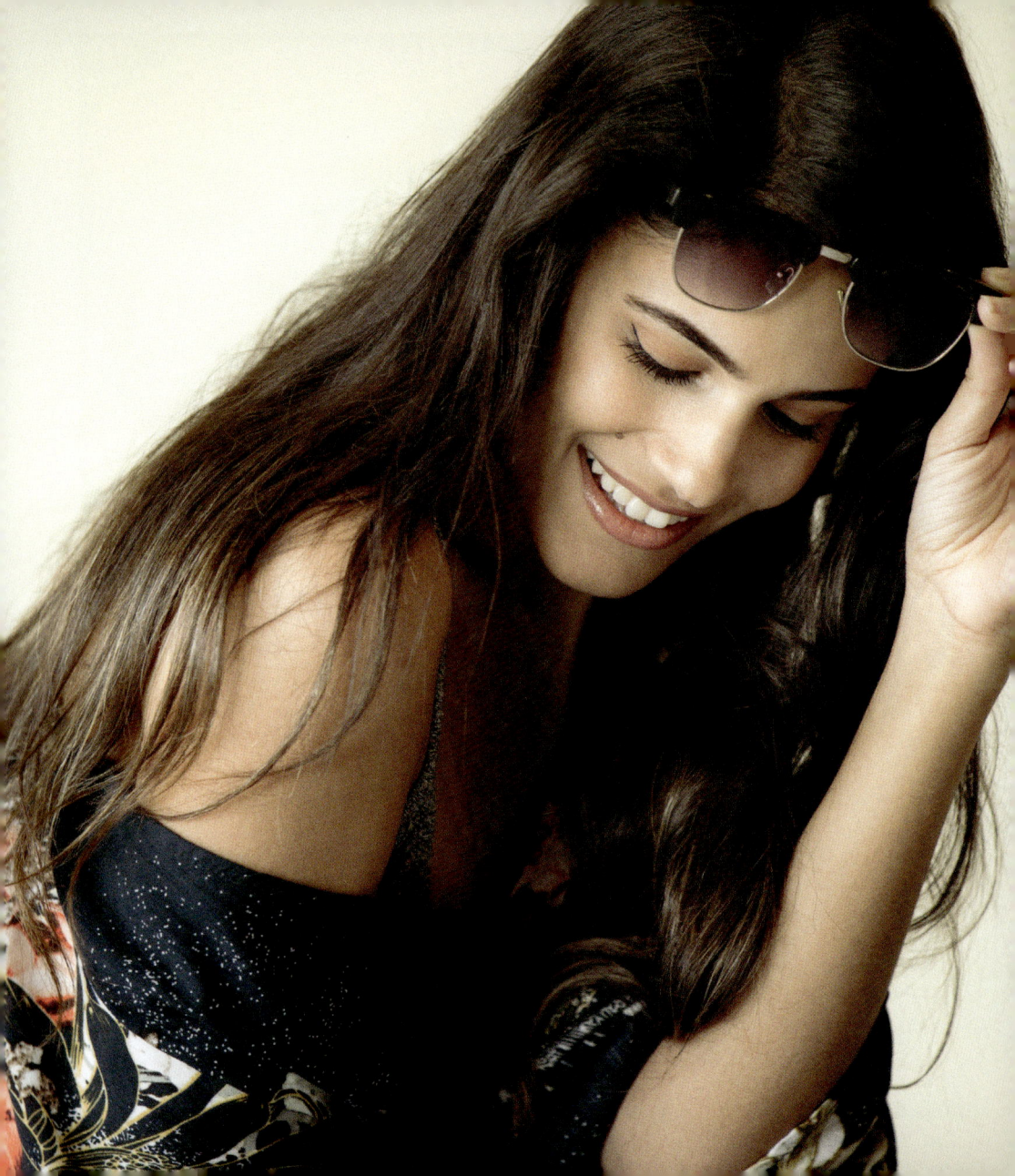

Chapter Nine

Portrait Recipes
The Ingredients for Making Great Portraits

I saved this chapter for last because…it's the last chapter. What this chapter is about is showing you a behind-the-scenes production shot of what goes into making a particular type of portrait. Then, I break it all down by giving you a description of what you're seeing, then the camera settings I used, and then my personal notes on how to get that type of shot. I finish up with a rundown of the post-processing I used, which I describe in the form of a black-and-white picture of a fence post. I know what you're probably thinking at this point: "Scott, what you just described was actually helpful and descriptive for what's to come in this chapter, and frankly, that's a let down to me, your valued reader, who was expecting so much less." I know. I also feel like I let you down, but this chapter intro isn't over yet— I still have an opportunity to take it on a wild goose chase that fulfills the important role these mindless intros have in the overall success of this book. But, I'm not going to do that (gasp!). No, because for the first time ever, I just delivered something of actual value in an intro, and I must admit, it feels kinda good. So good, that I now want to make up for all those other babbling intros by sharing something with you that I learned the hard way. Something I wish someone had told me when I was just starting out in portrait photography, because it literally would have propelled me forward by years, and I really think I can do that now for you. I can be that person who doesn't feel like you have to "pay your dues" and learn things "the hard way" just because I had to. No, I'm going to be the guy that breaks that rule, and I'm going to tell you, flat-out, unabashedly, that single thing that will make the most difference in your portrait photography, and it's something I didn't cover anywhere in the book, but it's honestly more valuable than any of it, and it's simply this….

Overhead Sun Portrait with Diffuser BTS

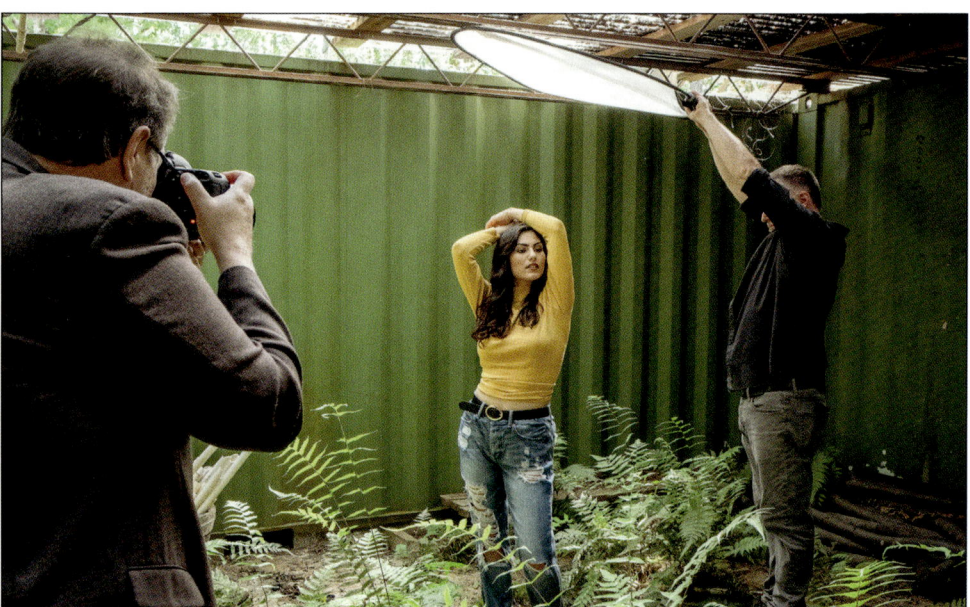

BEHIND THE SCENES: Here, our subject is posing in an old storage unit where the roof is mostly off, but there was enough light that it looked like it might make some great light for a portrait. Especially when we saw the color on the walls—it was just too perfect a match with the yellow shirt our subject was wearing—and I loved the pattern on them. But, when we took our first test shots, the sun was right overhead and it was clipping everything—the top of her head, her arms, everything was pretty much blowing out—and if I used exposure compensation, it just made the scene darker, and the highlights were still too bright. That's when we pulled out the 1-stop Lastolite TriGrip Diffuser and held it directly above our subject's head (as seen here), and that alone created some absolutely beautiful light.

CAMERA SETTINGS: For the final image on the facing page, I used an 85mm f/1.2 lens, but the shot was taken at f/1.8 because I didn't want such a shallow depth of field that if my focus was not 100% on the money, it was probably going to be visibly out of focus. So, I went with f/1.8. Once we softened the light, I had to crank up my ISO to 400, so I would have enough shutter speed to hand-hold. I was shooting (as always) in aperture priority mode and at f/1.8 at 400 ISO, and the camera chose a shutter speed of 1/100 of a second for a proper exposure. After taking a test shot, I thought the image was a little bit too bright, so I used exposure compensation (see page 22) to override what my camera thought was the proper exposure and darken the scene by 1/3 of a stop. That did the trick.

Final Image

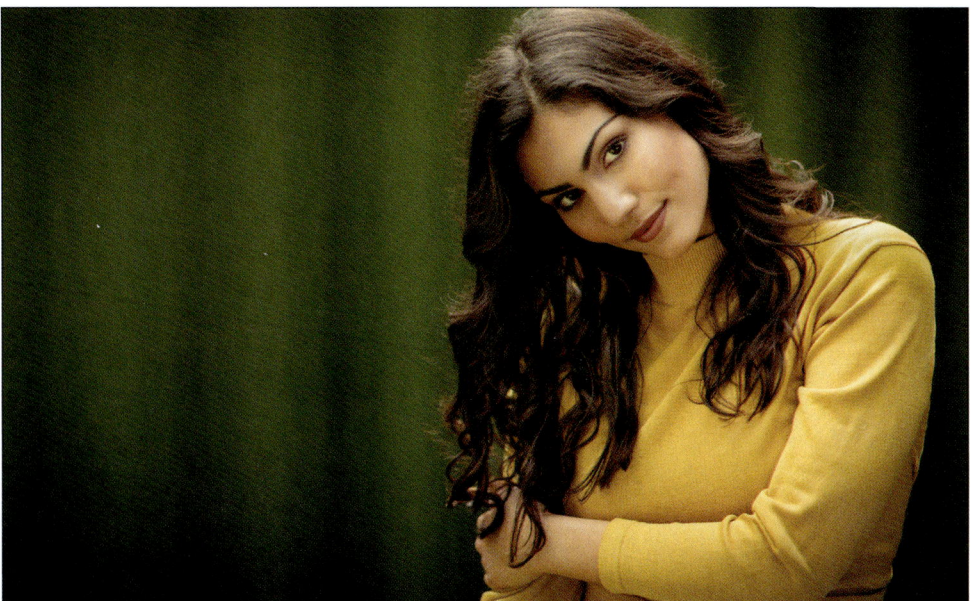

NOTES: You can see what a difference that 1-stop diffuser makes. Still a tad bright on her shoulder on the right here, but I can live with it. You can see the soft sunlight lighting the top of her head and both sides of her hair, so it's like you have a hair light on her, as well. Composition-wise, I intentionally framed the shot with her way off to the side, leaving lots of negative space (an empty area of your image, which draws your eye immediately to your subject). Also, we have really nice separation from the background. She's only standing six feet or so from the wall, but at an f-stop of f/1.8, that's more than enough to put the green wall in the background out of focus.

POST-PROCESSING: To make the light look more dramatic, in Lightroom, I first went to the Effects panel and added a post-crop vignette to darken the edges all the way around the image. Then, I took the Graduated Filter tool, darkened the Exposure by about –1.00 stop, and dragged the gradient from the left edge of the image all the way to where she starts. That darkened the left side of the image, which helps, yet again, in drawing your eye toward the subject. Then, I switched to the Adjustment Brush, increased the Exposure amount to 0.50 and painted over her hair on the left side of the image. By tilting her head to the side, it created some shadows on that side of her hair, and painting over it opened up those shadows, added some highlights, and made the light look a bit more interesting overall. Lastly, in the Basic panel, I increased the Contrast amount to make the colors nice and vibrant.

Large Area Portrait with Diffuser BTS

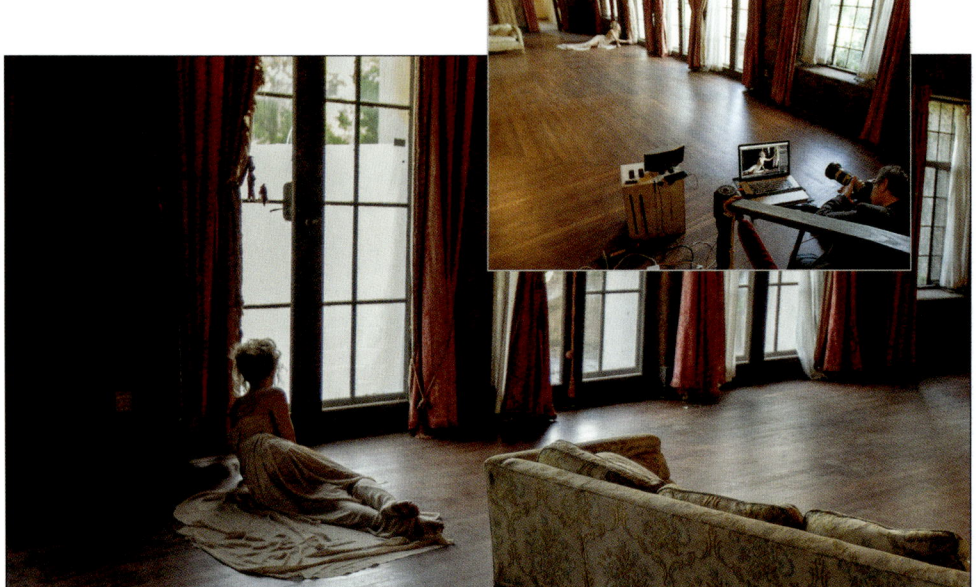

BEHIND THE SCENES: Our subject is lying on the floor in a big beautiful room lined with floor-to-ceiling French doors, and the light is just pouring in everywhere (we'll cover how to deal with that on the next page). I'm off to the far right, and I'm shooting sitting on the floor (you can see my shooting position in the inset top right). I'm shooting tethered into Lightroom, so when I take a shot it shows up full size on my 15" laptop. Seeing your images at that size, while you're shooting, is addicting because you'll catch so many mistakes (like slightly soft or out-of-focus shots), while you can still fix them. You'll also see your shadows better and your subject's expressions—I can't recommend it enough. The other thing you can see in the inset, sitting on the apple box next to me, is a speaker for playing music during the shoot.

CAMERA SETTINGS: For the final image on the facing page, I'm shooting with a 70–200mm f/2.8 lens at 70mm. I had to get far back from my subject to get her, and the environment, fully in the shot to tell a story with this image. I could have gotten closer with a wide-angle lens, but then your subject looks a bit distorted, and it's generally not flattering to them. Plus, you lose the wonderful lens compression of a longer lens, so I prefer to not go wide in situations where you want the subject to look awesome. I'm at 200 ISO, which is higher than I needed, since I'm shooting on a tripod; I should have been at 100 ISO. I'm shooting in aperture priority mode, so the camera chose a shutter speed for me of 1/13 of a second. Way too slow to hand-hold, but again, I'm shooting on a tripod.

Final Image

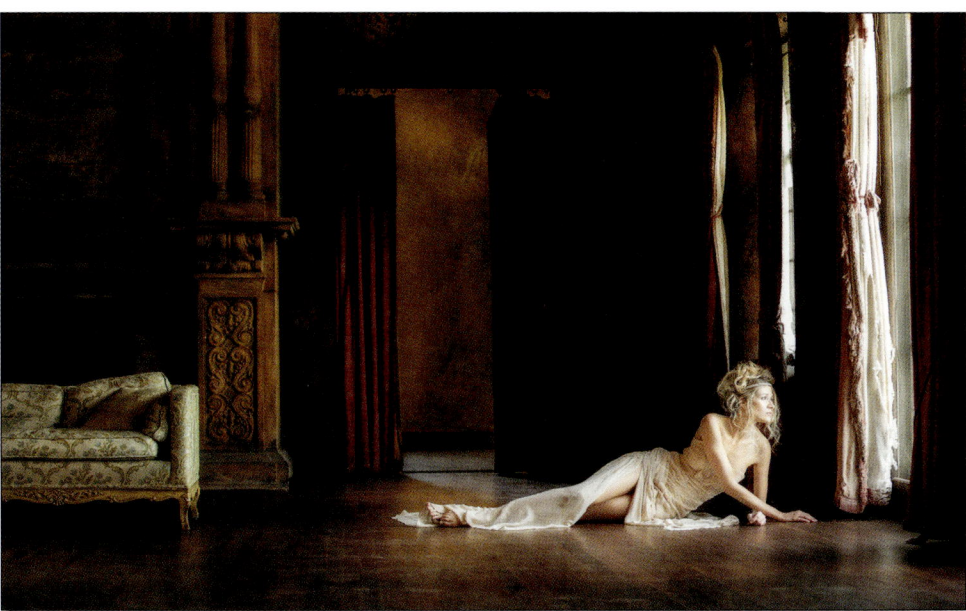

NOTES: The challenge with this shot is taming the light coming in through the row of windows. I took a test shot, and the light was so bright it was blowing out my subject's face (clipping warnings were going off left and right). But it's an easy fix: take a look back at the BTS production shot on the previous page, and you'll notice that we used gaffer's tape to put a shower curtain liner over the window to spread and diffuse the light (see page 39). This translucent liner does an amazing job of turning that huge window of harsh light into a big, beautiful softbox. That did the trick.

POST-PROCESSING: I wanted to make sure you would see lots of detail behind our subject, so the image had lots of depth. In Lightroom, I opened up the shadows a bit by dragging the Shadows slider to the right. I pulled back the Highlights slider to keep the light on her from getting too bright, and I increased the overall contrast (dragging the Contrast slider to the right quite a bit). Lastly, I darkened the edges all the way around the image using the technique from page 147. Just a little sharpening in the Detail panel and you're done (I increased the Sharpening Amount to 65 to give it a nice, punchy amount of sharpening).

Backlit Sun Flare Portrait BTS

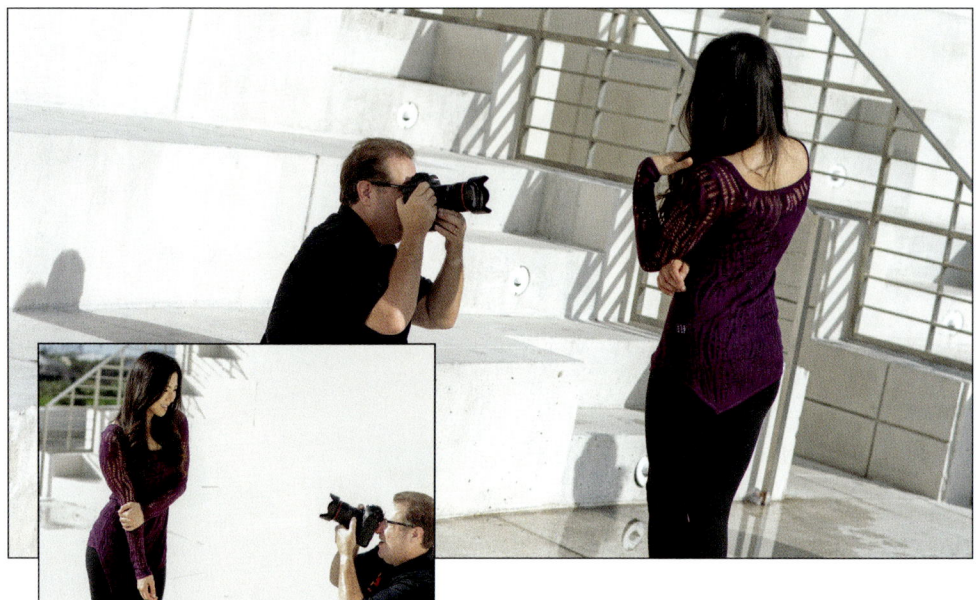

BEHIND THE SCENES: We're shooting in an open-air amphitheater on a hot, sunny Florida day. It's later in the day, so the sun is lower in the sky, and I can get down low and try to position the sun directly behind my subject. What I'm trying to do is to get the edge of the sun to touch part of my subject to create a sun flare. When that happens, instead of the sun being just a giant nebulous ball of bright, you start to get little beams or sprites (I'm not sure what the official name is) coming off it, and it looks a lot more interesting.

CAMERA SETTINGS: For the final image on the facing page, I'm using a wide-angle lens because it's much easier to get lens flare effects with a wide-angle lens than it is with a longer lens. I'm shooting with a 24–70mm f/2.8 lens at 24mm. This is my all-time least favorite lens (so much so that I sold this lens since this shot was taken), but it was the only wide-angle I had with me that day…so…ya know, "you dance with the one who brung ya" (or something like that). I'm at f/2.8 (I would have gotten a lot more sun rays if I had been at f/16), and I'm at 100 ISO. I'm shooting in aperture priority mode, so my camera set my shutter speed for me at 1/4000 of a second. My subject is backlit and she's pretty much a silhouette, so I used exposure compensation to make the scene much brighter than my camera thought it should be. I increased it to +1.3 stops brighter, so my subject wouldn't be a silhouette and I'd get that blown-out look in the image.

Final Image

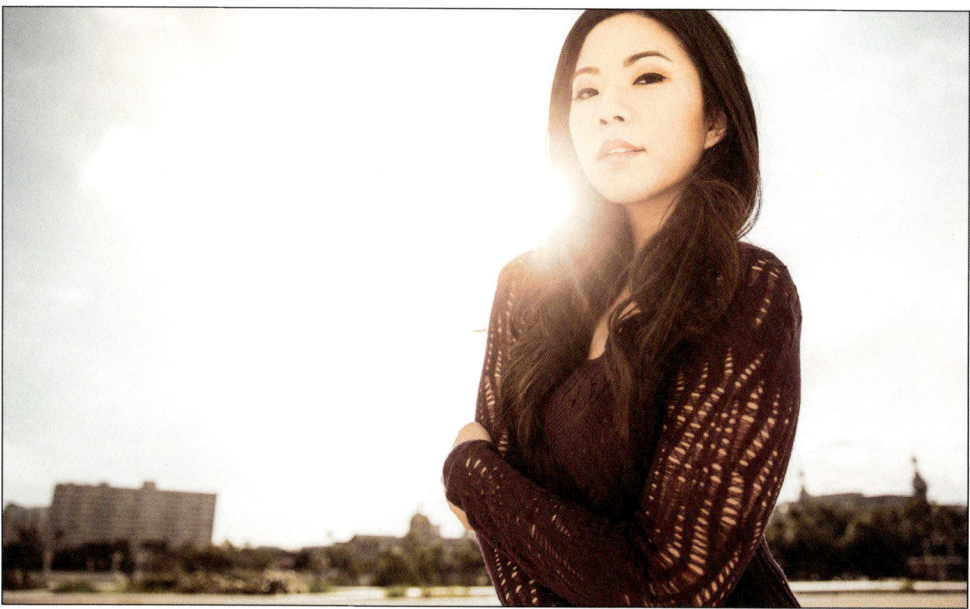

NOTES: I go out of my way not to shoot people from a low angle like this because it's generally not a flattering angle whatsoever, and I also try not to shoot people with an unflattering lens like a 24–70mm. But, in this case, we're going for a specific look (the blown-out look), with a bit of an environmental portrait to it (note the city skyline across the river), with a specific position for the sun (touching our subject, and even to get that I had to get down on my knees, which is something I don't relish, and that's being kind).

POST-PROCESSING: I'm going for the washed-out, blown-out look, so in Lightroom, I cranked up the Highlights and lowered the Contrast quite a bit. To bring a little more detail out in my backlit subject, I also increased the amount of the Shadows slider (dragging it to the right). To warm up the photo, I dragged the Temp slider over to the right toward yellow. But, for that to really have any effect, I would have had to wait another hour or so until the sun started actually getting close to sunset, and not just shooting late in the afternoon, because the sky still has a lot of blue it in.

Backlit Indoor Window Light Portrait BTS

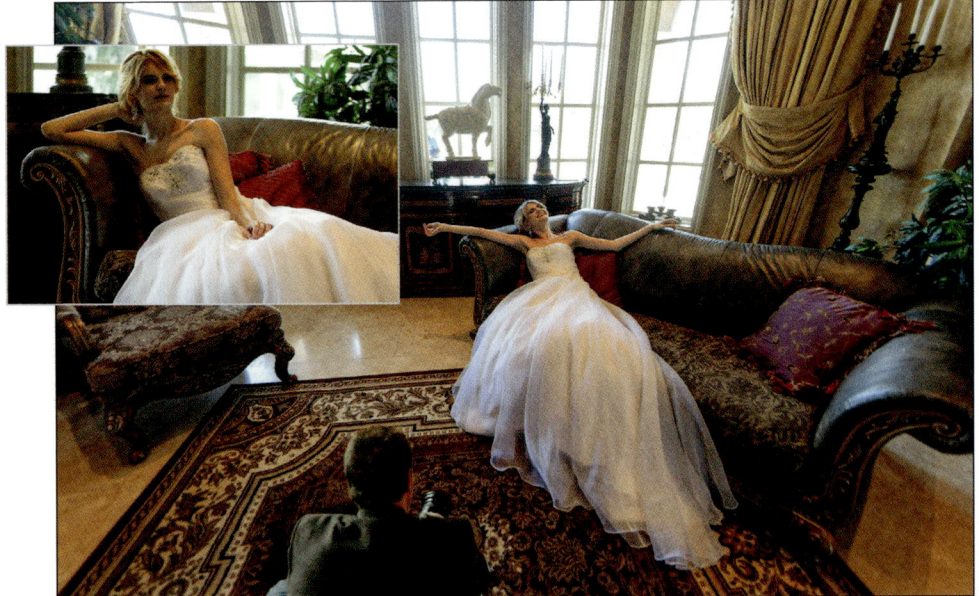

BEHIND THE SCENES: Here, our subject is lounging on a large leather couch in front of a large bank of windows. She's completely backlit, and her face is mostly in shadows, as seen in the inset above left. By the way, if you look at the image in the inset, you'll notice that for some reason her face isn't sharp; it's quite a bit out of focus actually, but her hand is tack sharp. Not sure what I was thinking. Plus, she's got a greenish tint. It's all bad. Also, in the main behind-the-scenes photo above, look at her dress. You can see all the different weird color casts we're getting from light bouncing around the room.

CAMERA SETTINGS: For the final image on the facing page, I shot this with an 85mm f/1.2 lens at f/2.8. I wasn't going for the creamy out-of-focus blurry background on this, but even at f/2.8, if I had gotten in a lot closer, I would have had that type of background. I was trying to capture the full extension of her pose, with enough of her gown in the shot that you could tell she was a bride. It's kind of an environmental portrait without going wide. My ISO is 320, and I'm shooting in aperture priority mode, so my camera chose a shutter speed for me of 1/160 of a second, but those settings gave me the awful exposure you see up in the inset above (known heretofore as the "lame shot"). The weird thing is it's not going to take much to get us from lame shot to the shot you see on the opposite page. A little change of a camera setting, a little color cast removal in Lightroom, and a few other little tweaks and we're there.

Final Image

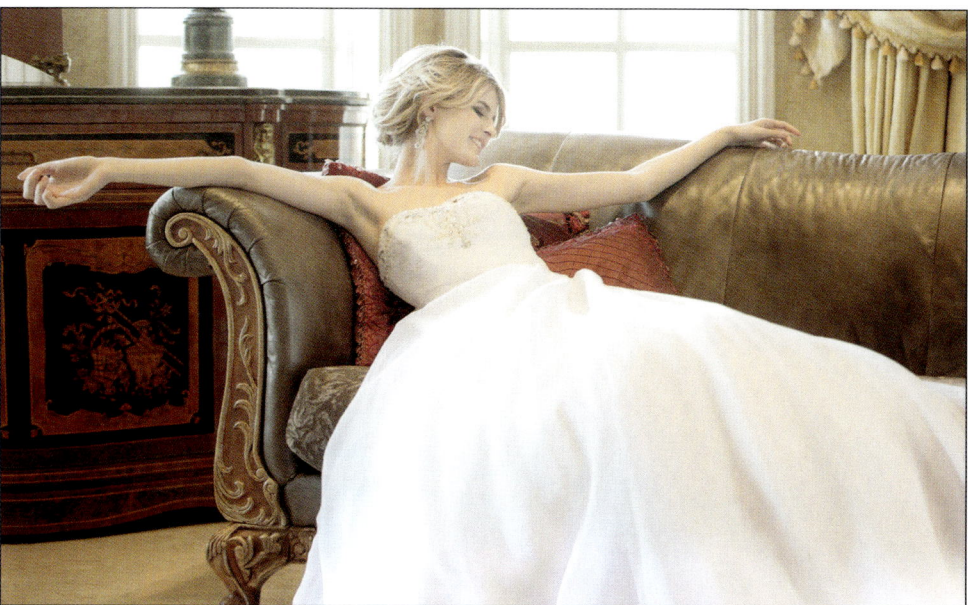

NOTES: When I took a test shot and the "lame shot" appeared on the back of my camera, I wanted to pick up everything and move to a different location. But, I thought those windows blowing out to solid white in the background could look cool, so I stuck around. The first thing was to get the bride out of the shadows. Remember back on page 76 when you're shooting out in direct light, so you put your subject's back to the sun, and then intentionally overexposure the shot by a bunch using exposure compensation? So, what happens when you do that? The background gets a lot brighter (possibly making those windows blow out to solid white, yes?) and your subject gets a lot brighter, taking her out of the shadows and lighting her beautifully. How much did I have to bump up my exposure compensation to get this gloriously high-key blown-out look? Nearly 3 full stops (yikes!). Well, 2.7 to be exact. Also, doing this sent my shutter speed down to 1/30 of a second, so I had to hold very still, which I did. Yay me.

POST-PROCESSING: The post was surprisingly easy now that everything was so bright. First, I had to get rid of all the color casts on her bridal gown, so in Lightroom, I got the Adjustment Brush, dragged the Saturation slider nearly all the way to zero (but not all the way or it would paint in gray), and painted over her gown. As I did, the casts were removed and what was left was a white dress. Booya! Then, I desaturated her skin as well (see page 135), and finally I created a new Adjustment Brush fix, cranked the Highlights slider way up, and painted over the windows to make them fully blown out, so you couldn't see any detail outside them.

Direct Sun Location Portrait with Diffuser BTS

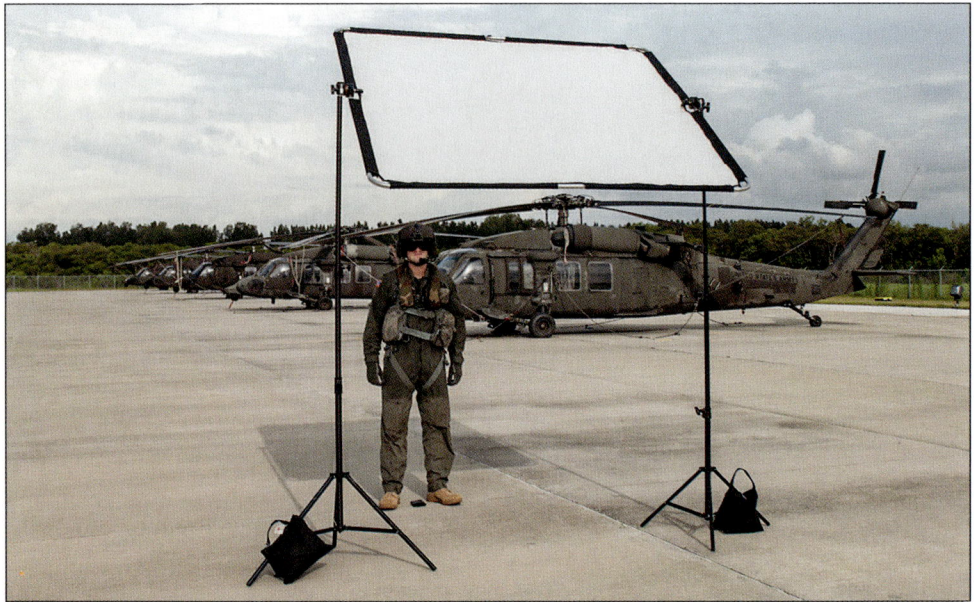

BEHIND THE SCENES: Our subject is a US Army rescue helicopter pilot, and we're shooting at the Army airfield, out on the ramp, on a hot summer's day. We're using a large scrim to diffuse the sun, giving us a softer, better quality of light. This is a much larger version of a 1-stop diffuser (see page 63). This one is made by British company Lastolite, and it's supported by two light stands (note the sandbags on each of the stands to keep this rig from flying away and damaging some expensive copters). On top of each light stand is a rotating head that lets us tip the scrim in the direction of the sun (you can see it's shadow on the ground just behind him).

CAMERA SETTINGS: For the final image on the facing page, I used a 70–200mm lens at 180mm. I also took some shots with a wide-angle lens at 24mm (seen in the inset). I chose a wide-angle lens because I wanted it to be an environmental portrait (the helicopter in the background is important to the story), and since I'm not trying to make a beautiful portrait—I'm trying to tell a story—I'm okay with using a non-flattering wide-angle lens, using an f-stop that keeps the background in sharp focus (like f/11), and shooting at 24mm.

Final Images

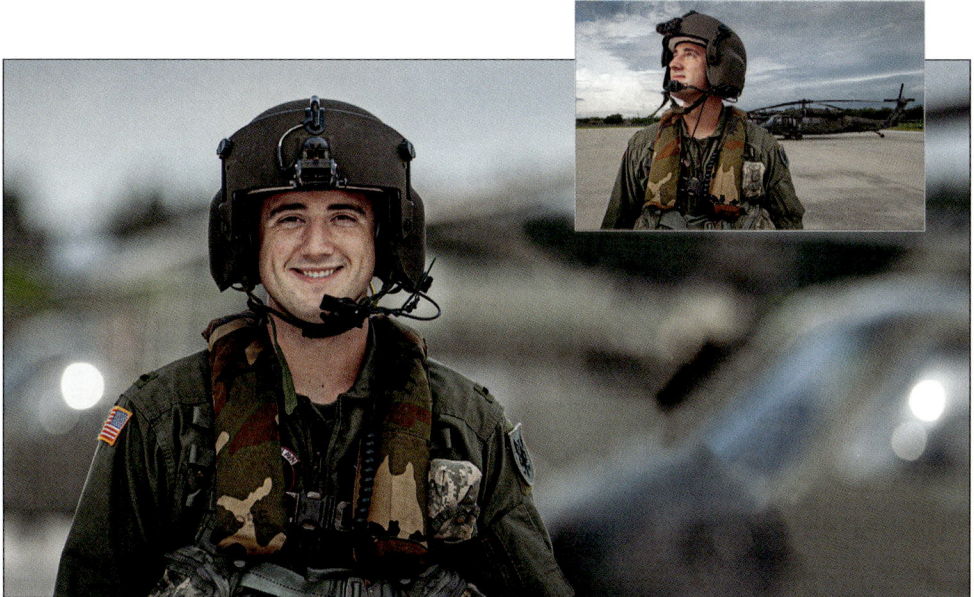

NOTES: The reason for the larger scrim is because I wanted to shoot small groups and some full-length shots (I wound up doing both), while still having them in nice, soft light. For some of the shots, we pulled out a circular reflector to send a little light back toward our subject. However, light reflects big time, and there's a ton of bright sun hitting the asphalt and bouncing back up toward our subject, so we didn't have to use the reflector a lot.

POST-PROCESSING: I edited the image in Lightroom (but you can do these exact same edits, and get the exact same results, using Camera Raw) by lowering the Highlights a bunch (to –75. His face was kind of shiny and sweaty, so that helped pull it back a bit), increasing the Contrast (to +10) to help make the image look a little more punchy, and cranking up the Texture to help accentuate the detail in his flight suit (I set it to +35). But, then I took the Adjustment Brush and painted over just his flight suit with the Texture set to 50 and the Clarity set to 25 to bring out even more detail (I felt that the first +35 of Texture alone I applied in the Basic panel wasn't intense enough). Then, I clicked on New, lowered the Texture to 30, the Contrast to 15, and painted over the sky behind him to give it some additional "oomph!" To make the sky darker, I switched to the Graduated Filter tool, set all the sliders to zero, then dragged the Exposure slider to –1.00 and dragged the gradient from the top of the image down to about an inch above the horizon line. Lastly, at the bottom of the Graduated Filter panel, I chose **Color** from the Range pop-up menu, and then clicked the eyedropper in the sky beside his helmet to have Lightroom remove the darkened sky from his helmet. That's it.

Harsh Direct Light Portrait with Diffuser BTS

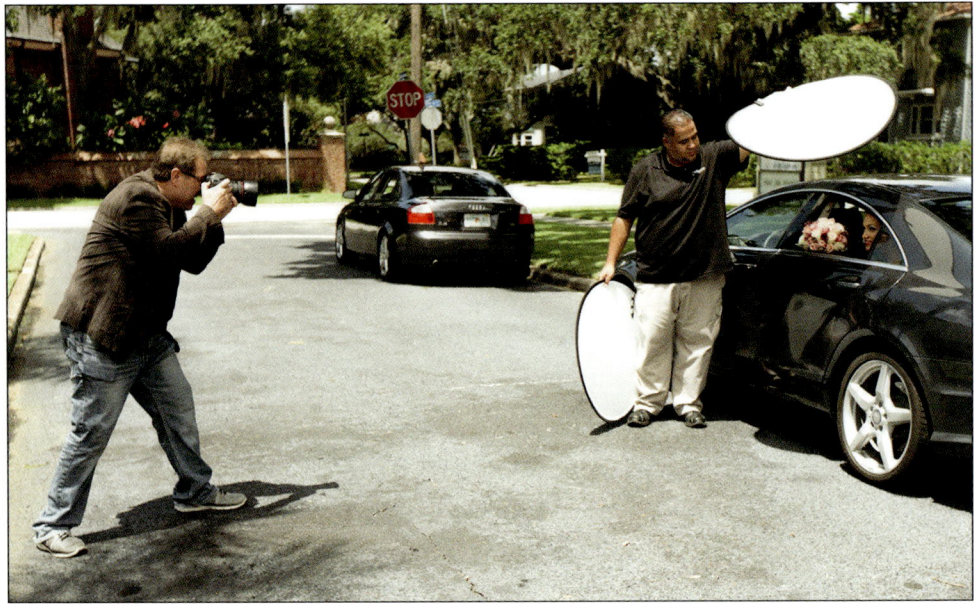

BEHIND THE SCENES: We're on location and our bride is in the backseat of a car. She has rolled down the back window and she's looking out toward the camera. The sun is beaming directly into the car, she's squinting in the bright sunlight, and the light on her is harsh and very unflattering. Here, I have an assistant holding a 1-stop diffuser (like the one on page 56) between the high overhead sun and the window of the car. That diffuser softens and spreads the light to make it soft and beautiful.

CAMERA SETTINGS: For the final image on the facing page, to put the background out of focus, I used an 85mm f/1.2 lens, taken at f/1.4, which is lower than I prefer to shoot because the depth of field is so shallow that if I'm off even a tiny bit with my focus on her eyes, the shot will be out of focus. I prefer f/1.8, but I probably didn't realize at the time that I was shooting at f/1.4 or I would have raised it. My ISO was 100. I was shooting (as always) in aperture priority mode, and at f/1.4, my shutter speed was a fast 1/2500 of a second.

Final Image

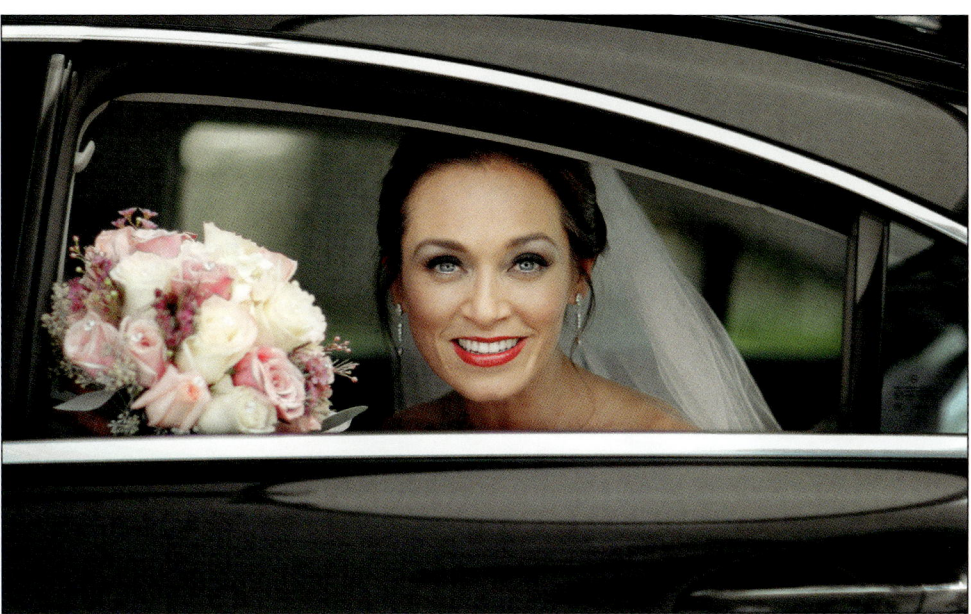

NOTES: You can actually see the 1-stop diffuser reflected in the car. No one ever noticed that, but of course once you see it, you can't un-see it. You can see from the position of the light that it's high noon and the sun is right overhead, which creates the worst shadows in the eye sockets and under the chin. But, with the diffuser, the light is soft, even, and beautiful.

POST-PROCESSING: The issue here was her veil. I was shooting with my camera set to Auto White Balance, which is what I typically choose while shooting outdoors. But, in reality, because of the 1-stop diffuser, her veil isn't outdoors, it's in the shade. When you're set to Auto White Balance, anything in the shade is going to turn bluish, and sure enough, her veil was bluish. So, in Lightroom, I got the Adjustment Brush, increased the amount of yellow using the Temp slider (I dragged it to the right), and I painted over the veil, which removed the blue tint. I also had to create a new Adjustment Brush fix, where I lowered the Highlights amount quite a bit, and then painted over the bouquet to lower the brightness—it was still very bright and you don't want to draw attention off the bride and over to the bouquet.

Dramatic Window Light Portrait BTS

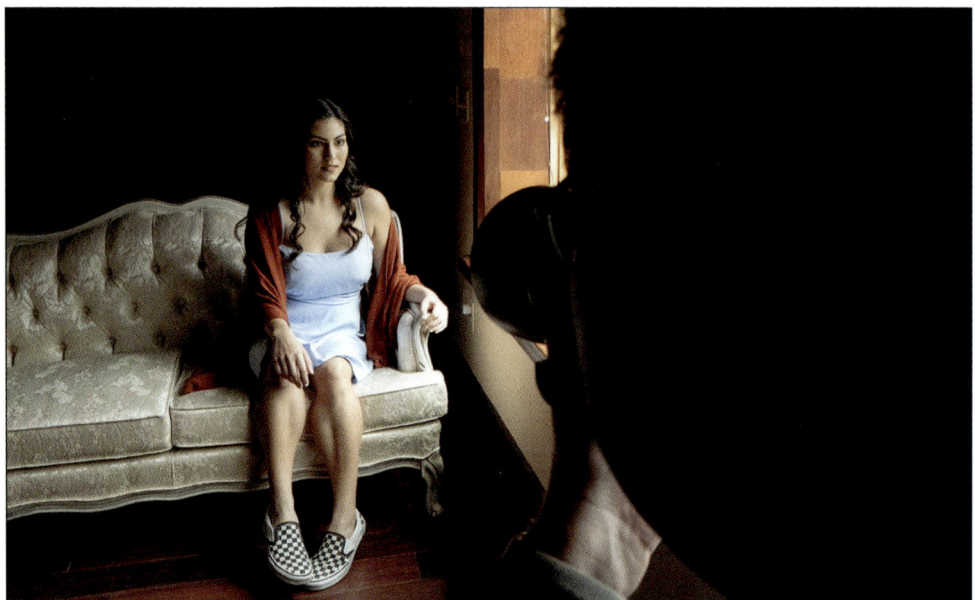

BEHIND THE SCENES: Here's a dramatic window light portrait, taken next to a nice big window on kind of a rainy day. The reason that's nice is the light, which usually would be bright and harsh and direct and yeech, is actually beautifully soft and wrapping. I have my subject seated on a couch just a few feet from the window. If the light had been more direct and harsh, I would have either moved the couch back six feet or so from the window, or I would have moved the couch behind the window by a couple of feet, so we'd get the edges of the direct light, for a softer and smoother effect. In this case, the light was awesome on its own (in short, we got lucky), so we could just pull the couch right on up to the window.

CAMERA SETTINGS: For the final image on the facing page, to put the background way out of focus, I used an 85mm f/1.2 lens at f/1.8. My ISO is set at 100. I'm shooting in aperture priority mode, and at f/1.8, my camera chose a shutter speed of 1/400 of a second, which is more than enough for hand-holding and getting a sharp shot. Although the light wasn't harsh at all, it was bright, so I had to use exposure compensation to darken the scene for more of that dramatic window light look. So, how far did I have to darken a scene like this? I took it down almost 2 full stops (1.7 stops). By the way, here's a handy thing to know: when you darken the scene using exposure compensation like this, it actually raises your shutter speed.

Final Image

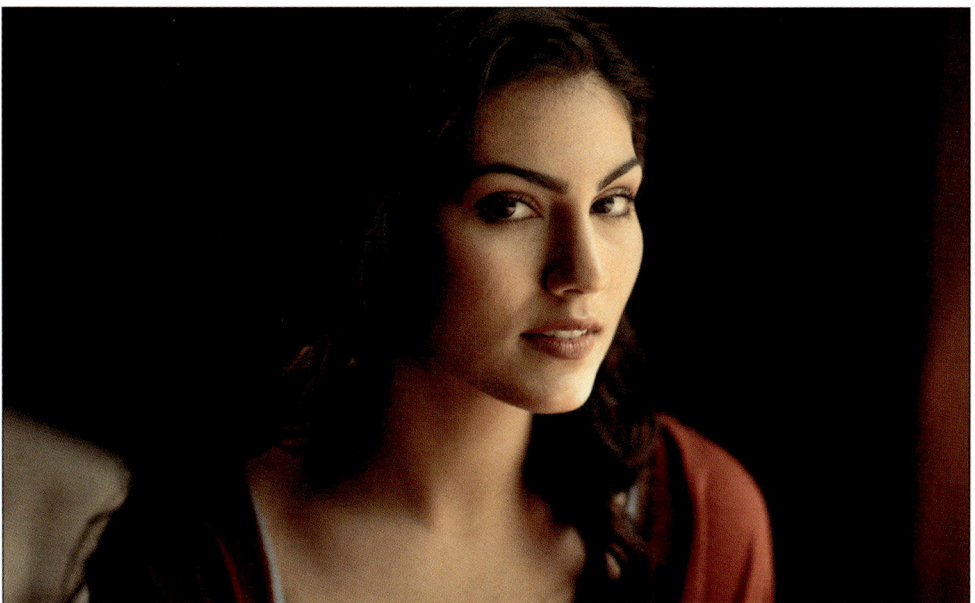

NOTES: Look how crazy soft the window light is here. This is the stuff we're looking for. Look how she's positioned to make the most of it, where the light is wrapping around her face, so some of it falls on her cheek opposite the window. Also note that I'm short lighting her (see page 112) by shooting into the shadow side of her face (the side with all the shadows on her face is the side closest to my camera). I think this is the most flattering way to photograph most people, and it's my go-to style of lighting. If I wanted to broad light her (see page 113), to give her a more rounded face (just a heads up: most people don't want a rounder face), I would have had her turn her body away from the window, and then look back at the camera. Now the brightly lit part of her face would be closest to the camera, and the shadows on her face would be on the other side, farthest from the camera. I don't often intentionally broad light my subject, but sometimes you have no choice based on location, position, or if the person has a long, narrow face.

POST-PROCESSING: In Lightroom I had to open up the shadows a bit, so her dark hair didn't disappear into the background. After I did that, I took the Adjustment Brush, increased the Highlights and Exposure amounts a bit, and painted over her hair to help bring out the highlights (I do this quite a bit on portraits. It makes hair look better, shinier, and it makes the lighting look even better). Lastly, I added a little darkening of the edges all the way around the image using the technique on page 147.

Classic Window Light Portrait BTS

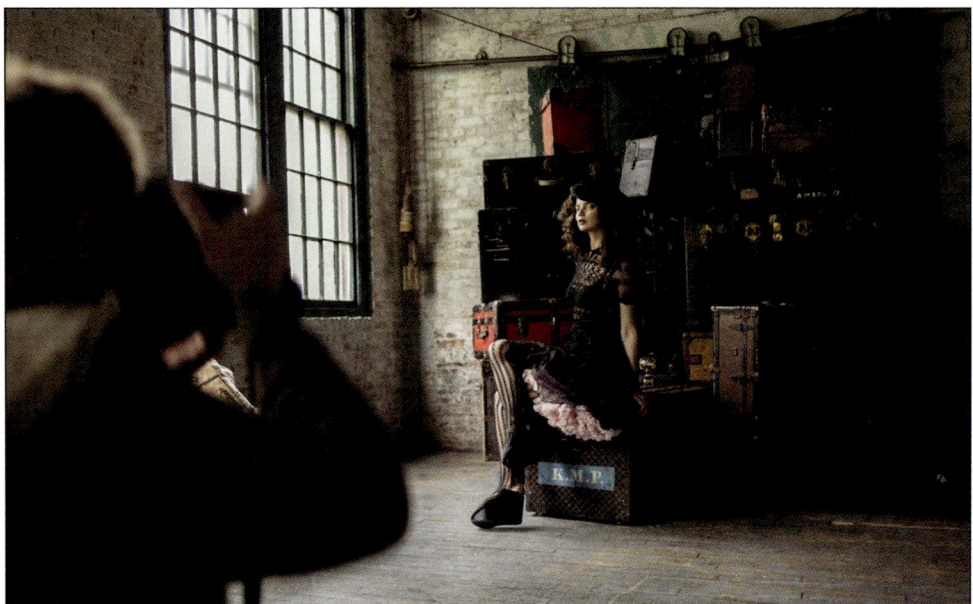

BEHIND THE SCENES: Here, our subject is in an old warehouse and light is streaming in from the windows up above. As you can see, I'm parallel to the windows, and she's not looking at them. We're letting the light from the windows side-light our subject.

CAMERA SETTINGS: For the final image on the facing page, I'm shooting with a 70–200mm f/2.8 lens at f/2.8, zoomed out to 70mm. My ISO is set at 1000, which is higher than normal, but I'm shooting with a camera body that is so clean at high ISOs like this (it's a Canon 1Dx, in case you were wondering) that I won't worry about raising it up one bit. Why, at f/2.8 and 1000 ISO, did I have to raise it up at all? We'll get to that on the next page. I was shooting in aperture priority mode, and at f/2.8 and 1000 ISO, my camera set my shutter speed to 1/50 of a second for a proper exposure. That is an awfully slow shutter speed to be hand-holding. Even though my lens has built-in Image Stabilization, and should be able to stabilize the camera no problem, I'd rather just shoot at a higher shutter speed like 1/125 of a second or faster. How do I get there? Well, I can't go any lower with my f-stop than f/2.8, so the only way to get there is to raise my ISO even farther. I could have easily gone to 1600 ISO, and that would've probably raised my shutter speed enough to where I'd feel comfortable. I still got a sharp shot, but I have others from this same set that were a bit soft or straight-up out of focus. That wouldn't have happened if I'd cranked up the ISO to where it needed to be.

Final Image

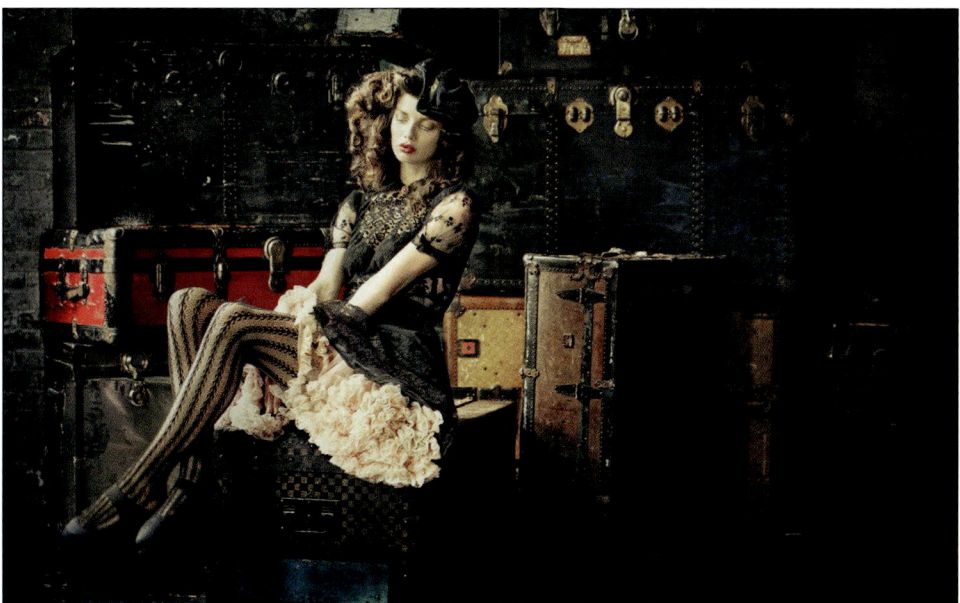

NOTES: If you look at the behind-the-scenes production image on the facing page, you'll notice how far back we built this scene with all those steamer trunks. We put them way back there, so we didn't get harsh direct light through those windows. Getting back far from the windows like that makes a huge difference in the quality of light from those windows. Back there, it's beautiful! It's soft, wrapping, gorgeous, but it's also not nearly as bright as it would be if we were much closer to those windows, so there's a trade-off. If you get back that far from the window to get that softer, more gorgeous light, it's not going to be as bright back there, so you're going to have to crank up your ISO to like, I dunno, 1000 ISO or more, so you have enough light to have enough shutter speed to hand-hold your shot and get it really sharp. If your camera creates too much noise at high ISOs, just shoot on a tripod and that would solve the problem right there.

POST-PROCESSING: There are four things going on here in post: (1) I used Photoshop's Healing Brush tool to remove any words that appeared on the luggage. If we see text in a photo, we're trained to read it before we look at anything else, so it all had to go. (2) Some of the trunks got too dark and kind of got lost in the shadows. So, before I went to Photoshop, in Lightroom, I increased the Shadows slider amount, and then used the Adjustment Brush, with the Exposure amount increased, and painted over some of the steamers to brighten them up. (3) I darkened the edges all the way around (see page 147) and (4) I added some cinematic color grading to finish it off (see page 143).

Cloudy Outdoor Portrait BTS

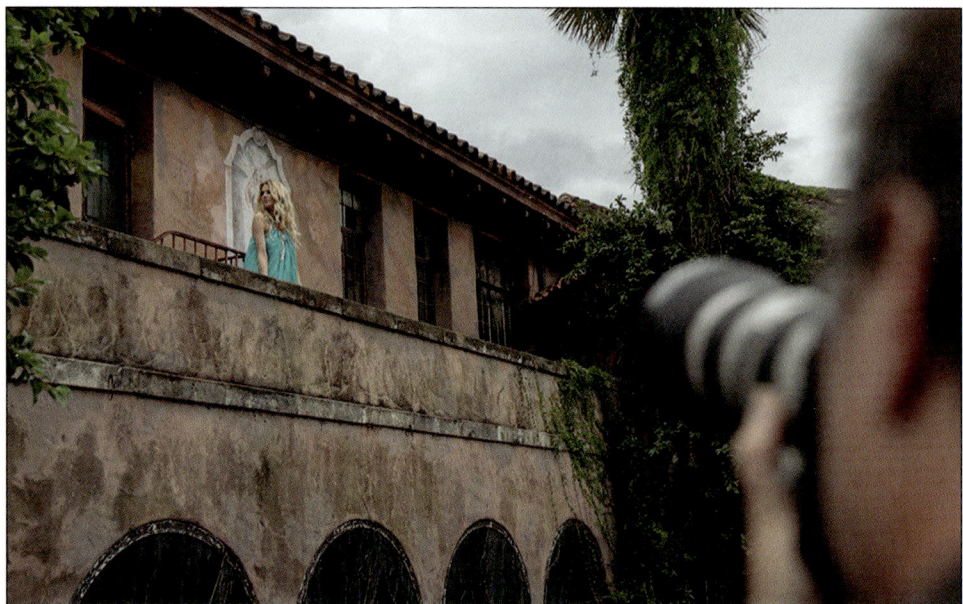

BEHIND THE SCENES: Here, our subject is in an old, abandoned mansion. She's up on a balcony, overlooking the grounds, and I'm down lower, shooting from a landing on a staircase, so I'm not fully at ground level. It's a cloudy, overcast day, which creates what is referred to as "nature's softbox." The light is fairly even and soft, which is a good thing because when it's really cloudy like this, the light is not harsh, but it's not super-directional either, so it's a bit flat. That's why I thought I could get away with doing this environmental-style portrait, where your subject is far away and awesome light isn't always so critical. Plus, I might be able to use a little Photoshop magic to take the lighting up a notch.

CAMERA SETTINGS: In the behind-the-scenes production shot above, I'm using a 70–200mm f/2.8 lens, but that's not actually what I took the final image with. For the final image on the facing page, I used a 16–35mm f/4 at around 29mm, which as you know, is a very odd mm and a sure sign of the coming zombie apocalypse. I shot it at f/2.8 (with a wide angle like that, everything will still be in focus, and it allows me to shoot without boosting my ISO like crazy, but I did boost it just a little to 200 ISO). Shooting in aperture priority mode at f/2.8 and 200 ISO, my camera set my shutter speed at a zippy 1/1600 of a second, which tells you one thing: I should have lowered my ISO back to 100, and I'd still probably be around 1/1000 of a second.

Final Image

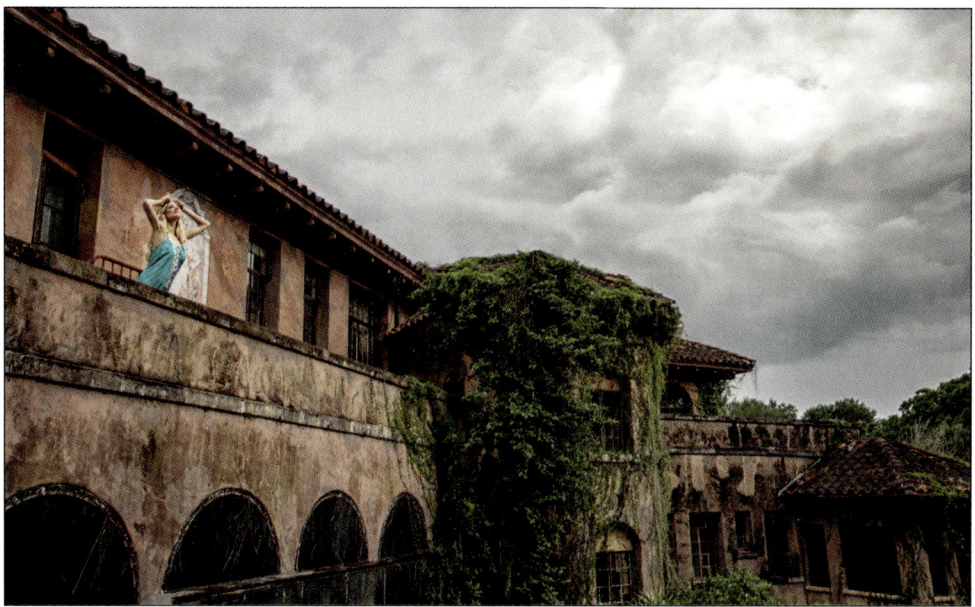

NOTES: Big, busy scenes like this are more challenging than you'd think. The challenge is having your subject stand out, while not having the scene so busy that they get lost in the frame. The first part was to have our subject wear a color that would stand out. My go-to color for that is red, but with the reddish tones already all over the building, we thought a bright blue would stand out nicely, especially since we didn't have a red dress anyway. That certainly helped sway the judges. I think we were particularly lucky that somehow a trickle of light cut through the clouds and landed right on our subject to help her stand out even more, and if you're thinking that it really didn't happen that way and it's some sort of Lightroom or Photoshop trick, then…well…you're right. Look at the sky in the behind-the-scenes shot, and then look at the sky in the final. Look at the color of the old mansion in the BTS shot, then look at how much more vibrant the color looks here. Hey, what happened to that ugly palm tree sticking up from the top of that tower? I'll tell you what happened—Photoshop happened.

POST-PROCESSING: To create the pool of light over our subject, and darken the sky and everything around her, I used the Lightroom (or Camera Raw) spotlight technique on page 148. It worked like a charm (I just put a very small oval right over her). To pump up the vibrant colors, I increased the Vibrance and the Contrast amounts (in the Basic panel) quite a bit, which boosted the colors. How did I make the sky look angry? I used the Adjustment Brush, with a lot of Texture and little bit of Clarity, to darken the clouds. To finish things off, I jumped over to Photoshop and used the Clone Stamp tool to clone nearby areas of clouds over that tall, ugly palm tree to cover it up.

Direct Sunlight Portrait BTS

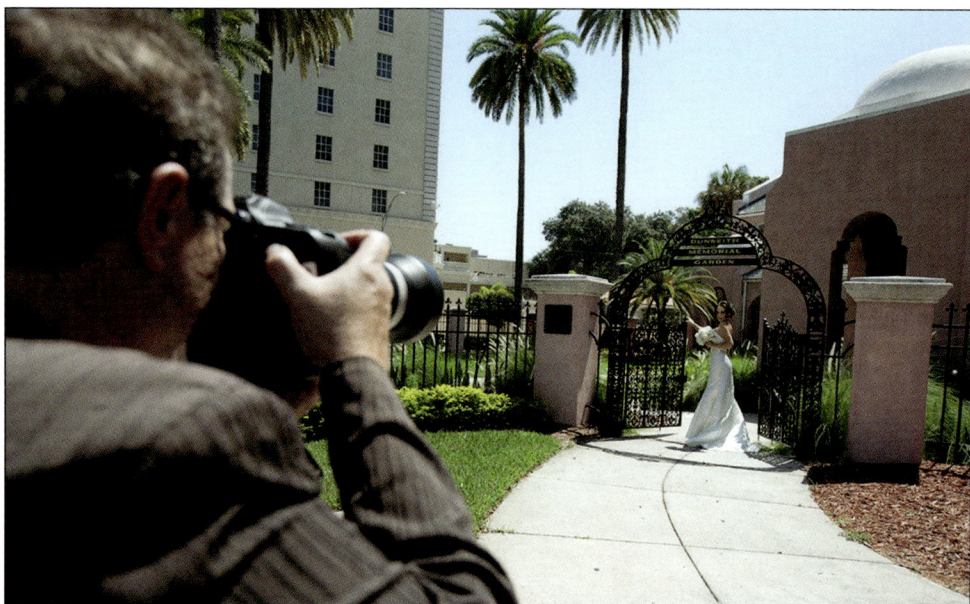

BEHIND THE SCENES: I positioned our bride at the gates outside the church here. It's a bright, sunny day, and I don't want to keep her outside in this heavy dress too long or she'll start to sweat...errr...I mean "glow" from the summer heat. There's nothing really there to shade her, so we're going to have to tame the light ourselves.

CAMERA SETTINGS: For the final image on the facing page, I'm standing way, way back and zooming in with a 70–200mm f/2.8 lens at 180mm. I'm shooting in aperture priority mode, and at f/2.8, my camera set my shutter speed for me at 1/2000 of a second. I'm at 200 ISO, but of course, I would have preferred to have set my ISO at 100 (that's the lowest, cleanest ISO on my particular make and model of camera body), and I still probably would have had well over 1/1000 of a second shutter speed (way more than I need). So, why was I shooting at 200 ISO? I forgot to change it back to 100 ISO when we stepped outside the church. Hey, it happens. What's the noise difference between 200 ISO and 100 ISO? Negligible at best. So, why did I tell you I messed up in the first place, since nobody would know? It's because, in this case, I got lucky and it really didn't matter, but it doesn't always work out that nicely.

Final Image

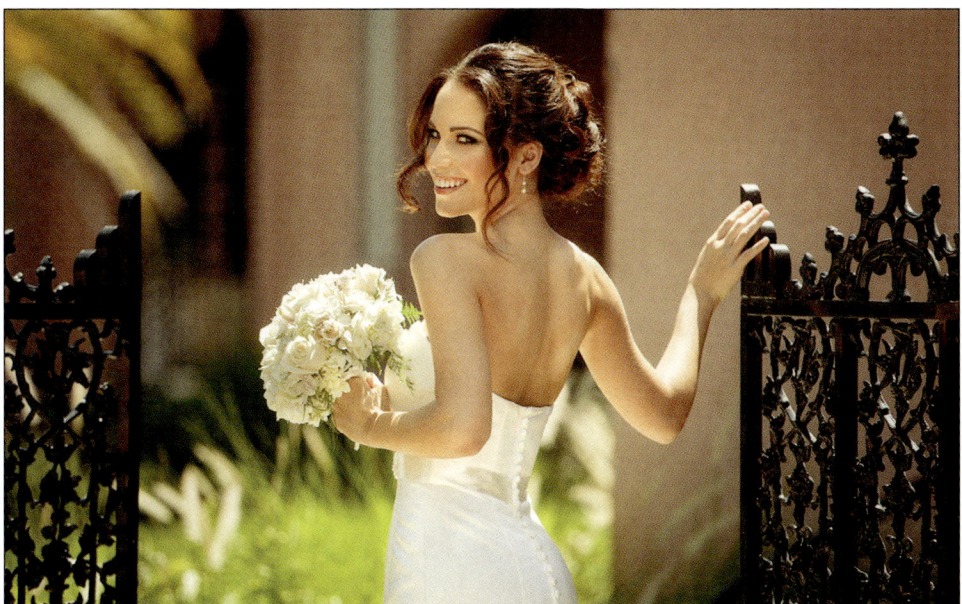

NOTES: The reason I'm standing so far back from my subject is because it allows me to shoot what kind of looks like a wide-angle shot. But, from that far back, I'm able to zoom in tight (to 180mm), which helps (with the f/2.8 f-stop) put the background nicely out of focus, creating the separation between the bride and the background. The second thing to note here is that my bride is facing the sun, which is very high in the sky (you can see it lighting most of her bouquet). So, to create that soft, beautiful light we're looking for, I had her turn her head back toward me, facing away from the sun so she's backlit, and I can use the sun as a rim light, lighting the top and sides of her hair, her shoulders, and so on. Having her turn her head back like this did a great job of getting her face out of the direct sun. However, everytime I look at this shot, what kills me is that her arm on the right side of the image is still getting direct sun. If I could have had her drop that arm, then boom—problem solved. But, I liked her gesture so much with her arm on the gate that I didn't change her pose.

POST-PROCESSING: Because the bride is facing away from the sun, and she's backlit, she isn't as bright as I'd like her to be. So, in Lightroom, I cranked up the Shadows slider a bit to bring her out of the shadows. I also used the Adjustment Brush to brighten her face (like I showed on page 146). I also darkened the edges of the image all the way around (see page 147), and I increased the Contrast quite a bit, which makes the whites whiter, the blacks blacker, and the overall color more vibrant.

Glass Door Light Portrait with Diffuser BTS

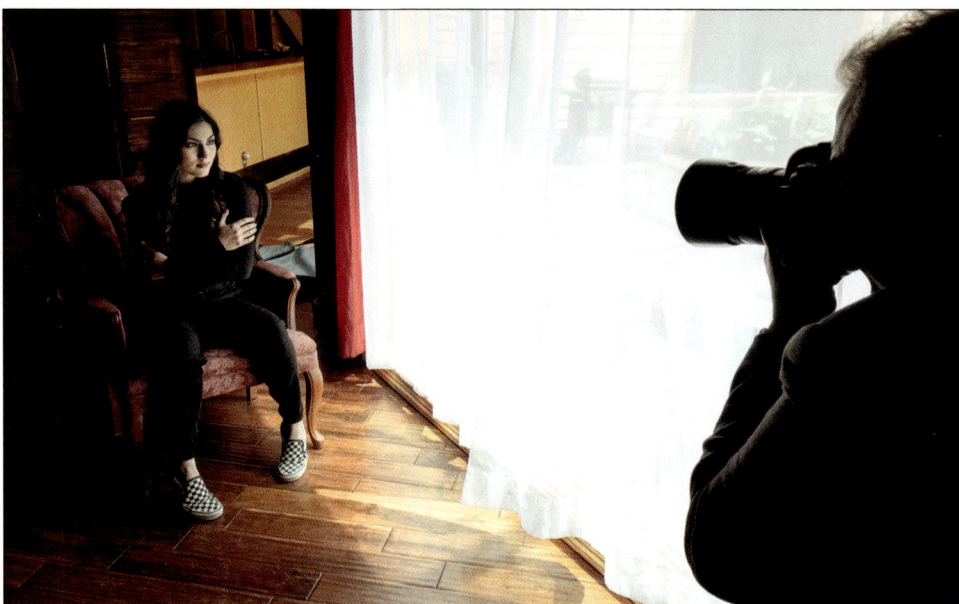

BEHIND THE SCENES: We're doing a window light shot at a friend's house here, but he doesn't have that smaller high-up window I'm looking for, so instead, we're using the large floor-to-ceiling sliding glass doors that lead out to his pool. I borrowed a really interesting chair, with a great color and interesting pattern, for my subject to sit on. In this behind-the-scenes photo, I'm doing a test shot standing, but I wound up sitting on a bar stool (so I'm shooting from slightly above eye height), and that's the angle you're seeing in the final image on the facing page. Also, to keep from seeing his kitchen in the background, we moved a tri-fold decorative panel into place behind her.

CAMERA SETTINGS: For the final image on the facing page, to put the background out of focus, I used an 85mm f/1.2 lens, taken at f/1.8 (see page 180 in this chapter for why I shoot at f/1.8 rather than f/1.4 or f/1.2). The light was fairly diffused and it wasn't very bright, so I cranked my ISO up just a bit to 200 ISO. As it turned out, I didn't need it because at f/1.8, shooting in aperture priority mode, my shutter speed was 1/400 of a second, which was actually way more than I needed (I only need around 1/125 of a second). There were several times during this shoot that I had a higher shutter speed than I needed with a higher ISO getting me there. A quick solution would have been for me to turn on my camera's Auto ISO feature (see page 20) and then choose 1/125 of a second as my minimum shutter speed. That way, it would only raise my ISO if my shutter speed fell below 1/125 of a second. Ahhhh, hindsight (and all that stuff).

Final Image

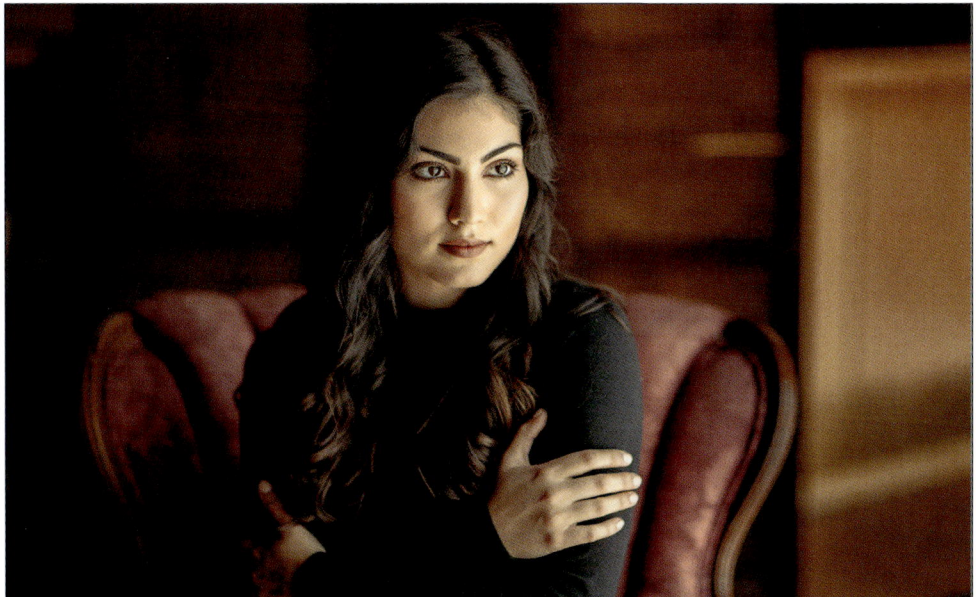

NOTES: Once I had my camera settings kind of dialed in, I took a few test shots and I wasn't thrilled with the softness of the light—meaning the light coming in through the giant sliding glass doors was harder and a bit harsher than I would like. So, I pulled the sheers closed (they had been open, so my subject was receiving direct light) to help diffuse the light, which is a great way to quickly provide better, softer light. Closing the sheers, though, also cuts the intensity of the light, which is why I kicked up my ISO to 200—I was afraid the lower light would drop my shutter speed too much. Another thing I was dealing with was the light hitting the hard wood floor and bouncing some of that light back up toward my subject. I usually don't mind having a little light bounce off the floor because it helps fill in shadows under the eyes and the neck, but in this case, so much light was bouncing up that it added a bit of an up-lighting effect that is not awesome, so I had to address it in post (as mentioned below).

POST-PROCESSING: My post-production challenge here was the kitchen cabinet on the far right. You're probably thinking: "Yeah, it's bright, but it's not too bad," but that's only because I darkened it big time in post. I used Lightroom's Graduated Filter tool, by lowering the Exposure to –1.50, and then dragging a gradient from the wall on the left just past the edge of her chair to darken that whole side and tone down the brightness from that kitchen. I also had to use the Adjustment Brush with the Exposure set to 0.50 to paint over the top half of her face to try to offset the bright light reflecting up from the floor.

Window Light Bridal Portrait BTS

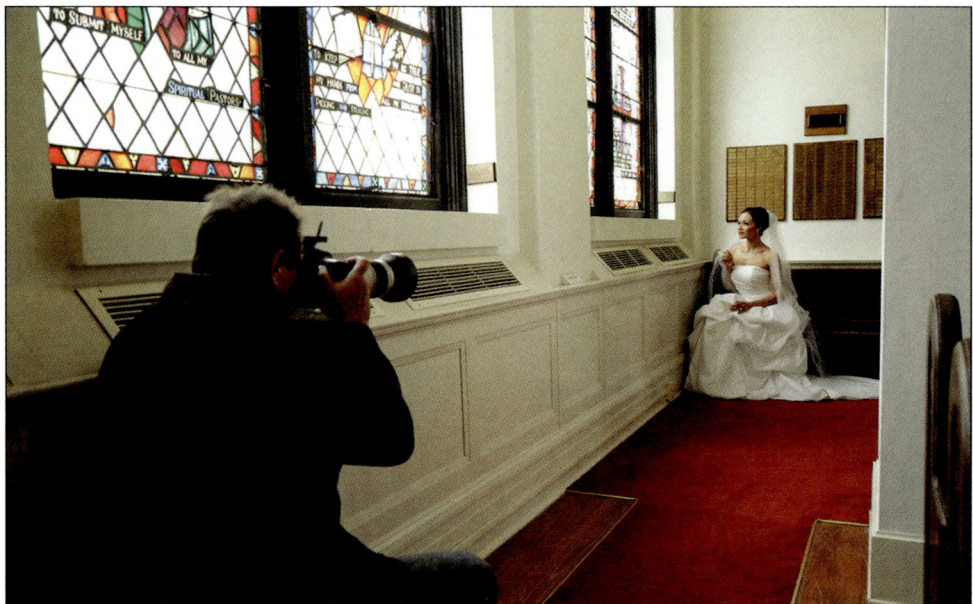

BEHIND THE SCENES: Here is our subject sitting on a bench (okay, it's probably a pew, but it's all by itself, separated from the other pews, so I'm going with bench). Our bride is sitting down and, ideally, you want to shoot from eye level or just above—if I shot this from a standing position, while she's sitting, it might be too high an angle (remember, eye height or ideally a little higher). So, in this case, I wound up sitting on another bench (okay, they're pews. They're pews) to take the shot. Also, while there is a wireless transmitter sitting on my camera's hot shoe (you can see the little antennae sticking up), I'm not using a strobe or flash here. The transmitter is off—this is a 100% natural light shot (no flash needed).

CAMERA SETTINGS: For the final image on the facing page, it was taken using my go-to portrait lens, the 70–200mm f/2.8. My f-stop is f/2.8 (because I'm shooting in low light—more on that in a moment). My ISO is 1600 because the window light was very soft and subtle—there's not a lot of light in there, so I had to crank it up. I'm shooting in aperture priority mode, so the camera chose a shutter speed of 1/250 of a second. I probably could have shot this at a slower shutter speed, like 1/125 of a second no problem, so actually, I could have dropped my ISO to around 800 ISO (which would have given me a cleaner shot).

Final Image

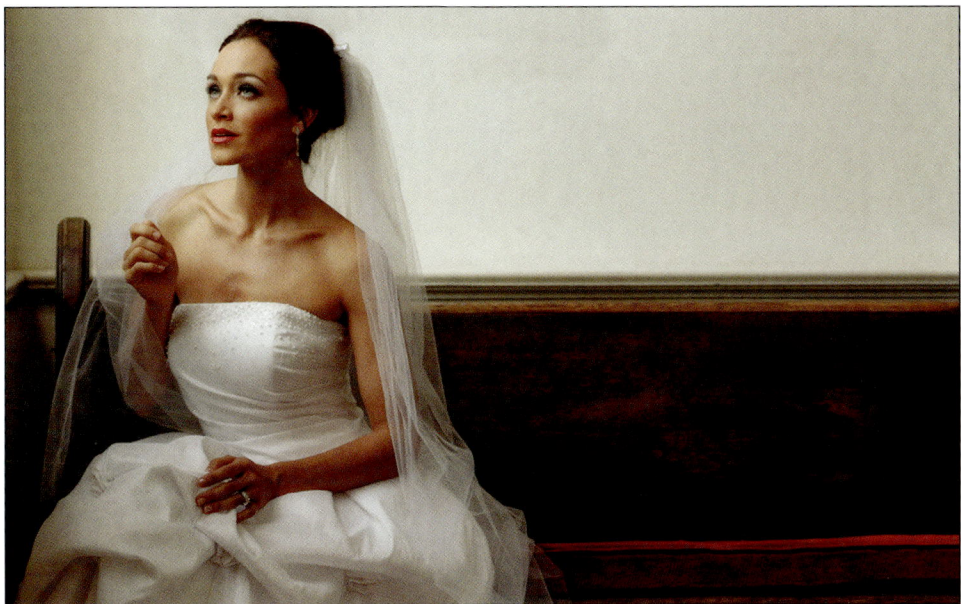

NOTES: The windows in this church couldn't have been at a better height for a window light shot. If you look at the behind-the-scenes shot on the facing page, you can see that they are up a little higher than the bride, so the light falls on her from a slightly higher angle and that helps make for some beautiful light. But, there's another wonderful benefit to these windows: because of their position, the light "falls off" naturally, meaning her face is beautifully and fully lit, then the lights starts to fall off as it hits her décolletage (five points for using a cool big word) and chest, and then it continues to fall off and get subtly darker and darker as it moves down her gown. Also, how am I able to get her so close to the window without the light being harsh? Two reasons: the glass itself is textured, and there's an overhang on the outside of the church that keeps the light from being so direct. It's soft and beautiful, and I soon as I saw it I thought it would make a great spot for a portrait.

POST-PROCESSING: Just the regular portrait retouching stuff I've outlined in the Post-Processing chapter, but I do want to note that I also added a soft glow effect to this image as well (the one from page 133) to give the image a bit of a dreamy look.

Low-Perspective Bridal Portrait BTS

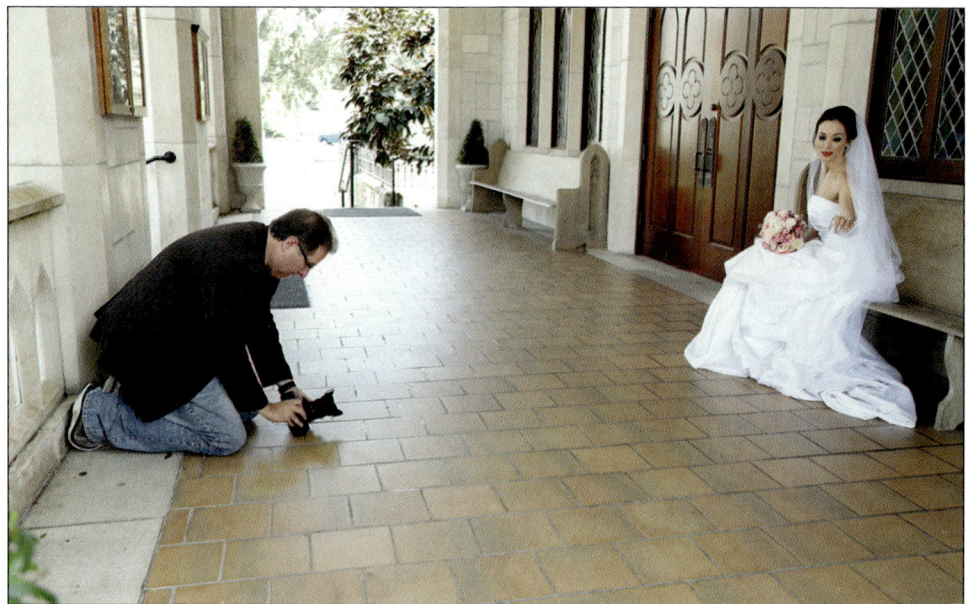

BEHIND THE SCENES: Here, our bride is sitting right outside the church doors on a bench with a large overhang above her, covering the entryway. We have a lot natural light pouring in from the side, but since she's so far away from the light, it's really soft and beautiful. I did not have my trusty Platypod with me (it's what I mount my camera and ballhead on for low-angle shots), so I got down on my knees and aimed my wide-angle lens upward toward our bride.

CAMERA SETTINGS: For the final image on the facing page, I'm using a 16–35mm f/4 wide-angle lens, and I'm all the way out 16mm. The reason I'm shooting with such a wide-angle lens is that I want to include the church in the shot for more of an environmental portrait (the bride outside the church) rather than a tighter shot that's more flattering. Because wide-angle lenses like this can cause body parts to distort, I tried to keep the bride pretty close to the center of the shot (without being dead center) because the center of the frame is the part of a wide-angle lens that has the least distortion.

Final Image

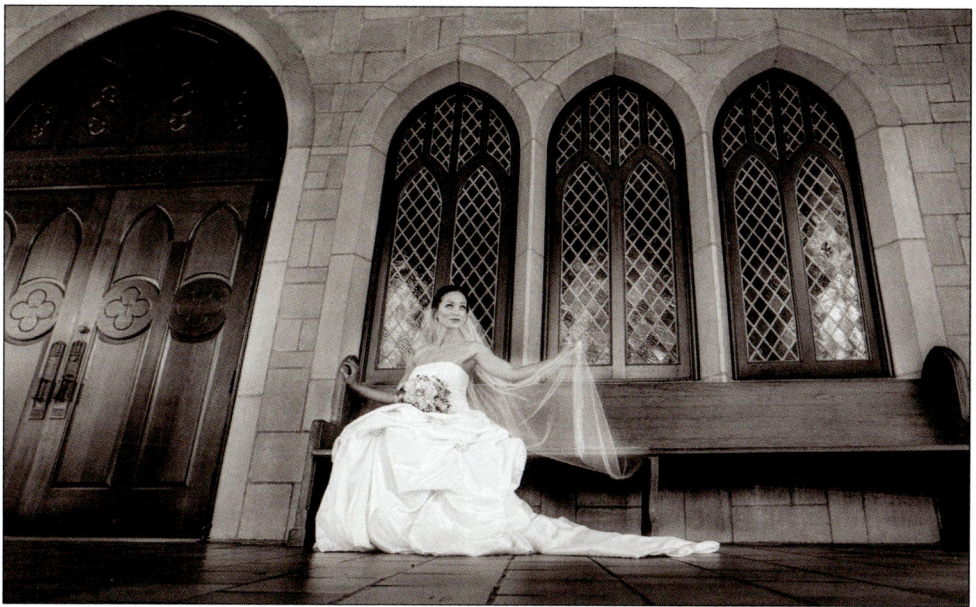

NOTES: The reason for shooting at such a low angle with a wide-angle lens like this is to create more of an epic look. Notice the tiles on the floor—not only do they lead the viewer's eye right toward the bride, they actually render a reflection, as well (this reflection is a benefit of shooting at a low angle like this. Wood floors and tile that otherwise don't look reflective often give a nice reflection when you're down at such a low level).

POST-PROCESSING: In Lightroom (you can also do all of this in Camera Raw), I first converted the image to black and white by clicking on the icon that looks like four little rectangles near the top right of the Develop module's Basic panel, which brings up the Profile Browser. I then scrolled down to the B&W profiles and chose one that looked good (hover your cursor over each of the 17 different black-and-white conversions until you see one that looks good to you). With the image converted to black and white, I added the nice brownish duotone-style tint by scrolling down to the Split Toning panel and, in the Shadows section, moving the Saturation slider to 18 and the Hue slider to 41 (you may choose a different Hue setting, depending on your image). I don't mess with the Highlights section at all or the Balance slider. Lastly, back in the Basic panel, I added a lot of Contrast and a lot of Texture to bring out the detail in her dress, the walls, and tile. I also added a little bit of Clarity, which helps make the tiles on the floor look a little shinier (Clarity is great for adding shine. Try it on water or metal).

Open Shade Portrait BTS

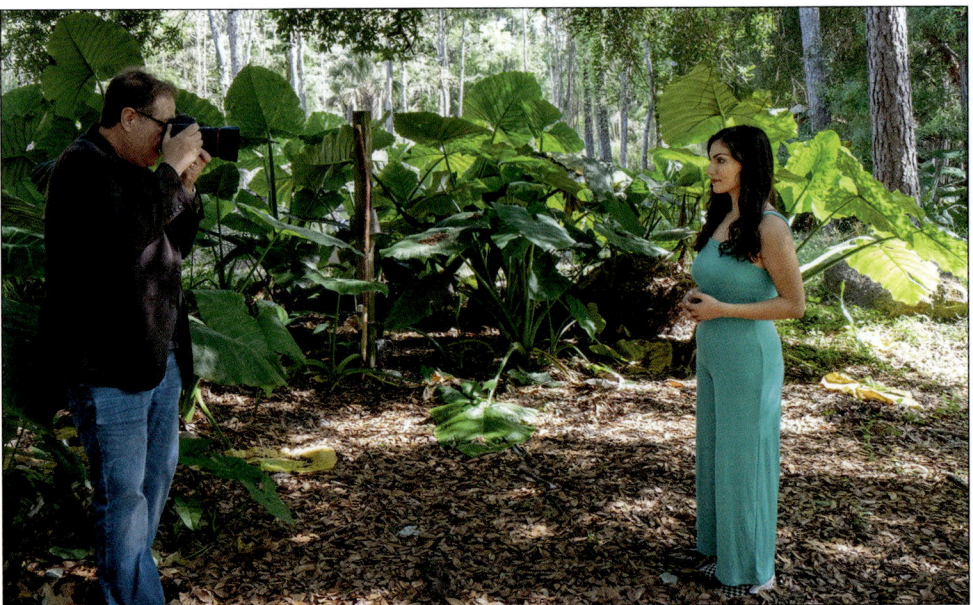

BEHIND THE SCENES: Here, our subject is standing under a large tree to help give us some better light than just the harsh direct sunlight where we're shooting.

CAMERA SETTINGS: For the final image on the facing page, to put the background way out of focus, I used an 85mm f/1.2 lens, but the shot was actually taken with my f-stop at f/1.8, which still creates a very shallow depth of field. I generally don't shoot at f/1.2 or f/1.4 because it makes your depth of field so shallow that you're likely to get a lot of out-of-focus shots unless you absolutely nail that focus every time. Why risk it? It's hard to notice a big difference (if you see any difference at all in the amount or quality of background blur) between shooting at f/1.8 versus f/1.2, so why risk having a bunch of shots that wind up soft or out of focus? That's why f/1.8 is my go-to f-stop on an 85mm lens. I'm shooting in aperture priority mode, and at f/1.8, my camera chose a shutter speed of 1/125 of a second. That's a decent shutter speed for hand-holding my camera and still getting a sharp shot. If my shutter speed had gone any lower, I would have raised my ISO to get it up to at least 1/125 of a second.

Final Image

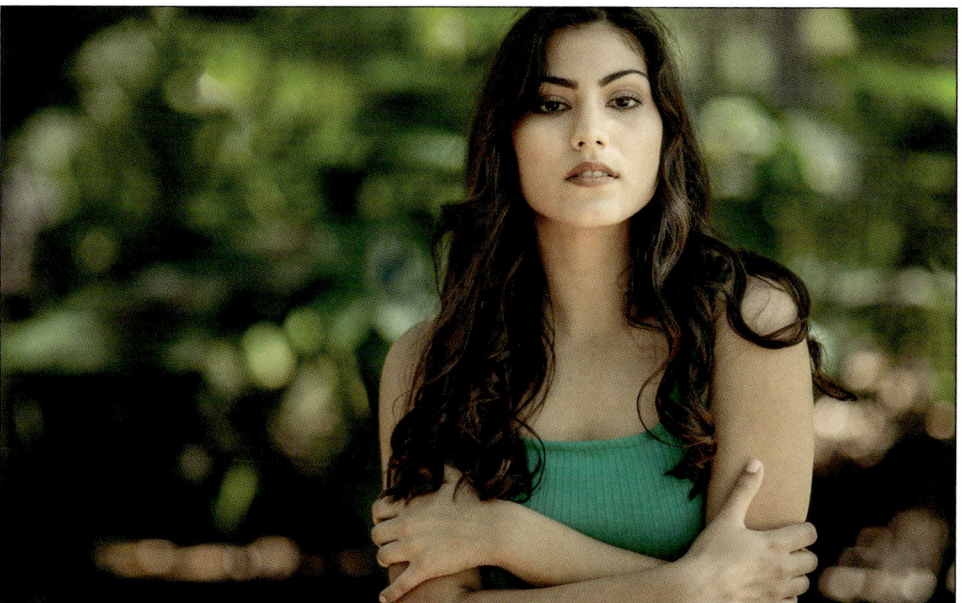

NOTES: The key here is to position your subject so they're in smooth, even light, not dappled light (see page 64). I kept the lens up to my eye and directed my subject to move to the left, right, whatever, until she didn't have any annoying dapples of light sneaking through the tree. Once I had that soft, even light, I took the shot.

POST-PROCESSING: There were two main things I had to deal with: (1) All the green foliage behind her and above her gave her skin tone a bit of a greenish/yellowish tint. So, in Lightroom, I took the Adjustment Brush, lowered the Saturation amount to –25, and then I painted over her skin to desaturate it a bit, which removed that tint. Her skin was still a little dark, so I used the skin brightening technique I showed you on page 150 in the Post-Processing chapter (in short: I went to the HSL/Color panel, clicked on the Luminance tab, and dragged the Red and Orange sliders to the right). The second issue (2) was that the background was too bright and had lots of white "hot spots," drawing your eye. So, first, with the Adjustment Brush, I painted over the background with the Exposure slider set at –1.00 to darken it up. Then, I jumped over to Photoshop and used Content-Aware Fill to get rid of those super bright areas: Using Photoshop's Lasso tool **(L)**, I drew a selection around a bright spot, then I went under the Edit menu and chose **Fill**. When the Fill dialog appeared, I made sure **Content-Aware** was selected from the Use pop-up menu, then I clicked OK and the bright spot was gone. I then moved on to another spot and repeated the process until they were all gone. No retouching on the face, etc.

Epic-Style Indoor
Window Light Portrait BTS

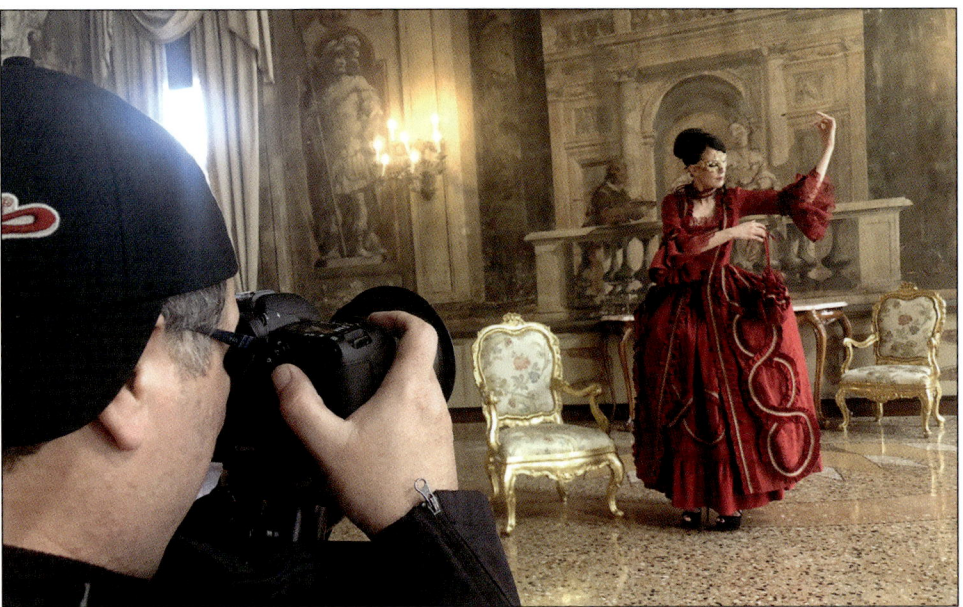

BEHIND THE SCENES: Here, our subject is in a hotel ballroom in Venice, Italy. We rented a Carnival costume and mask, and shot with nothing but natural light, because the light in this second story ballroom was just beautiful.

CAMERA SETTINGS: The final image on the facing page is an environmental portrait where the setting is very important to the story you're telling with your subject, so I'm using a very-wide-angle lens. This was shot with the widest full-frame lens they make—the Canon 11–14mm ultra-wide-angle lens—at 11mm. It's. So. Wide! Because it's a wide-angle lens, which tends to distort anything that's not right in the middle of the frame, I tried to put our subject right in the middle. I want everything in focus from front to back, and I could have used an f-stop like f/11, which is made for stuff like that, but I'm hand-holding, so I don't want to shoot at 4000 ISO. The good thing about super-wide-angle lenses is you don't have to shoot at f/11 or f/16 to have everything in focus. You can shoot at more wide-open f-stops, and that's what I did here. Even though I shot this at f/4, everything is in focus from front to back. Even at f/4, I had to raise my ISO to 1250 to be able to get to 1/125 of a second for a sharp hand-held shot, but take a look at the shot—you don't really see any noise.

Final Image

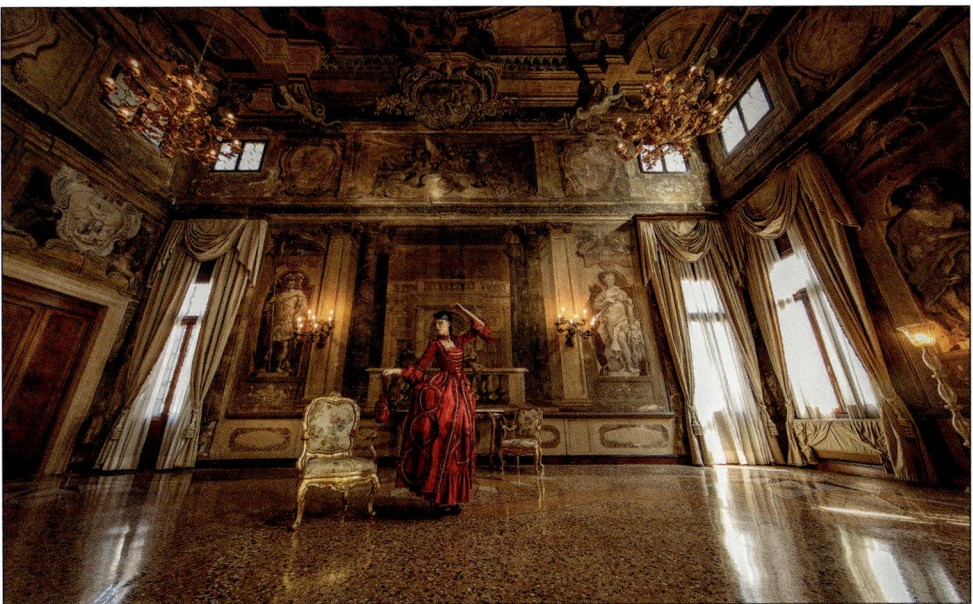

NOTES: A couple of important things to note: Look how far our subject is from the windows that are mostly lighting her—the side window on the far right and the windows up high above those on the sides. The back windows aren't helping much, but there are more windows in front of her that are helping to light the room overall, and some of that light is bouncing off the floor, which is helping, as well. One thing that is making the light nice is those sheers in front of the windows. When I walked into the ballroom, it was the first thing I did—I ran around closing all the sheers to make the quality of light better in the room. Lastly, I wound up sitting on the ground to make this shot, so the floor would become more of a factor in it, and it reflects the chair and the windows better. The 11mm lens is really creating the epic here, and when you get low with a super-wide-angle lens, that's when the magic happens.

POST-PROCESSING: In Lightroom, the first thing I did was to lower the Highlights all the way around. A lot of light was streaming in, blowing out all the windows, and I felt it was taking the focus off our subject, which is never good. Also, I raised the Texture amount a lot, and then increased the amount of Clarity to about 1/3 of the Texture amount to add shine to everything. Those two sliders work well together. I darkened the edges all the way around the image (see page 147). Then, I took the Adjustment Brush, increased the Exposure amount to 0.30 and, with a very small brush, I painted over our subject, so she would have that extra pop of light to draw your eye. My final step was to drag the Contrast slider (in the Basic panel) to the right to boost the overall contrast in the image.

Index

1-stop diffusers, 56–57
50mm lenses, 7
70-200mm zoom lens, 2
85mm f/1.8 lens, 3
135mm portrait lens, 4

A

Adjustment Brush, 132, 135, 139, 141, 146, 151
aperture priority mode, 17, 19, 22, 23, 76
aperture (f-stop) setting, 18
arm poses, 124, 126
Auto Eye AF feature, 28
Auto ISO setting, 20
Auto White Balance, 165
autofocus feature, 28

B

B&W profiles, 179
backdrops, painted, 50
backgrounds
    bright spots in, 91, 181
    contrasting colors in, 78
    distracting elements in, 89
    lens compression and, 11
    painted backdrops as, 50
    shadow patterns as, 49
    soft or out-of-focus, 9, 18, 90
    textured, 149
backlit subjects
    direct sunlight and, 173
    sun flare portrait with, 158–159
    window light and, 44, 160–161
bending body parts, 126
black reflectors, 60
black-and-white conversions, 179

blank expression, 118
blemish removal, 136
blend modes
    Overlay, 149
    Screen, 134
    Soft Light, 139
blinkies, 23
blog of author, 114
bridal portraits
    low perspective for, 178–179
    window light for, 160–161, 176–177
bright spots in background, 91, 181
brightening
    eyes, 141
    faces, 146
    skin, 150, 181
broad lighting, 113, 167
Brush tool, 134, 139, 149

C

camera
    hand-holding, 19, 31
    shake reduction features, 13
Camera Raw
    brightening eyes in, 141
    brightening faces in, 146
    brightening skin in, 150
    desaturating skin in, 135
    sharpening portraits in, 140
    spotlight effect in, 148
    sunburst effect in, 132
    White Balance tool, 69
Camera Raw Filter, 132, 134
camera settings, 16–31
    aperture, 18
    clipping warning, 23
    exposure compensation, 22
    focus-related, 25–28

IS or VR feature, 31
ISO, 19, 20, 21
RAW format, 16
shooting mode, 17
shutter speed, 19–20
white balance, 24
Canon lenses, 3, 4
Caponigro, Paul, 100
catchlights in eyes, 88
child portraits, 97
chin down technique, 115
cinematic color grading, 143
classic window light portrait, 168–169
clipping warning, 23
Clone Stamp tool, 145
clothing choices, 79, 104
cloudy outdoor portraits, 67, 170–171
Cloudy white balance, 24, 67
Color Lookup adjustment layer, 143
colors
    cinematic, 143
    contrasting, 78
composition guidelines, 82–97
    bright spots in background, 91
    catchlights in eyes, 88
    child photographs, 97
    cutting off top of head, 85
    distracting background elements, 89
    environmental portraits, 96
    eyes positioned in frame, 83
    full-length photos, 92
    higher angle shots, 93
    intimate portraits, 82
    low perspective shots, 92
    placing subjects in frame, 84
    points for framing subjects, 94–95
    simplifying the scene, 90
    space left above head, 86
    visual space in frame, 87
connecting with subjects, 100
Content-Aware Fill, 181
contrasting backgrounds, 78

D
dappled light, 64
Daylight white balance, 24, 52
desaturated skin look, 135
Detail panel, 140
diffusers, 56–57
    direct sun location portrait with,
        162–163
    glass door light portrait with, 174–175
    group shots using scrims as, 63
    harsh direct light portrait with,
        164–165
    large area portrait with, 156–157
    overhead sun portrait with, 154–155
direct sunlight
    behind your subject, 72–73
    diffusers used in, 56, 154–155,
        164–165
    harsh window light from, 34, 36
    lens flare effects from, 75
    location portrait with scrim in,
        162–163
    overexposing subjects in, 76
    recipe for shooting in, 172–173
    rim or hair light from, 72, 74
    shade near edge of, 65
    spilling onto subject's face, 73
direct-at-the-camera pose, 108
directing subjects, 107
directional light, 68
distance
    Minimum Focusing, 10
    subject-to-background, 9
distortion
    50mm lens, 7
    wide-angle lens, 5
distracting background elements, 89
documentary-style portraits, 7
Doorhof, Frank, 151
doorway portraits, 48
dramatic window light portrait, 166–167
duotone-style tints, 179

E

edge darkening vignette, 147
edge-of-the-seat pose, 125
effects
    cinematic color grading, 143
    soft glow, 133, 177
    spotlight, 148, 171
    sun flare, 134
    sunburst, 132
    vignette, 147
emotion and expression, 110
environmental portraits, 96
    backlit sun flare effect for, 159
    cloudy outdoor setting for, 170
    epic-style indoor window light
        portrait, 182–183
    scrim used in direct sun for, 162
    wide-angle lenses for, 5
epic-style window light portrait,
    182–183
exposure compensation feature, 22
expression
    dealing with blank, 118
    emotion and, 110
Eye AF feature, 28
eyes
    brightening, 141
    catchlights in, 88
    enhancing irises of, 139
    expression and emotion in, 110
    focusing on, 25–28, 110
    minimizing whites in, 111
    positioning in frame, 83

F

Face-Aware Liquify feature, 144
faces
    adjusting, 144
    brightening, 146
facial lighting
    roundish faces, 112
    thin faces, 113
    tilting face up for, 117

Fade dialog, 137, 138
fashion accessories, 129
fast lenses, 3, 4, 12, 26
filters
    Camera Raw, 132, 134
    Gaussian Blur, 133
    Lens Flare, 134
    Liquify, 144
finger poses, 128
flat-footed poses, 121
Fluorescent white balance, 24
fly-away hair removal, 145
focusing
    autofocus feature for, 28
    choosing the eye for, 27, 110
    focus and compose technique for, 25
    for group shots, 29–30
    single-point mode for, 26
Forward Slash key [/], 136, 137
f-stop (aperture) setting, 18
full-length photos, 92

G

gaffer's tape, 39
Gaussian Blur filter, 133
glass door light portrait, 174–175
gold reflectors, 51, 58
Gravity Backdrops, 50
gray cards, 69
group shots
    diffusing outdoor, 63
    focusing for, 29–30

H

hair
    adding volume and movement to,
        119
    removing fly-away, 145
hair light, 72, 74
hand directions, 107
hand-holding cameras, 19, 31
hand poses, 127–128

hard light, 74
head of subject
    cutting off top of, 85
    space left above, 86
Healing Brush tool, 136, 137, 138
highlight profile portraits, 43
highlight warning, 23
hot spots in background, 181
HSL Adjustments panel, 135
HSL/Color panel, 150
Hurley, Peter, 114

I

Image Stabilization (IS) feature,
    13, 31
intimate portraits, 82
iris enhancement, 139
ISO setting
    Auto ISO option, 20
    shooting at lowest, 21
    shutter speed and, 19, 20

J

jawline technique, 114

K

kelbyone.com website, xii
kicker light, 74

L

large area portrait, 156–157
Lastolite gear
    Gray/White Balance Card, 69
    Skylite Scrim, 63, 162
    TriGrip Diffuser, 154
legs
    thinner-looking, 123
    tips for shooting, 121
lens compression, 2, 4, 11

lens flare
    getting into photos, 75, 158
    reducing with lens hood, 8
    sun flare effect, 134
    sunburst effect, 132
Lens Flare filter, 134
lens hoods, 8
lenses, 2–13
    50mm, 7
    70-200mm, 2
    85mm f/1.8, 3
    135mm, 4
    fast, 3, 4, 12, 26
    IS or VR feature, 13
    Minimum Focusing Distance, 10
    telephoto, 5, 11
    tips on buying, 12–13
    wide-angle, 5–6, 11, 75, 96, 182
    zoom, 2, 9, 10, 11
light
    dappled, 64
    directional, 68
    hard, 49, 74
    low, 13, 18, 53
    rim, 72, 74, 173
    soft, 66, 74
    window, 34–53
    See also direct sunlight
lighting
    broad, 113, 167
    Rembrandt, 42
    short, 112, 167
    side, 41
Lightroom
    blemish removal in, 136
    brightening eyes in, 141
    brightening faces in, 146
    brightening skin in, 150
    desaturating skin in, 135
    iris enhancement in, 139
    sharpening portraits in, 140
    shiny skin spot reduction in, 138
    smoothing skin in, 151
    soft glow effect in, 133
    spotlight effect in, 148

Lightroom *(continued)*
    sunburst effect in, 132
    vignette effect in, 147
    white balance fixes in, 69
    wrinkle or mole reduction in, 137
    See also post-processing
Liquify filter, 144
location portraits
    in direct sun with diffuser, 162–163
    See also environmental portraits
looking off-camera pose, 109
low perspective shots, 92, 178–179
low-light situations
    aperture setting for, 18
    IS or VR for, 13
    tripods used in, 53

M

Matisse, Henri, 89
Minimum Focusing Distance, 10
Minimum Shutter Speed setting, 20
mole reduction, 137
Move tool, 134
multi-point focusing feature, 26
multi-row group shots, 30

N

Nikon lenses, 3, 4
north-facing window light, 38
nose thinning pose, 116

O

off-center composition, 84
opacity adjustments, 137, 149
open doorway portrait, 48
open shade portrait, 180–181
outdoor photography, 56–69, 72–79
    1-stop diffusers for, 56–57
    best time to shoot, 77
    black reflectors for, 60

    cloudy day shoots in, 67, 170–171
    contrasting backgrounds for, 78
    creating shade for, 62
    dappled light avoided in, 64
    diffusing group shots in, 63
    directional light used in, 68
    full shade used in, 66
    gold and silver reflectors for, 58
    lens flare effects in, 75
    light-colored clothing for, 79
    overexposing subjects in, 76
    positioning reflectors for, 61
    rim or hair light in, 72, 74
    shade near edge of sunlight for, 65
    sun behind subjects in, 72–73
    white balance trick for, 69
    white reflectors for, 59
out-of-focus backgrounds, 9, 18, 90
overexposing subjects, 76
overhead sun portrait, 154–155
Overlay blend mode, 149

P

painted backdrops, 50
Patch tool, 138
Perfectly Clear retouching plug-in, 142
photo shoots
    directing subjects during, 107
    reviewing photos during, 105
    shots between poses in, 106
photogenic people, 101
Photoshop
    blemish removal in, 136
    brightening eyes in, 141
    brightening faces in, 146
    brightening skin in, 150
    cinematic color grading in, 143
    desaturating skin in, 135
    facial adjustments in, 144
    fly-away hair removal in, 145
    iris enhancement in, 139
    sharpening portraits in, 140
    shiny skin spot reduction in, 138

soft glow effect in, 133
spotlight effect in, 148
sun flare effect in, 134
sunburst effect in, 132
textured backgrounds added in, 149
vignette effect in, 147
white balance fixes in, 69
wrinkle or mole reduction in, 137
See also post-processing
Pinterest website, 102
plug-in, Perfectly Clear, 142
portrait recipes, 153–183
backlit indoor window light portrait,
160–161
backlit sun flare portrait, 158–159
classic window light portrait, 168–169
cloudy outdoor portrait, 170–171
direct sunlight portrait, 172–173
dramatic window light portrait,
166–167
epic-style indoor window light
portrait, 182–183
glass door light portrait with diffuser,
174–175
harsh direct light portrait with
diffuser, 164–165
large area portrait with diffuser,
156–157
location portrait in sun with diffuser,
162–163
low-perspective bridal portrait,
178–179
open shade portrait, 180–181
overhead sun portrait with diffuser,
154–155
window light bridal portrait, 176–177
portraits
characteristics of memorable, 100
cinematic color grading of, 143
ingredients for making, 153–183
sharpening applied to, 140
poses
arm, 124, 126
chin down, 115

creating lists of, 102
direct-at-the-camera, 108
face up toward the light, 117
hand and finger, 127–128
jawline technique, 114
leg, 121, 123, 126
looking off-camera, 109
nose thinning, 116
seated, 125
sideways shoulder, 120
taking shots between, 106
waistline thinning, 122, 124
positioning
reflectors for outdoor portraits, 61
subjects for window light portraits,
41
Post-Crop Vignetting options, 147
post-processing, 132–151
blemish removal in, 136
brightening eyes in, 141
brightening faces in, 146
brightening skin in, 150
cinematic color grading in, 143
desaturating skin in, 135
facial adjustments in, 144
fly-away hair removal in, 145
iris enhancement in, 139
retouching plug-in for, 142
sharpening portraits in, 140
shiny skin spot reduction in, 138
smoothing skin in, 151
soft glow effect in, 133
spotlight effect in, 148
sun flare effect in, 134
sunburst effect in, 132
textured backgrounds added in, 149
vignette effect in, 147
white balance fixes in, 69
wrinkle or mole reduction in, 137
See also Lightroom; Photoshop
props and accessories, 129

R

Radial Filter tool, 148
rapport building, 103
RAW format, 16
recipes for portraits. *See* portrait recipes
reflectors, 58–62
    black, 60
    gold, 51, 58
    lighting backlit subjects with, 44
    opening up shadows with, 51
    positioning of, 61
    shade created with, 62
    silver, 51, 58
    white, 51, 59
Rembrandt lighting, 42
researching subjects, 100
retouching plug-in, 142
reviewing photos, 105
rim light, 72, 74, 173
round face subjects, 112

S

scottkelby.com blog, 114
Screen blend mode, 134
scrims
    direct sun location portrait with,
        162–163
    shooting group shots using, 63
    See also diffusers
seated pose, 125
shade
    creating with reflectors, 62
    finding near edge of sunlight, 65
    portrait shot in open, 180–181
    shooting in full, 66
Shade white balance, 24, 52
shadows
    background patterns of, 49
    black reflectors for creating, 60
    depth and dimension added with, 68
    reflectors for opening up, 51
sharpening portraits, 140

sheers, closing, 40, 175, 183
shooting mode, 17
shooting tethered, 156
shoots. *See* photo shoots
short lighting, 112, 167
shoulders, sideways, 120
shower curtain liner, 39, 157
shutter speed
    hand-held cameras and, 19
    IS or VR for slow, 13
    ISO setting and, 19, 20
    Minimum setting for, 20
side-lighting, 41
Sigma Art 135mm f/1.8 lens, 4
silhouettes, 44, 158
silver reflectors, 51, 58
simplifying the scene, 90
single-point focusing mode, 26
skin retouching
    blemish removal, 136
    brightening skin, 150, 181
    desaturated skin look, 135
    shiny spot reduction, 138
    smoothing skin, 151
    wrinkle or mole reduction, 137
sliding glass door portrait, 174–175
smoothing skin, 151
soft backgrounds, 9, 18
soft glow effect, 133, 177
Soft Light blend mode, 139
Sony 135mm f/1.8 lens, 4
split-lighting look, 41
Spot Healing Brush tool, 145
Spot Metering mode, 74
Spot Removal tool, 136, 137, 138
spotlight effect, 148, 171
subjects
    blank look on faces of, 118
    building rapport with, 103
    directing during shoots, 107
    looking directly at the camera, 108
    photogenic people as, 101
    props or accessories for, 129

researching and learning about, 100
sun flare effect
    backlit portrait for, 158–159
    post-processing images for, 134
sunlight. *See* direct sunlight

T

telephoto lenses, 5, 11
tethered shooting, 156
textured backgrounds, 149
thin face subjects, 113
thinning poses
    for legs, 123
    for waistline, 122, 124
tinting images, 143, 179
TriGrip Bracket, 57
TriGrip diffuser, 57, 154
tripods
    IS or VR feature and, 31
    window light portraits and, 53
Tungsten white balance, 24

V

Vibration Reduction (VR) feature, 13, 31
video resources, xii, 114
vignette effect, 147

W

waistline thinning poses, 122, 124
web resources, xii, 114
Westcott gear
    5-in-1 Reflector Disc, 56
    Scrim Jim, 63
white balance
    camera settings for, 24
    window light portraits and, 52
White Balance Selector tool, 69
White Balance tool, 69
white reflectors, 51, 59

whites of the eyes, 111
wide-angle lenses, 5–6, 11, 75, 96, 182
window light portraits, 34–53
    background shadow patterns in, 49
    backlighting subjects in, 44, 160–161
    bridal portraits as, 160–161, 176–177
    changing light as issue with, 47
    classic, 168–169
    closing the sheers for, 40, 175
    direct sunlight as bad for, 34, 36
    dramatic, 166–167
    epic-style, 182–183
    facing subjects toward windows in,
        45
    highlight profile lighting for, 43
    moving away from the window for,
        36
    moving behind windows or doorways
        for, 37
    north-facing windows and, 38
    painted backdrops used in, 50
    positioning subjects for, 41
    qualities of windows for, 46
    reflectors used for, 44, 51
    Rembrandt lighting for, 42
    shower curtain liner for, 39
    sliding glass doors for, 174–175
    tripod used for, 53
    turning off room lights for, 35
    white balance setting for, 52
wrinkle reduction, 137

Z

zoom lenses, 2, 9, 10, 11

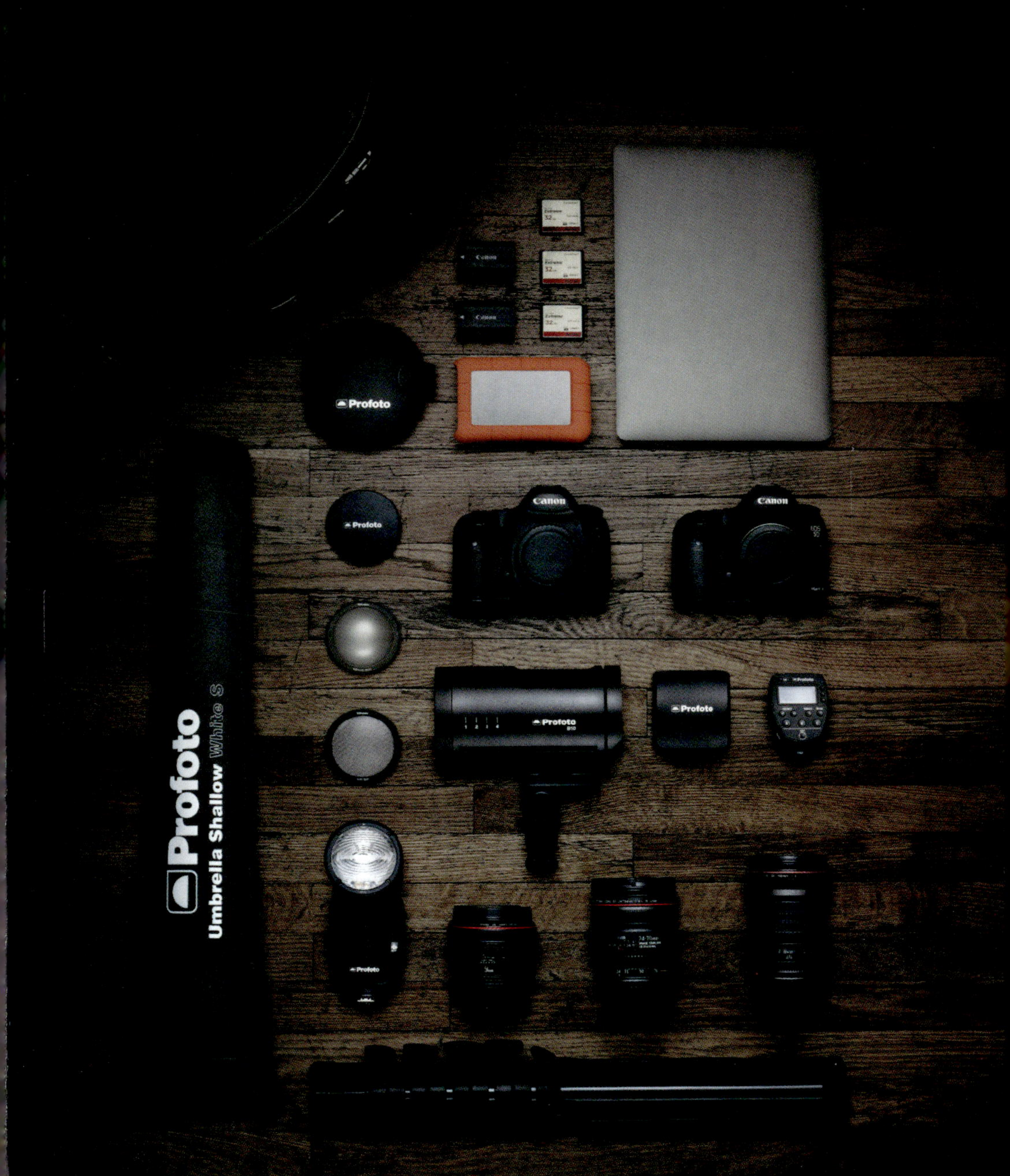

The power of small
Profoto B10

Can you spot our new light? It's in the middle just below the first camera. So yes, the Profoto B10 is small, yet it's more powerful than five speedlights and compatible with more than 120 light shaping tools - so it delivers beautiful light. This is small without compromise; and on-location - size matters.

Discover the B10 at profoto.com

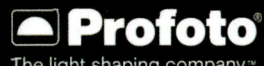

The light shaping company™

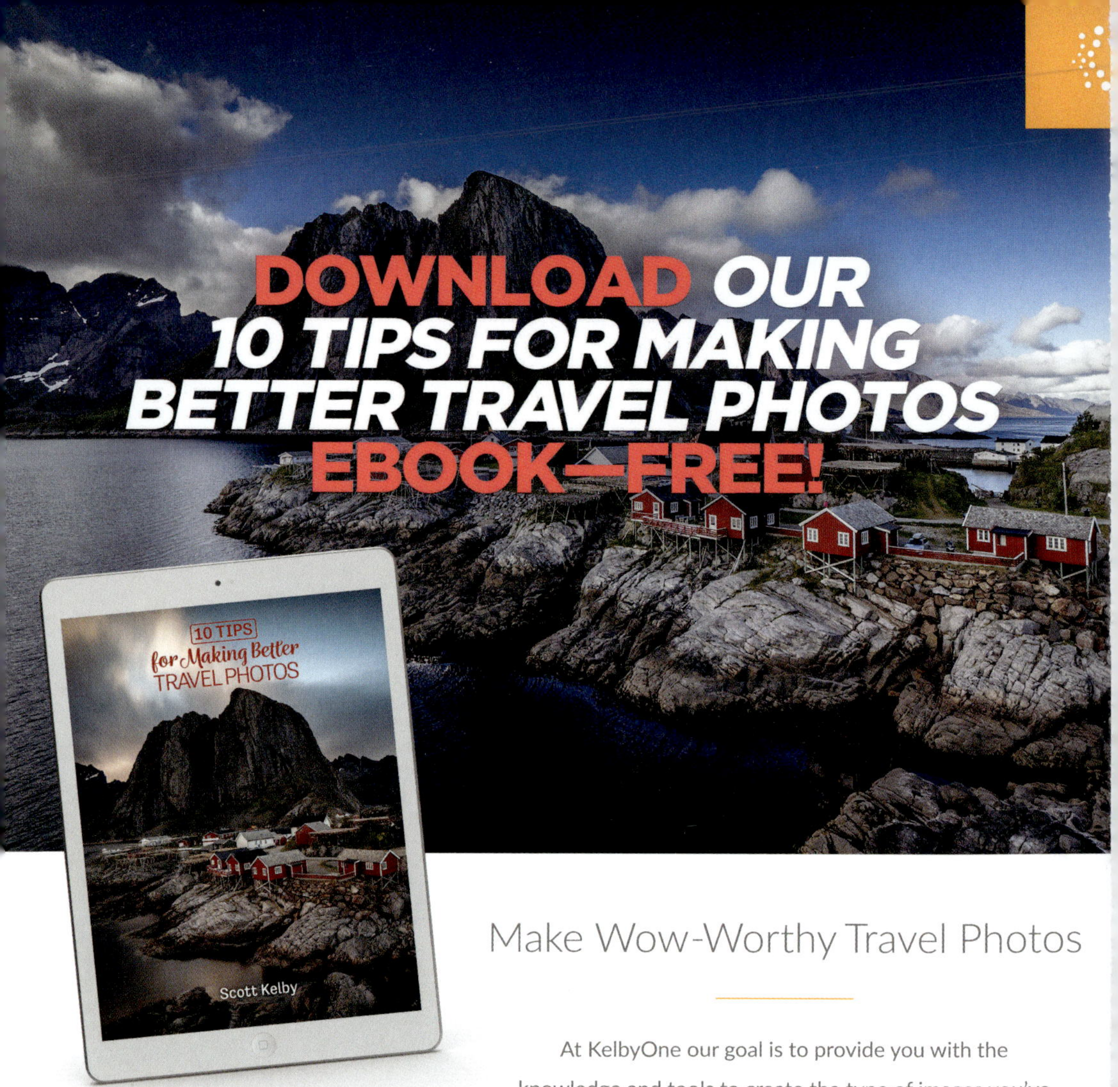

DOWNLOAD OUR 10 TIPS FOR MAKING BETTER TRAVEL PHOTOS EBOOK—FREE!

Make Wow-Worthy Travel Photos

At KelbyOne our goal is to provide you with the knowledge and tools to create the type of images you've always dreamed of. This is why we like to occasionally provide free presets, brushes, eBooks and more. Get this eBook from Scott Kelby, travel photographer and author, and conquer your travel photography. Scott will outline everything from overcoming overcast days, when to shoot, what to shoot, what to bring, how to get better results during an urban shoot, and so much more!

visit kel.by/travelebook to redeem your free eBook

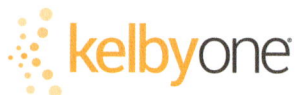